Luke is the most exceptional and talented charcuterie maker I know and one of the finest chefs I have had the pleasure of working with. His passion shone through from the moment I met him. He is now sharing this passion for his craft and his industry secrets with the world through this great book.
TETSUYA WAKUDA, author and chef,
Tetsuya's and Waku Ghin

Quality Meats the book, much like Luke Powell himself, is all about pin-point detail and generosity with the know-how. Luke has given us a delicious new reference to understand and enjoy the transformative nature of meat and food preservation.
DAN HUNTER, author and chef, Brae

This book is destined to be a reference for all things charcuterie for a new generation, packed with a lifetime of knowledge. Luke has really mastered the art. Whether you're a home cook or a professional, you need this book!
DANIELLE ALVAREZ, chef and author,
Recipes for a Lifetime of Beautiful Cooking

Luke Powell is a very talented and driven chef who I've worked with many times over the years. I am so proud of the direction he took when he opened LP's Quality Meats. He had a vision and uniqueness that created a successful niche in the Sydney food scene, and LP's is synonymous with quality, creativity, and innovation. This book is testament to all of that and will be a well-worn tome for years to come.
MARTIN BENN, chef and author, *Dinner Party*

I first fell in love with a quality meat from Luke Powell when I discovered his gently-spiced mortadella pleated into a little fluffy cloud of a potato bun at Mitch Orr's ACME around a decade ago. It was such a simple, cheerful snack but that tenderly-crafted morta knocked it into the realm of the truly exceptional. ACME is no more, but I still get my LP morta fix on the regular — layered like blush-pink bedsheets accessorised with green-olive buttons on the pizzas at my forever favourite pizzeria, Bella Brutta in Sydney's Newtown. To this day, I rarely meet an LP's meat in a restaurant that I don't end up ordering. This excellent and accessible book lets you peek beneath the pepperoni to find out exactly why LP's Quality Meats is so proudly name-checked on menus all over the country.
ALEXANDRA CARLTON, food writer and Oceania Chair, World's 50 Best

This book is a must-have for anyone looking to enhance their charcuterie skills, but even more importantly, to put huge smiles on faces at the dinner table. Luke is one of the most talented and humble people I know. Few possess an innate ability to harness the exacting technique of fine dining and apply it towards butchery, to create a warm culinary hug in every dish. This unique skillset of crossing over from one of Australia's best chefs to butcher makes him the undisputed Sausage King down under.
ANTHONY HUCKSTEP, food writer and host,
Deep in the Weeds podcast

QUALITY MEATS

QUALITY MEATS

THE HOME GUIDE TO
SAUSAGES, CHARCUTERIE,
SMOKED MEATS & MORE

LUKE POWELL

with
David Matthews

murdoch books

Sydney | London

CONTENTS

INTRODUCTION	6
THE BASICS	14
SAUSAGES	16
CURING & FERMENTING	58
LEVEL UP: SALAMI	80
TERRINES & PÂTÉS	92
RAW, GRILLED & ROASTED	116
SMOKING	146
LEVEL UP: SMOKED BRISKET	178
VEGETABLES	190
SAUCES & STAPLES	216
DESSERTS	238
ACKNOWLEDGEMENTS	262
INDEX	264

INTRODUCTION

This is a book about meat, but in many ways it could be about cooking anything. What fills these pages is a collection of recipes drawn from 25 years of cooking, with roots in all kinds of kitchens. It's about meat, yes, but in many ways it's about what came before, about the training, collecting, refining and adapting I've done with so many skills and dishes I've learnt along the way.

Each part of this book is tied closely to LP's Quality Meats, the restaurant and smallgoods supplier I opened in Sydney in 2014. The recipes include some of my all-time favourites from our kitchen, as well as bestsellers from our smallgoods arm. My hope is that this book will serve as a window into LP's, as well as a guide to leaf through and cook from. It's also a tribute to the wonderful people I've worked with throughout my career, and the lessons and techniques they've passed on. The mentoring I've had and the fundamentals I've learnt are the reasons I can say I'm anything of a success. And that, of course, starts with my mum.

The early days

I grew up in Petone, a suburb of Wellington in New Zealand. This was the 80s and 90s, and you wouldn't exactly call Petone a culinary wonderland, but my mum was a wonderful home cook, and I loved joining her in the kitchen. When I turned 13, she organised a part-time job for me in the holidays, washing dishes at Cobar Restaurant, on the beach in Days Bay.

I still remember how shocked I was on my first day stepping into this adult world – the swagger of the chefs, how they spoke and joked and talked about their lives after work. I loved it. Every weekend for two years I'd turn up in my chef's whites – I'm talking 40 minutes on the bus in a skull cap, neckerchief, apron, the works – even though I was only doing the dishes. I was captivated, and as soon as I could train, I did, dropping out of school at 15 to start a full-time chef's course at Hutt Valley Polytechnic.

That was my grounding, but it was a move up the beach to a small restaurant called Brasserie 16, where I'd work under French chef Sandrine Urvois, that was fundamental. Sandrine was the most wild and eccentric person I'd ever met. She was boisterous and loud, and had a deep passion for French culture and cuisine. I loved working for her, and she taught me so much – braising, estouffade, confit, you name it. She also taught me, after I burnt them about 20 times, to always set a timer when you're roasting nuts. But what stuck with me most was how often she tasted everything.

After a year and a half, Sandrine and her partner Kirk encouraged me to try something new, and set me up with a job at a restaurant in Wellington called The White House, run by Paul Hoather. This was real fine dining, driven by New Zealand produce: we'd serve whitebait, pāua (abalone) and venison, and Paul would take me fishing or diving for shellfish. He was a real outdoorsman, so apart from the fishing, he'd often go out hunting with his two English pointers, then come back with a pheasant or two, ready to be hung, plucked and put on the menu.

Paul's cookbook collection was epic. I'd often spend time flicking through cookbooks from Est Est Est or Tetsuya's, both of which were among Australia's most influential restaurants at the time – Est Est Est with a take-no-prisoners unbridled commitment to perfection, Tetsuya's with its intricate plating and melding of French and Japanese traditions. It was like peeking into another world. Paul knew his stuff and was well connected, so three years in, he organised for me to fly to Sydney and do a three-week stage – basically an unpaid internship – at Rockpool, run by Neil Perry and at that time still in its original location on George Street. I packed up, checked into a backpackers in Chinatown, and walked down to The Rocks to go to work.

A taste of Sydney

The first morning I arrived, I immediately knew I was out of my depth. The chefs were immaculate, the copper pans were polished and perfectly hung up. Cooks would pass me things to try that had such intense, complex flavours. A sauce for the poached bar cod dish, with coconut milk, garam masala, turmeric, fresh makrut lime leaf and Thai basil. Or an entrée of tea-smoked duck, handpicked mud crab, lychees and cashew nahm jim. Having grown up in a place where I'd never experienced any of these flavours, or even had access to a Chinatown, my mind was blown.

When the stage ended, I knew I had to come back to Sydney as soon as possible, and within a few months I'd packed up and moved my life over. Thankfully, I was fortunate to land an interview with Martin Boetz at Longrain, the city's renowned Thai restaurant. I was completely enthralled by the complexity of his food, marked by seasonings that were so intentional and intense. I loved working with the team, and I learnt so much, but I had a strong yearning to be back in a fine-dining setting.

Ever since I'd first found that Tetsuya's cookbook, I'd dreamt of working there. But after my Rockpool experience, I didn't think I'd be good enough to land a job at Tets, so instead I applied for a position at The Boathouse on Blackwattle Bay, where Martin Benn, who'd previously led the kitchen at Tetsuya's, had just been appointed head chef – I thought if I couldn't get a job at Tetsuya's, the next best thing would be to work for someone who'd run the kitchen.

If I had any defining feeling about starting at The Boathouse with Martin, it was that I had a lot to learn. It was a good fit, though – Martin's guidance and instruction were always methodical and straight, and even if I felt like my skills didn't always allow me to deliver on the expectation, he was patient (albeit direct) – if something wasn't correct. I also respected and appreciated his undeviating philosophy of cooking. I was learning plenty, and would have happily stayed with Martin there, but suddenly, after just seven months, he told me that he was returning to Tetsuya's, and that there would be a position for me if I came with him. It honestly felt like winning the lottery, and I jumped at the opportunity. But things were about to get very real.

Tetsuya's

My first days at Tetsuya's were about as intimidating as it gets. When I met Tetsuya Wakuda for the first time I choked up and didn't say anything. I just stood and shook his hand. This was a restaurant that was number four on the World's 50 Best list and was fully booked for months in advance. Each day, the entire menu was prepared from scratch by a brigade of 25 incredibly driven, purposeful chefs, with just a few portions kept aside to cover for any mistakes. Everyone in that kitchen was aware of the expectation, and it was run tightly and with precision. After service, the breakdown and cleaning was meticulous, with every inch of the kitchen, top to bottom, cleaned and then polished every single night. The whole team knew the routine and it would be performed like clockwork every single service. I felt like I was the clunky gear in a well-oiled machine.

Tetsuya's was hard. Each chef was a part of a team that ran a section, with each section typically tasked with crafting just one dish. When I was made responsible for one myself, I'd struggle to get it ready for service each day, then I'd miss my call for dishes to be sent. It was tough in other ways, too: compared with the places I'd worked previously, where I might've had responsibilities across a large section of the menu, at Tetsuya's I was preparing the same dish – perhaps the tuna tartare on sushi rice with avocado, or the confit ocean trout – day in, day out. It was monotonous, but slowly I started to feel the rhythm and became attuned to the subtle differences and details of each plate.

After 10 months, which can be a long time when you're working as hard and as long as chefs do, I couldn't shake the feeling that I should look further, travel wider, and move to London. I resigned, and moved back to New Zealand while I sorted out my visa. It was a funny time – I started working for an Italian chef, Maria Pia de Razza, at her trattoria in Wellington. Maria reminded me so much of Sandrine, and she was an amazing cook. She cooked with passion and tradition, braising veal shoulders and roasting ducks, or making pasta and saucing it with ragù that had simmered all night. She frequently reminded me that 'This is not cheffy food.' I loved it. But somehow, I had the feeling that I'd left Sydney too early. Instead of moving to London, I called Martin and said I wanted to come back to Tetsuya's.

Martin welcomed me back, and I started to really love the work. Not long after that, he ended up leaving to set up Sepia, but Darren Robertson (who later went on to open Three Blue Ducks), took over as chef de cuisine, and I was promoted to sous-chef.

The opportunities working at a place like Tetsuya's were incredible; Tetsuya was one of the most famous chefs on the planet and was invited to cook all over the world, and he'd take different chefs to join him on his overseas trips. We'd go to the US, the Middle East, Asia. It was awesome. And the cooking was as precise and as technical as ever.

It was a holiday to the States that changed things for me. I spent some time in San Francisco, eating at restaurants that specialised in beautiful, produce-driven Californian cuisine, then on the back of it, I flew to Chicago for a week-long stage at Alinea, which was deep into molecular gastronomy. The night before I started, I shared a meal there with my friend James Parry, who would go on to open Sixpenny in Sydney.

It was a mind-blowing dinner. We had 25 courses, each dish featuring a range of different textures and techniques, and I had no idea how anything was made. The biggest impression the place left on me, though, was that it felt more like a laboratory than a kitchen. Every ingredient had its texture warped by blending it up and adding hydrocolloids, or by turning it into a gel or freezing it with liquid nitrogen. The contrast with San Fran was stark, and even though I appreciated the incredible technical aspects, I couldn't help but feel it sacrificed the integrity of the ingredients for the sake of technique. This feeling would stick with me, and guide me in my next moves.

By this stage, I'd been at Tetsuya's for three years, and although I could have happily stayed, it felt like the right time to leave; I needed to see some more restaurants, and began looking at other places that were on the 50 Best list. Spain, at the peak of molecular gastronomy but also very grounded in real, elemental cooking, felt like the right place. And it was Mugaritz, in the Basque Country, that I settled on, where James Parry also happened to be working. A few poorly translated emails and miscommunications later, I turned up on their doorstep ready to begin a six-month stage.

Spain

At Mugaritz, I was part of a large brigade of chefs from all over the world: 28 stagiaires, plus eight full-time chefs. It was an amazing restaurant, and with so many hands, any wild idea could be executed. It was incredible. The dishes were so detailed and thoughtful, and seeing how they got to those ideas with their research and development team was equally astounding. I remember there was a course of sea bass with a zucchini garnish

that looked like risotto, except the risotto was made from seeds collected from roasted giant zucchini by seven of us huddling around boxes of the stuff and carefully scraping them out with teaspoons. (Side note: we had zucchini soup for staff meal every single day I was there.) The produce was incredible, too: the team would skip over the border to France to buy vegetables; we visited the farm up the mountainside near the restaurant where our foie gras was produced; the squid would arrive still pulsating and changing colour.

I didn't speak Spanish, so I struggled a lot during service – I'd miss my calls to send plates out – but the team was always patient, and I have the fondest memories of spending that time with them and living in the Basque region. It's something I'll never forget.

Still, sometimes life comes at you, and three months into my stage, Tetsuya rang. Darren Robertson was leaving his post, and Tetsuya asked me if I'd take the position. With the blessing of Mugaritz's head chef, Llorenç Sagarra, I ended my stint in Spain early and flew back to Sydney, primed to take on my first head chef role.

Return to Tetsuya's, and the seeds of LP's

When I arrived back at Tets, a lot of the old crew were still there, so it was an easy transition. Of course there were days when the weight of responsibility made me anxious, but coming fresh from Spain, I was so inspired by what I'd seen and eager to get into this new role and try things out. Looking back, it's an unusual mindset to have had, especially when Tetsuya's was so established. Still, we found some kind of happy medium. I loved working there, I loved the restaurant, and I loved being able to talk with Tetsuya. He's a fascinating man, a legend of gastronomy, who has such an incredible palate and eye for detail, and a truly unique sense of taste and vision.

I stayed in that role for another two years, but having cooked at Tetsuya's for six years all up, I started to get itchy feet again, thinking it was time to do my own thing. The more I thought about it, though, the more the idea began to get into my head that I didn't actually know how to cook. As a young chef, I'd worshipped the restaurants on the World's 50 Best list, fine-diners where precision and high-wire technique was the name of the game. But working only in those kinds of restaurants, you miss out on a lot: I could cut a piece of fish to an exact weight, slice chives with millimetre precision, but if I had to braise a lamb shoulder or roast a large cut of beef, I felt like I'd probably stuff it up.

I dreamt of opening somewhere where I could almost retrain myself in all the skills I felt like I'd missed out on. But before I jumped, I decided to go on one last trip – this time to New York and Montreal – to see some sights and find some inspiration. As part of the trip, I organised a month-long stage at Blue Hill at Stone Barns, run by Dan Barber in upstate New York. It was incredible, and the chef, Adam Kaye, mentioned to me that if there anything in particular I wanted to learn about while I was there to please let them know.

The property, a working farm, had so much beautiful produce, and there were so many different projects going on – the chefs would make charcoal, pick grapes. One day, Adam took me into the wine cellar, which had an attached maturing room filled with what seemed like 100 smoked specks that the team had made with pigs from the farm. Then he showed me where they were making salami, sausages and boudin noir. I asked Adam, 'Can you please show me how to do all of this?' It was amazing that just meat, salt and time could produce such complex and delicious products. For me, this was it. I was hooked.

Opening LP's Quality Meats

When I arrived back in Sydney, I was hungry to take the next step. I was kicking around doing odd jobs in friends' kitchens, trying to navigate the complexities of leases, DAs, liquor licences and the rest, when I had a meeting with Elvis Abrahanowicz who, with Sarah Doyle and Joe Valore, ran Porteño, a Latin American steakhouse in Surry Hills. I loved their food and I loved their venues. I'd already told Sarah what I was thinking, and when I sat down with Elvis for coffee, I went through it again: a place where I wanted to smoke meats, make charcuterie, the whole business. I expected to have to elaborate more, but he just stopped me and said: 'I spoke with Joe, and we're doing it.' We shook hands, and that was it.

I can't express enough how grateful I am to these guys. Without them, the restaurant would never have come to fruition. We discussed plans and locations, and they held my hand through the entire build, guiding me over the millions of hurdles that come with opening a venue. And there are hurdles. LP's took about a year to build. We had to import our Southern Pride smoker from the States and get it firing. And the opening, in 2014, coincided with the start of the NSW lockout laws, something that made running licensed venues even more demanding – we even had to post a bouncer outside the entrance. Still, it probably added to the wild roadhouse vibe.

We opened LP's with a focus on smoking meats and making our own charcuterie, but really it was an environment to hone skills and break out of the fine-dining mould. Somewhere to practise 'real' cooking, serving food that wasn't overfussed or overworked. At the start, we had just three of us in the kitchen, myself, Shannon Debreceny and Kimmy Gastmeier, prepping a menu featuring a range of smoked meats – chickens, beef short ribs – then a smoked sausage, those trashy-but-so-good dinner rolls, mashed potato and gravy, kale with chickpeas and anchovy caramel, as well as plenty more. Kimmy would be hand-rolling puff pastry, making sourdough bread and constructing beautiful tarts.

Needless to say, we were busy. And it was a beast of a place that heaved when it was full. Some nights the team wouldn't even get a chance to look up – Shannon would be carving smoked meats non-stop, and the music would be cranking. It was a rollicking carvery.

As much as that was the tone, we tried to stay away from being pigeonholed as an American-style barbecue joint, and we always thought there was so much more we could do with the smoker. But given how busy we were, it was hard to shake that format and evolve. Still, we managed to pick up a few awards and the restaurant, above all, was a success.

Selling smallgoods

As the years rolled by, we got to grips more with the smoker, our flavours were brighter and clearer – but mostly, we began to refine our charcuterie and smallgoods to a point where they were beginning to feel like proper products. It sounds funny, but when you see a finished product that looks and feels just like something you'd buy from the shops, it's remarkable. If there was a difference, it was that ours had their own unique process behind them, were small batch and put quality first. Just like the real thing, but better.

We didn't do it on our own, though. Shannon and I went down a mortadella rabbit hole after reading Paul Bertolli's *Cooking By Hand*, for example, and we were always referencing and discovering more books. This was when things started to get more serious. Mitch Orr, who was running ACME at the time, asked if we could sell him mortadella. Folded into a fluffy potato bun and sauced with tomato relish, this went on to become a defining snack on his menu. Monty Koludrovic, at The Dolphin Hotel, plated sheets of our mortadella with a garnish of fried olives in the Wine and Dining Rooms. As demand started to increase, our little Robot-Coupe food processor couldn't keep up, so we started to upgrade our equipment.

Suddenly, we had larger companies wanting to buy our products. When they asked us to send through our licence and HACCP plan, though, we just looked at each other: 'What the hell is that?' Turns out, you're not supposed to sell meat to anyone without a licence… This is the point where we got our meat-processing plant licence. We started to seriously make smallgoods on top of running the restaurant. It was full on, and we ran out of space almost immediately.

Renovating, and a new direction

At the end of 2019, we decided to close and renovate. The plan was to reduce the size of the restaurant space – we got rid of around 60 seats – and in its place build a refrigerated workspace and a larger coolroom to store raw ingredients, then add fermenting and maturing rooms so we could make and sell salami.

Wholesale was doing well, until Covid hit, then we had to close, reopen and do takeaway, and everything else we could to keep things going. Once we could properly open the doors again, we managed to keep both sides running, and the smallgoods were better than ever. With the renovation, we got an ice-crushing machine so that we could add ice to our forcemeats without burning out any more Thermomixes crushing up blocks. This also meant we could shuck huge platters of oysters to serve on ice; the coolrooms let us source more fruit and vegetables from small growers, and we could make charcuterie in greater quantities, meaning we could stay ahead.

During this same time I'd begun talking to another cook, Isobel Little, who was working in London but was keen to join the team as our head chef. Isobel wanted to stretch her culinary legs, take control of the kitchen and push it in a slightly more refined direction.

Working with Izzy was easy. We gelled so well, and the changes were simple to achieve and execute because of the reduced restaurant capacity. Under her watch, it felt like there was a lightening of the menu – we didn't smoke the meats for such a prolonged time, and the smoke itself became more of a nuanced seasoning. Where previously we'd used the vegetables and sides to bring relief from the richness of the meats, now the light, clean theme seemed to flow through the whole menu – there was a softening of our approach, and a greater clarity of flavour.

We began to cook a hell of a lot of dry-aged steak and whole fish over the charcoal, and the only smoked meat we consistently offered became the smoked prime rib. This felt like the best iteration of the restaurant, and in a sense how it was always meant to be – it had just taken some growth for us to get there. We were doing production Monday to Thursday, then Thursday to Sunday we'd open for service, and the whole venue felt great. We would have guests come in for leisurely late lunches and sit in front of the gently lit window looking into a room filled with drying saucisson. They'd start with some oysters and a plate of charcuterie, then share a whole grilled turbot or a big steak with horseradish, with sides of lightly smoked potatoes and a bright green salad. After a crème caramel and a coffee they'd fill a bag with cold cuts, sausages and saucisson, and then stroll out into the evening. What a dream.

We operated like this for just over a year, but as time went by, we were feeling the pinch on both sides. We could've done with another day of service, and we also could've done with a few more days to increase production. Something had to give, and even though we were loving the new incarnation of the venue,

I didn't feel like we were able to give either side the room to do it justice. As much as we loved the restaurant, it felt right to give the smallgoods side room to grow and see where we could go with it. We spoke to the team, and as reluctant as we all were, we were unanimous in agreeing it was the right move. It was a hard decision, but we all felt that we needed to explore this concept. We closed the restaurant for good in 2022. Since then, our focus has been on making our smallgoods the best they can possibly be. But this isn't the end.

LP's, now and into the future

With the physical and mental room to grow, we've been able to focus on the different ways to sell our products, new techniques, new sizes and new packaging. We've also been able to engage with more venues, which means we get to see how others choose to serve and cook our stuff. In that way, LP's is busier than ever.

A few years ago, we also opened a pizzeria in Newtown called Bella Brutta. Bella instantly became LP's best customer. Salumi plates are offered at the start, then the pizzas – which get pushed to the limit of charry blisteriness – might be topped with sliced pepperoni, salami or piles of thinly sliced mortadella that get draped over cheesy, garlicky bases.

LP's is also a business with plenty of friends reaching out to us to join in with events and collaborations, and our set-up means we're now free to take LP's offsite and cook elsewhere, whether it's the Adelaide Hills, events around Sydney, or even Singapore. We also have a fortnightly stall at Carriageworks Farmers Market in Eveleigh that stocks the whole range of LP's products, which is also a beautiful way to hear about what people are doing with all the goods.

We've been lucky enough to build a huge following with our products, from retail customers through to restaurants, delis and cafés. And it always makes us so proud to see our products on menus named as LP's mortadella or saucisson. All this from a guy who used to spend his days cutting chives to the millimetre at Tetsuya's. It's been a journey.

This book

These pages contain a collection of knowledge that I've accumulated from decades working in kitchens and products that we've served or made over the years at LP's Quality Meats. As such, it's geared towards meat cookery and the realm of smallgoods and charcuterie. While there are plenty of people in the world who have a much broader knowledge in these areas than I do, what I hope this book offers is a range of techniques and recipes that empower you to perfect your meat cookery and meat products at home.

Everything that follows has been refined over thousands of services and working hours, and I'm pleased to say that with care and attention, they're all achievable for the home cook. Some of the techniques in the book may seem daunting at first, but once you understand the basics, you'll realise they're actually very accessible; even recipes that appear complex often require very little hands-on time. Also scattered throughout are some finer details that are there as a reference, an explanation or simply for inspiration.

You'll notice that throughout this book, meat is often cooked in large cuts and birds or fish are often cooked whole, and they're served simply, with just a few accompaniments. During my career, I've learnt to let produce speak for itself, without overcomplicating things (see page 119 for more on that). I have, however, adopted a rather heavy hand when it comes to seasoning with salt and acid – I love salt and biting acidity. This means that vegetables or salads are often dressed with both vinegar (which is rich and delicious) and lemon (which brings freshness and brightness). It's the best of both worlds. Push these to their limits, and they'll produce mouthwatering results, and make those plates even more effective when you serve them alongside the richer, heavier dishes in this book.

Finally, it's worth noting that I've never quite been able to shake the fine-dining background. We've always tried to make things look as good as they can in the restaurants, and I still can't help myself when it comes to cutting chives perfectly. If you're cooking from this book, though, one thing to keep in mind is not to get

carried away with the aesthetics. There's no wrong way to cut parsley and no-one is going to critique you if things aren't perfectly consistent, nor will it affect the flavour. I love the rustic charm of home cooking, where nothing has to be presented perfectly and the focus can be where it always should be: on how things taste. Relax, and enjoy the process.

THE BASICS

Many of the recipes in this book don't need much in terms of equipment to make them tick. I believe that using the right tools for the job not only makes things smoother, but the results are often better – or at least more consistent. You certainly don't need all these tools, although if you're planning on making sausages, fermenting meats or jumping into the smoking chapter in earnest, it pays to at least be across them. Here's where you'll also find information on some crucial ingredients – salt included – that play key roles in many of the recipes.

Scales

Scales are very important, not only for smallgoods production but all aspects of cooking. Where possible, I steer away from using volume as a measurement for recipes as I find using weight is much more accurate.

I use a variety of scales, including some that take heavier weights for raw meat or large batches of ingredients, smaller scales that measure smaller quantities in grams, and microscales, used for measuring small amounts of curing salts or other seasonings with precision. We've given ounce measurements in decimals in order to be as accurate as possible.

Knives

Sharp knives are essential in any kitchen. Dull knives are not only frustrating, they're also dangerous: exert too much pressure when you're cutting and accidents can happen.

You don't need to spend thousands on bespoke knives; a well-sharpened and well-maintained boning knife will be more than enough to get all the meat processing jobs done. Get your knife professionally sharpened from time to time, or buy some sharpening stones and a steel and learn how to do it yourself.

Thermometer

Investing in a good-quality probe thermometer is well worth it. It's essential for checking the internal temperatures of smallgoods when they finish cooking, and for monitoring the cooling process. It's also useful when roasting or grilling meats. I might have come from the school of poking and prodding things with my fingers to assess the doneness, but I've learnt that intuition will never get you as far as fact. I love Thermapen probe thermometers. They're on the expensive side, but give you an instant result.

I also recommend buying an oven thermometer to validate your oven's thermostat. You'd be surprised how many ovens run hotter or colder than what's written on the dial.

Brining needle

A brining needle, which is effectively a big syringe with a perforated needle on the end, is essential for brining meats, and will help ensure that the brine is evenly distributed, avoiding the chance of a patchy finished product. Brining needles are inexpensive and readily available online or in kitchenware stores.

Mincer

If you're serious about making sausages, I'd recommend getting a small electric mincer. These make sausage making a lot easier and also make a wonderful tool for passing tomatoes and vegetables for ragùs and sauces. Most mincers come with different-sized plates, which determine the texture of the mince. The plates we use are a 3 mm (⅛ in) fine plate, 5 mm (¼ in) medium plate and 10 mm (½ in) coarse plate.

Filler

The very first sausages I made were made using a small piston filler. In fact, the sausages in this book were made with that very filler. If you're going to pursue sausage making at home, buy a decent benchtop piston filler, which is operated by putting the sausage mix into the hopper and then turning the crank to extrude the meat through the nozzle to fill your casing.

pH meter

This is used to measure the pH level – or acidity and alkalinity – of a product. It's essential to monitor the pH during the fermentation process of salami making. There are different brands on the market; we use Hanna Instruments.

Fermentation chamber

A fermentation chamber is used in salami making to provide the perfect conditions to kickstart fermentation. The particular culture you're adding to your salami will dictate the temperature and humidity you'll need to maintain. For our salami or saucisson recipe, you're looking to hang the sausages at around 25°C (77°F) with up to 90% humidity to get the bacteria in the culture working at their peak.

Maturing chamber

When making salami and dry-cured meats, you'll need a refrigerator or room set to specific conditions to allow the products to dry correctly. The ideal conditions are around 10–16°C (50–61°F) and 75–85% humidity. It doesn't take much for the conditions in any chamber to fluctuate, so it's necessary to check the progress frequently to make sure things aren't too dry or humid.

There are products available on the market that are used to hold, dry and mature meats, as well as thrifty DIY options – look online for different ideas and plans.

Smoker

We have a few smokers at LP's. Our main one is our massive Southern Pride smoker, which has become synonymous with LP's. We couldn't live without it. There are plenty of options for home use, many of which are discussed in more detail in the smoking section of this book (see pages 153–155).

Salt

Salt... what an ingredient! I use a variety of different salts for different purposes. For all my baseline cooking, like seasoning water for blanching or making brine, I use fine salt, because it dissolves easily. I am, however, apprehensive about using fine salt for seasoning salads, meats and other dishes because I find it too astringent and overpowering.

For curing meats or for smallgoods I like to use flossy salt, which has a larger grain that's similar to kosher salt. You can buy it online. For cooking, or for seasoning salads, meats and basically everything else, I use flaky salt, which has crystals in the shape of fine blossoms, sheets or pyramids. It typically flakes through the fingertips nicely, which gives a feeling of accuracy when seasoning.

Sodium nitrite and sodium nitrate

These two curing salts are used to produce smallgoods and charcuterie. Sodium nitrite is used in cured products that are cooked, such as bacon, ham, corned beef and various sausages, and is sometimes sold as curing salt number 1. In all the recipes that contain nitrite in this book, it is optional. However, the products will not keep their attractive pink hue or preserving properties, and will lose some of the sharp flavour normally associated with cured foods.

Sodium nitrate, on the other hand, is used in dry-cured products, such as salami, prosciutto and 'nduja. It's sometimes sold as curing salt number 2. For the recipes that contain nitrate (pages 83 and 89), this is a mandatory addition that safeguards against botulism (see pages 80–81).

Nitrate and nitrite are usually sold as blends mixed into regular salt. Sometimes these blends can have different amounts or ratios added, so it's crucial to check the packet instructions to ensure the correct amount is used, and to make sure all food safety practices are followed (see pages 80–81). Both these products are available online through butcher supply stores.

Dextrose

Dextrose is a simple sugar that's derived from corn or wheat, and is almost identical to glucose. It's 100% fermentable, so it's brilliant in fermented-meat products as a way to feed starter cultures and achieve acid production and a pH drop. Find it in health food shops or online.

Crushed ice

Some of the recipes in this book – mainly the sausages – contain crushed ice, which helps to increase myosin development and elongate the mixing time (giving you a better texture), and also keep everything cold. At LP's we have a dedicated ice machine that produces flaked ice. At home you can often blend up small quantities of ice in a blender or a Thermomix – some are even designed to do it. In a pinch – or if you're having a bad day – you can also wrap the ice in a clean towel and hit it with a rolling pin.

Cultures

Cultures are isolated strains of beneficial bacteria or moulds that are useful in fermented smallgoods production to ensure the strains that take hold are the ones you want. There are many different types that give different results, such as lowering pH or speeding up fermentation. You can order specific cultures from butcher or smallgood supply stores. Please take note of the manufacturer's instructions as the ratios and quantities needed can vary.

Sanitising spray

For our meat production, we use a commercial food-safe sanitiser that we spray on all our equipment and surfaces after we've cleaned them with hot soapy water. Sanitiser ensures most bacteria are killed on any surfaces that will come into contact with our products to keep them food safe.

At home, and especially whenever you're working with mincers and sausages, it's a good idea to clean all your equipment with hot soapy water, then spray it with sanitiser after use, just to be safe.

CHAPTER ONE

SAUSAGES

CONTENTS

INTRODUCTION 19
SAUSAGE BASICS 22
SAUSAGE CASINGS 24

SALSICCIA 26
COOKING AND STORING SAUSAGES 30
BRATWURST 32
   BRATWURST WITH PICKLED CABBAGE AND MUSTARD 32
COTECHINO 35
   COTECHINO WITH LENTILS AND SALSA VERDE 36
MORTADELLA 38
PEPPERONI 43
   PEPPERONI PIZZA 44
BOUDIN NOIR 47
   BOUDIN NOIR WITH FRIED EGGS AND BROWN SAUCE 47
SCHINKENWURST 48
FRANKFURTS 51
   HOT DOGS 51
CHEESE KRANSKY 52
PIG'S-HEAD SAUSAGES 55
   PIG'S-HEAD SAUSAGE MUFFIN 56

If I think about my earliest memories of barbecues as a child, I remember loving sausages. There's something so perfect about a hot sausage served in a slice of bread. Whether it's with tomato sauce, mustard, onions or just straight up, it's always undeniably delicious.

When sausages are made with consideration and care, they can be the perfect mouthful, encompassing meat, fat, spice, salt, snap and bite in one package. A well-put-together sausage is instantly recognised by our palate as something delicious that ticks all the boxes of good taste. Sausages are also a comforting and humble food, something that can be eaten at any time of day.

While the most basic definition of a sausage is minced meat encased in the intestines of an animal (not necessarily of the same species), sausages come in all shapes and sizes, and can be found in some form in almost every corner of the planet. Think of Germany's extensive repertoire of wursts, of Thailand's fermented sai krok Isaan, of China's sweet lap cheong or Hawaii's preference for Spam. A cheese board in Australia or New Zealand might well feature cabanossi. In France, saucisson is just one link of many.

The list of what is and what isn't a sausage is vast and full of diversity. Hamburger patties aren't considered sausages, for example, but a patty of breakfast sausage, which has distinct sausage spicing and no casing, and might be served in a sandwich or an English muffin (see page 56), somehow is. Is haggis a sausage? Are rissoles or ćevapi? Is breakfast cereal a soup?

Regardless of style, in many instances sausages have their origins in peasant cooking – throughout history, they've had a close association with preservation and thrift, hence the prevalence of trim, skin, blood and bits, and a casing made from intestines.

Today, butchers and charcutiers still use trim and offcuts in the production of both fresh and cured sausages. If you like meat, it's good to remember that aside from being delicious, sausages play an integral part in using the whole animal. And, since sausage making has often been a way to make use of less

SAUSAGES

desirable cuts, or to preserve or extend provisions, it's still intrinsically linked to our growth as humans. Even as the craft has developed and approached art at the heights of gastronomy, the sausage remains fundamental and, ultimately, humble. You should care about sausages.

At LP's, we've always been inspired most by European sausage varieties, and I've turned to books for inspiration and methods. I was gifted Ryan Farr's *Whole Beast Butchery* when I left Blue Hill; I've also studied his *Sausage Making* book. Brian Polcyn and Michael Ruhlman's books *Charcuterie* and *Salumi* have been constant references, while Elias Cairo, of Portland's Olympia Provisions, is my sausage hero. I not only love his book, but his work in general, and I've watched more than a few of his YouTube videos. Then there's all the inspiration that comes from simply eating, travelling and tasting: the French charcutiers, beautiful sausage displays at artisan butchers, where craft and craftmanship is on full show.

When LP's first opened, we had a plan that we were going to make a number of different smoked products and, needless to say, sausages were going to feature heavily. We had a few pieces of equipment, including a hand-and-knee-operated piston filler with a 20-kilogram capacity. At the time, we thought all of this equipment felt like overkill for what we were going to be doing. As we would later find out, it was nowhere near enough.

In those early days, we would make our sausages during the day and smoke them each afternoon for service that night. Our sausages were good, but at times we did experience inconsistencies, particularly with texture. Occasionally we would have very greasy sausages or a poor bind. However, with time and refinement through repetition, and as we learnt about the importance of strict temperature control and the order in which ingredients are added, our products improved dramatically.

Today, the repertoire of sausage products we make at LP's is the result of a decade of testing different recipes and refining the ones that we love. Unfailingly, we've found that the simpler recipes end up being the best, exhibiting a clarity of flavour that a complicated muddle of spices and flavours tends to suppress. We like to focus on the flavour of meat and salt, with the seasonings designed to elevate and complement, not overtake.

As a chef, I have always approached making sausages in the same way as any other dish. I think about how to make the flavours pop, and mix the seasonings just before adding them to the meat mix. This means toasting and grinding spices, grating garlic and picking herbs right before mixing. It makes complete sense if you are wishing to make something of substance and bright flavour, however this isn't common practice in the world of

THE SAUSAGE REMAINS FUNDAMENTAL AND, ULTIMATELY, HUMBLE. YOU SHOULD CARE ABOUT SAUSAGES.

sausage making – a lot of producers will simply buy pre-made sausage 'meals' made from spice mixes, dried herbs and garlic powder. They taste stale and bland. If you're going to go to the effort of making your own sausages, freshly ground spices and seasonings are a must.

It then follows that the better quality meat you use, the better the result will be; just because something is made from trim or offcuts doesn't mean the quality should suffer. Buy the best you can, from a butcher you trust, and the results will speak for themselves.

Unlike the saucisson you'll find in the Curing & Fermenting chapter, all the sausages in this chapter are cooked in some way. And most, except perhaps the mortadella and the schinkenwurst, are best served hot – sausages are always better hot as the flavours awaken and become fragrant. I've given recipes throughout, but I still love eating sausages straight from the barbecue or smoker with nothing more than some mustard. (That being said, eating a cold sausage from the fridge post-barbecue – while leaning over the kitchen sink – is also immensely satisfying.)

When it comes to cooking a raw sausage on a barbecue or in the pan, or reheating a cold one, I like to use the absolute lowest setting. Otherwise it

IF YOU'RE GOING TO GO TO THE EFFORT OF MAKING YOUR OWN SAUSAGES, FRESHLY GROUND SPICES AND SEASONINGS ARE A MUST.

tends to colour too fast, or even burn, before the inside is heated through. This can be avoided by gently poaching sausages before grilling or frying them, allowing them to heat up slowly and ensuring the inside is hot and the sausages are plump and snappy. Ideal.

Imagination and visualisation lend themselves well to sausage making, which usually begins with a forcemeat – the uniform mixture of lean meat and fat that's made by grinding or sieving the ingredients to a smooth or coarse texture. Forcemeats are used to produce numerous items found in charcuterie, including quenelles, sausages, pâtés, terrines, roulades and galantines.

Once you've made some of the products in this book, you can really run wild. A lot of these products can be formed into different shapes to create different results. Once you've combined the pork and seasonings to make the forcemeat for mortadella, for example, you can then use the same mix to make beautiful tortellini in brodo. Or when you've made a sausage mix, you don't have to put it into a hog casing for traditional links. Instead, use a larger casing so you can cut yourself a sausage patty for a Sunday morning egg muffin.

Once you understand the methods and techniques, you can fully go down the rabbit hole: substitute different meats, tweak seasonings, tinker with different casings. The options, and the opportunities, are endless.

Sausage basics

Most of the sausages in this chapter follow the same general method as the salsiccia recipe on pages 26–29. Consider this your primer, then flip through the other pages to see how else you can put your new-found skills to use. Before we begin, though, there are a few variables that need to be kept in check to produce results consistently and safely.

Firstly, you need to make sure your work area and equipment are super clean. This means that everything should be cleaned with hot, soapy water and sanitised, ideally with an unscented spray, and wiped clean. Check that there's no residual meat or grime left on equipment from last time.

The general ratio for making sausages is 70 per cent lean meat to approximately 30 per cent fat. This can be adjusted and scaled for different results and recipes. It may seem like a lot of fat, but fat is an integral part of sausages, not only adding flavour but providing juiciness; dry sausages are not good.

FAT IS AN INTEGRAL PART OF SAUSAGES, NOT ONLY ADDING FLAVOUR BUT PROVIDING JUICINESS; DRY SAUSAGES ARE NOT GOOD.

Another rule in sausage making is that the meat needs to be kept as cold as possible the whole time you're processing it. This means minimising the time the meat is out of the refrigerator and chilling it whenever you're not working with it.

You can also keep the temperature down by refrigerating or freezing all the equipment you will be using – putting the mincer attachments, mixer bowl, paddle attachment and filler in the fridge or freezer to chill before use will help keep everything cold throughout.

You will notice that we add approximately 12 per cent crushed ice to all our sausage recipes. This isn't because we're following the shady-butcher, water-equals-profit model. Instead, it's done to keep the temperature down, which means we can lengthen the mixing time, resulting in a more integrated forcemeat. More importantly, the ice aids in a wonderful reaction: when meat is combined with salt and ice and mixed at 0–4°C (32–39.2°F), it promotes the extraction of a protein called myosin. Myosin makes the mixture feel sticky and tacky, and begin to appear thread-like. You may have noticed something similar if you've hand-kneaded meatballs or slapped together a dumpling filling.

One great feature of myosin protein is that it helps emulsify the lean meat with the fat, thereby allowing the meat to encapsulate and hold the fat in the sausage. The result is a tight emulsification that keeps the fat from running out during cooking, pricking or slicing. A sausage in which the myosin is well developed has a better texture, and is juicier and more delicious.

When mixing our sausages, we start with the meat, salt and crushed ice. After a couple of minutes of mixing, we begin to see the meat and salt work their magic as the myosin develops and the mixture becomes tacky and sticky; this is a sign that the forcemeat is developing myosin and will do its job of clinging to the fat.

The next step is to add what we call the 'spice kit', which in the salsiccia recipe would be the fennel seeds, pepper, chilli flakes and garlic. Whenever possible, the spice kit ingredients should be ground fresh and at the very last minute in order to preserve the bright, fresh flavours.

When the sausage mix has been mixing for a couple of minutes and the spices are evenly distributed throughout, it's time to add the fat. After a couple more minutes of mixing, check to see if the fat has been thoroughly mixed through – it's always satisfying to see a good definition of pieces of meat and fat in the finished sausage. It's then time to remove the forcemeat from the mixer and load the filler. If you're not filling the casing straight away, the mix can go back in the fridge.

Sausage casings

If you're a first-time sausage maker, it's likely that what will strike you most when you first fill sausages is the ridiculous feeling of the casings slipping and sliding wildly around the bench as they fill. That's the fun part, but before you thread your first casing onto the filling horn, there's an important question to ask: which casing is best?

There are a number of different products that can be used for encasing meat to make sausages. **Man-made casings**, such as collagen casings, are made from a natural membrane that sits underneath a cow's hide, which is then melted down and formed into casings of considerable length. They are very consistent in size, and the long length means sausage makers don't have to keep putting a new casing on the filling horn every couple of minutes. These casings have their place, but they can have a rubbery or chewy texture and can look a bit suspicious or fake. It doesn't feel like you are doing the sausage gods justice by using them.

24　　　　　　　　　　　　　　　　QUALITY MEATS

Some products use a **fibrous or synthetic casing**. These are designed to be removed before eating and can be used for cooked and dried products. They're also good for large products, such as mortadella, since natural casings don't get that large. Fibrous casings benefit from being soaked in warm water for 15 minutes before filling, which makes them a bit more supple so they can be filled to their full potential.

Finally, there are **natural casings**, which are simply the cleaned and salted intestines of animals. Apart from a few products that require fibrous casings (such as mortadella, as mentioned, and schinkenwurst), natural casings are my casing of choice. They have an irresistible texture and inimitable snap after cooking, and using them feels like the right thing to do. They're also easy to source – they're readily available online, and your local butcher will probably sell you some if you're in a pinch.

There are a couple of things worth knowing before you get started, which go all the way back to processing at the abattoir, where the intestines are cleaned and packed in salt before being graded into different widths, then repacked in salt ready for sale. Since they're a natural product and the grading is done by hand and eye, you'll find that natural casings can be slightly inconsistent in size, with a slight variance in the width of sausages even when made with casing from the same batch. It is the nature of the beast, so to speak.

Natural casings can also occasionally have varying visual characteristics, such as webbed patterns on the surface with little 'feathers' on them. These are tiny, naturally occurring threads that are all over casings. They can be painstakingly removed, and some butchers go down this path for visual appeal, but to me they're just indicative of a natural product, and once you cook the sausages, they sizzle off and disappear anyway. Embrace and respect the true nature of natural casings!

Almost all natural casings come packed in salt and can range in size from tiny little lamb casings to massive beef bungs. Regardless of the size or type, they must be rinsed to remove the excess salt and then soaked in ample fresh, clean water. This allows them to rehydrate and become supple and flexible so they can be filled tightly and to their full potential. If casings are not soaked thoroughly, they can be brittle and may burst during filling.

Casings can be a bit tricky to work with at times, and you may find yourself swearing as you try to untangle seemingly impossible knots. Be patient, and a plump, appealing sausage will be the delicious reward.

> **NATURAL CASINGS ARE MY CASING OF CHOICE. THEY HAVE AN IRRESISTIBLE TEXTURE AND INIMITABLE SNAP AFTER COOKING, AND USING THEM FEELS LIKE THE RIGHT THING TO DO.**

SALSICCIA

This is effectively an Italian-style pork and fennel sausage. It's a great go-to, not only for filling sausage casings that can then be poached, smoked or grilled, but for many other preparations, too – try it torn into chunks to toss through pasta or scatter over pizza, use it as a filling for sausage rolls or a coating for Scotch eggs… you name it. The flavours here are simple, but this base recipe has as many variations as you can imagine. If you're not a fan of fennel seed, take it out or replace it with cumin. Don't like spicy food? Lose the chilli. The door is open – dream big. You could be onto the next award-winning sausage.

You can ask your butcher to mince the meat and fat for you, but if you'd like to do it yourself, you'll need a mincer with 5 mm (¼ in) and 10 mm (½ in) plates and a sausage filler. If you don't have a filler, you can use a piping bag to fill your casings, securing the open end with a rubber band. You'll also need a stand mixer, ideally with the bowl and paddle attachment chilled.

Regardless of whether the sausages are going to be poached, smoked or cooked from raw on a barbecue (see pages 30–31), it's good to let them hang in the refrigerator overnight. This allows the seasonings to develop and flavour the sausages, but also allows any excess water from the filling stage to drip off, and the casing to dry out a little. The sausages can be hung together on a hook, but it's beneficial to use a rod so they can hang without touching, meaning air can circulate between each link. This will help the surface become tacky and form a pellicle – a fine film or coating that allows smoke to better adhere, resulting in an even, tanned colour; sausages that are smoked while wet will have a streaky, uneven appearance. Hung sausages will also 'bloom', meaning the casing becomes transparent and the filling becomes more visible and attractive.

MAKES 1 KG (2 LB 4 OZ)

1 metre (39½ in) of 26–28 mm (1 in) hog casing (see pages 24–25)
700 g (1 lb 9 oz) skinless pork shoulder, coarsely diced
300 g (10.5 oz) pork fat, coarsely diced
120 g (4.25 oz) crushed ice
17 g (0.6 oz) fine salt

SPICE KIT

4 g (0.1 oz) toasted fennel seeds
4 g (0.1 oz) freshly ground black pepper
1 g (0.05 oz) chilli flakes
1 garlic clove

1. Rinse the casing under a tap to remove excess salt, then soak it in a bowl of water at room temperature for at least 2 hours before use.
2. If you're going to mince the filling yourself, put the diced pork shoulder and pork fat in the freezer separately, along with the mincer attachment, mixing equipment and sausage filler attachments, about an hour before you start. You want the pork to be slightly crunchy, around 0°C (32°F), but not frozen. If you've bought minced pork shoulder and fat from your butcher, ignore this step and step 4.
3. Weigh out the spice kit. Toss the fennel seeds, pepper and chilli flakes together in a small bowl. (The garlic clove can be grated into the mixture with a microplane at the last minute, so hold off on this for now.)
4. Set up the mincer with the 10 mm (½ in) plate. Working quickly, take the pork shoulder out of the freezer and put it through the mincer. Return the pork to the freezer, then put the pork fat through the mincer using the 5 mm (¼ in) plate. You want the mincer to be cutting the fat so it comes through the plate in small pieces rather than looking like a squishy mousse; return it to the freezer if needed before trying again.

5. Put the minced pork shoulder, crushed ice and salt into the chilled bowl of a stand mixer fitted with the chilled paddle attachment. Mix slowly for approximately 2 minutes. You'll start to notice the mixture becoming sticky and tacky. This is the sign of successful myosin extraction (see page 23).
6. Turn off the mixer and add the spice kit, grating the garlic directly into the bowl, then turn the mixer back on until the spices are thoroughly mixed in, approximately 2 minutes.
7. Turn off the mixer and add the minced pork fat, then turn the mixer back on until the fat is thoroughly mixed in and you can see small, clearly defined chunks of fat throughout the forcemeat.
8. Turn off the mixer, remove the paddle and put the whole bowl in the fridge until you're ready to fill the casing.
9. At this stage you can check the seasoning by pinching off a small clump of sausage mix and giving it a quick sizzle in a frying pan. (This is wise if you're going to start making large batches – you don't want to get all the way to the filling step and then remember you forgot the salt.) Check how it tastes: you can add more seasoning if you like, otherwise take a note for next time to adjust the quantities to your preference.
10. Set up the chilled sausage filler. Make sure the horn and seals are assembled correctly so there are no leaks. Taking note of how big the mouth of your filler is, use a wet hand to scoop up an appropriately sized ball of forcemeat and slam it back into the mixing bowl to remove any excess air. Then, as accurately as possible, slam the ball of forcemeat into the mouth of the filler. (Try to get it into the filler cleanly and tightly to push out any air so that you don't end up with air pockets in your sausages.) Repeat until you've used all the mix or the filler is full.
11. Open one end of the soaked casing and pour in some water, allowing it to run all the way through from end to end to get rid of any salt on the inside of the casing. Slide the casing onto the filler, bunching it up on the horn, and tie off the other end with a knot. (You want most of the casing to be on the horn, with just a little overhang, so the sausage fills from the tied end first.)
12. Make sure the bench you're working on is wet – this will allow the sausage to slide around as it fills, mitigating the risk of the casing tearing. Begin to crank the handle on the filler, trying to be as steady and smooth as possible; it's best to use one hand to turn the filler and the other to

»

gently hold the casing on the horn as it fills and is pushed off. There needs to be a slight resistance to ensure the casing is firm, even and full of forcemeat, but not so tight that it's likely to burst. Keep in mind that you still need to be able to twist and link the sausages afterwards.

13. Once you've filled the casing, tie off the open end with another knot. The sausage is easiest to manage at this stage if you create a big spiral on the bench. Inspect the filled casing all over and look for air pockets. If you do find any air pockets, they can be pricked with the tip of a sharp knife – the air will then be expelled when the sausages are linked.

14. Begin linking by pinching about a hands-length down from the knot at the end of the sausage and giving two full twists. You can make the sausages whatever length you like, but there is definitely an appealing look to a sausage that's the traditional length of around 15 cm (6 in): it just looks right. You'll notice that this twisting tightens the sausage and makes the casing fill out slightly. Measure another length and pinch again, this time twisting the sausage in the opposite direction. (Twisting in alternate directions each time will mean the whole thing doesn't unravel when it's hung up to dry.) Continue linking along the entire length of the sausage.

15. Hang the sausages on a rod or hook in the refrigerator overnight, with a bowl underneath to catch any drips.

16. Cook the sausages following the instructions on pages 30–31.

SAUSAGES

COOKING AND STORING SAUSAGES

Once you've made your sausages, there are a few ways to cook them: poaching, smoking and frying or barbecuing from raw.

POACHING

This method involves gently cooking the sausages in a deep pot of water. You want the water sitting at around 80°C (176°F) and the pot to be of a decent-enough size that the sausages are not crowded and the water can move around and cook the sausages evenly. Drop the sausages into the water and adjust the heat to maintain a steady 80°C (176°F) temperature. Depending on the size of the sausages, poach them for 20–30 minutes or until the internal temperature of a sausage reads 65°C (149°F) on a probe thermometer.

You can serve the poached sausages as they are or give them a quick sizzle in a hot frying pan to add some colour.

SMOKING

To smoke the sausages, start a smoker or a barbecue and maintain the temperature at around 80°C (176°F). Add wood or woodchips to get a steady flow of smoke, then add the sausages. The sausages are ready when the internal temperature reads 65°C (149°F) on a probe thermometer; this will take approximately 1–1½ hours. (See pages 152–155 and page 165 for more detailed information about smoking.)

CHILLING AND STORING

Once the poached or smoked sausages have reached the correct internal temperature, the cooking process can be halted by plunging the sausages into a bowl filled with ice and water. Not only will this allow the sausages to stay plump, it also accelerates the cooling process to minimise the time the sausages are sitting in the bacterial danger zone of 4–60°C (39.2–140°F). The sausages can stay in the water for up to 5 minutes before being removed and hung up to dry in the fridge once again. (If you've smoked your sausages, don't worry about their beautiful tan washing off; it won't.)

The sausages can now be frozen for up to a month. Poached sausages can be kept in the fridge for up to a week, smoked sausages for up to 2 weeks.

REHEATING

Because poached or smoked sausages have already been cooked, there's a slower heat transfer compared with raw sausages, meaning it's important to heat them gently. If the heat is too intense, the sausages will burn on the outside before the inside is hot. The best way to proceed is to bring a pot of water to just below a simmer, then drop the sausages into the water to heat through for 5–10 minutes. This heats them slowly and plumps them up but also makes the casing super snappy. From this point, they'll only require the most minimal sizzle on a barbecue or in a frying pan.

COOKING FROM RAW

Of course, you can also cook the raw sausages in a frying pan or on a barbecue, just as you might with ones you've bought. One detail to note – and that is often overlooked – is that the heat should be kept low, otherwise the outside of the sausage can burn before it cooks through. Check your sausage is cooked by cutting a slice from the end and looking inside, or go all out (you've made these yourself, after all) and use a probe thermometer to check that the internal temperature has reached 65°C (149°F).

SAUSAGE SIZZLE

Once you've mastered sausage making, throwing a sausage party is a great way to try a few different types all at once. The key to a good time, though, is in the timing. Consider poaching some of the more delicate sausages beforehand so they only need a quick sizzle at the end, or start early and grill everything slowly over low heat, taking your time so they cook through without drying out and, of course, don't burn.

The best way to serve sausages is, obviously, gripped with a baseball mitt of sliced white milk bread (page 237) or on a soft white roll, topped with plenty of mustard like my beer mustard (page 228) or your favourite yellow American mustard (it has to be Golden State), and tomato sauce (I go for Heinz) or even barbecue sauce (page 220), should you feel the need.

BRATWURST

Sausages matter in Germany. There are laws about their purity, museums dedicated to them and more than a thousand kinds, with regionally specific variations. As famous as Volkswagen is for manufacturing cars, their Wolfsburg factory pumps out more currywurst – offered to its workers and sold in shops – than the company does vehicles. The sausage even has its own part number: 199 398 500 A.

This is to say that as simple as a bratwurst – Germany's most famous sausage – might seem, it's something to approach seriously, with a sense of respect. Ours are finely tooled to be light, with a prominent flavour of pork and subtle background spice. They are well suited to being doused with spiced ketchup and sprinkled with curry powder as with currywurst, but the best place to start, I think, is to simply grill them over charcoal. When the sun is shining, slowly grilling brats while drinking pilsner sounds like my idea of a good time. Serve your bratwurst with pickled cabbage, in bread or with potato salad. Just don't forget the mustard.

MAKES 1 KG (2 LB 4 OZ)

1 metre (39½ in) of 26–28 mm (1 in) hog casing
700 g (1 lb 9 oz) skinless pork shoulder, coarsely diced
300 g (10.5 oz) pork fat, coarsely diced
120 g (4.25 oz) crushed ice
18 g (0.6 oz) fine salt

SPICE KIT

40 g (1.5 oz) milk powder
5 g (0.2 oz) ground white pepper
2 g (0.1 oz) caraway seeds
1 g (0.05 oz) ground ginger
3 g (0.1 oz) mustard powder
1 g (0.05 oz) freshly grated nutmeg

1. Make the bratwurst by following the basic salsiccia recipe (page 26), using the ingredients listed here.
2. Cook and store the bratwurst following the methods on pages 30–31, according to your own preference. They will keep for up to a week in the fridge or a month in the freezer.

BRATWURST WITH PICKLED CABBAGE AND MUSTARD

Add the bratwurst to a pot of barely simmering water and gently heat them for 5 minutes. Meanwhile, drain some pickled cabbage (page 226) of most of its juice, then toss it with a drizzle of olive oil and a good grind of black pepper. Check the seasoning and add a little salt if needed. Pull the bratwurst from the water and give them a sizzle on the barbecue or in a frying pan to create some colour on each side. Serve the sausages with a pile of pickled cabbage and plenty of your favourite mustard – I recommend my beer mustard (page 228).

COTECHINO

This Italian sausage is seasoned with a heady mix of fragrant spices, along with the unusual ingredient of pig skin (the name cotechino comes from the word 'cotica', meaning rind). The skin is boiled before being added to the sausage mix, allowing it to soften and melt when the sausage is cooked, giving the sausage an incredibly rich and gelatinous quality.

Cotechino are typically cooked from raw in wet dishes where the gelatine melts into the cooking liquor, adding both viscosity and texture. We smoke them first to add another layer of flavour.

Start this recipe a day ahead to prepare the pork skin.

MAKES 1.25 KG (2 LB 12 OZ)

250 g (9 oz) pork skin
700 g (1 lb 9 oz) skinless pork shoulder, minced with 10 mm (½ in) plate
120 g (4.25 oz) crushed ice
20 g (0.7 oz) fine salt
1 g sodium nitrite — curing salt #1 (see page 15)
300 g (10.5 oz) pork fat, minced with 5 mm (¼ in) plate
1 metre (39½ in) of 26–28 mm (1 in) hog casing, rinsed of salt and soaked for at least 2 hours

SPICE KIT

10 g (0.4 oz) milk powder
5 g (0.2 oz) raw sugar
3 g (0.1 oz) ground white pepper
1 g (0.05 oz) ground coriander seeds
1 g (0.05 oz) ground cloves
1 g (0.05 oz) ground cinnamon
1 g (0.05 oz) ground cayenne pepper
1 g (0.05 oz) freshly grated nutmeg

1. Put the pork skin in a large saucepan and cover it with cold water. Bring to the boil, then turn down to a gentle simmer. Simmer the skin for approximately an hour or until you can fish it from the water and squeeze your fingers through it (be careful, it will be very hot). Once it's ready, remove the skin from the pot and place it in an uncovered dish in the fridge to cool overnight.
2. The next day, cut the pork skin into pieces that will fit into the mouth of your mincer. Mince the skin through the 5 mm (¼ in) plate, then chill until needed.
3. Weigh out the spice kit and toss the ingredients together in a small bowl.
4. Prepare the sausage mix by following steps 5–7 of the basic salsiccia recipe (page 27), using the minced pork shoulder, crushed ice, fine salt and curing salt (add the curing salt along with the fine salt). Beat until tacky, then beat in the spice kit, followed by the minced pork fat.
5. Once the fat has been mixed in, add the minced pork skin and mix slowly for a further 2 minutes or until thoroughly combined.
6. Fill, link and hang the sausages following steps 10–15 of the salsiccia recipe (pages 27–28) and making the sausages around 100 g (3.5 oz) each.
7. Smoke the sausages (see page 30), then chill in iced water, drain and refrigerate. The cotechino will keep for up to 2 weeks in the fridge or a month in the freezer. They're best gently reheated in a pot of water just below simmering point for 5–10 minutes, then sizzled in a frying pan or on the barbecue to add colour.

COTECHINO WITH LENTILS AND SALSA VERDE

Cotechino is traditionally eaten with lentils in Emilia-Romagna at Christmas and New Year. The lentils are said to represent Roman coins and to bring good fortune to those eating them. For me, the good fortune might just be the luxury of being able to enjoy this dish at any time of year.

SERVES 4

400 g (14 oz) green or Puy lentils
500 ml (17 fl oz) beef jus (page 235)
4 x 100 g (3.5 oz) cotechino
 (page 35)
Salsa verde (page 222), to serve

SOFFRITTO

1 carrot, finely diced
1 onion, finely diced
1 celery stick, finely diced
5 garlic cloves, finely diced
100 ml (3.5 fl oz) olive oil
5 fresh bay leaves
1 bunch thyme, leaves picked
1½ teaspoons tomato paste
 (concentrated purée)

1. Cast your eyes over the lentils to make sure there are no small stones in there. This is rare, but it happens. When you're sure they are free of debris, put the lentils in a saucepan and cover with cold water.
2. Bring the lentils to a simmer and gently cook for 30–40 minutes or until tender but still slightly firm inside. Stir and check them frequently by fishing one out and biting it. Strain the lentils through a sieve and spread them out on a tray to cool.
3. For the soffritto, put the carrot, onion, celery and garlic in a saucepan with a big pinch of salt and a grind of black pepper. Add the olive oil, bay leaves and thyme. Cook very gently and slowly over low heat. Think of it as trying to melt all the veggies down – they will become translucent and very soft. This should take 20–30 minutes. Add the tomato paste and cook for a further 5 minutes.
4. Add the lentils and beef jus to the soffritto and bring to a gentle simmer, stirring to combine well.
5. Meanwhile, add the cotechino to a saucepan of water and bring to a simmer, then cook for 5 minutes to heat the sausages through.
6. Remove the cotechino from the water and give them a quick sizzle on the barbecue or in a frying pan.
7. Taste the lentils and adjust the seasoning with salt and pepper.
8. Spoon the lentils into warm bowls, slice the cotechino and arrange them on top. Top with salsa verde, or serve it on the side.

MORTADELLA

Despite being revered in Italy, mortadella (pictured overleaf) and its variations (such as Devon or luncheon meat in Australia), were regarded with a little suspicion when I was growing up, and came with the reputation of being made from mystery meats. Fortunately, this isn't actually the case, and not only is well-made mortadella absolutely delicious, it's one of the world's most luxurious products.

There is an additional step to this sausage recipe that involves blending the mix in a food processor to make it very smooth before folding in the whole black peppercorns and cubes of pork fat. It can get a little messy as the mix is mousse-like and a bit sticky; take care to work as methodically and cleanly as possible.

MAKES 1 KG (2 LB 4 OZ)

- 50 g (1.75 oz) pork fat, cut into 1 cm (½ in) cubes, plus 260 g (9.25 oz) pork fat, minced with 3 mm (⅛ in) plate
- 730 g (1 lb 9 oz) lean skinless pork shoulder, minced with 3 mm (⅛ in) plate
- 250 g (9 oz) crushed ice
- 18 g (0.6 oz) fine salt
- 1.2 g sodium nitrite – curing salt #1 (see page 15)
- 4 g (0.1 oz) black peppercorns
- 1 metre (39½ in) of 110 mm (4¼ in) fibrous casing, soaked in warm water for 20–30 minutes

SPICE KIT

- 12 g (0.4 oz) caster (superfine) sugar
- 1 g (0.05 oz) ground cayenne pepper
- 1 g (0.05 oz) ground allspice
- 1 g (0.05 oz) ground cinnamon
- 1 g (0.05 oz) ground cloves
- 1 g (0.05 oz) freshly grated nutmeg
- 6 garlic cloves, finely grated

1. Blanch the cubed pork fat in a large saucepan of boiling water for 1 minute. Refresh in iced water, then drain well and dry on a clean tea towel. Place in an uncovered dish in the fridge until needed.
2. Weigh out the spice kit and toss the ingredients together in a small bowl.
3. Prepare the mortadella mix by following steps 5–7 of the basic salsiccia recipe (page 27), using the minced pork shoulder, crushed ice, fine salt and curing salt (add the curing salt along with the fine salt). Beat until tacky, then beat in the spice kit, followed by the minced pork fat.
4. Working in small batches so as not to overload the machine, transfer the mix to a food processor and blend until smooth. It should take around 2–3 minutes to form a homogenous texture with no visible pieces of meat or fat. Monitor the temperature with a thermometer while processing to make sure the mix doesn't exceed 11°C (52°F). If it's getting close to that, pop the processor bowl in the freezer for 20–30 minutes, then keep going.
5. Transfer the smooth forcemeat to a bowl and use a spatula to fold in the cubed pork fat and whole peppercorns.
6. Fill the mortadella following steps 10–13 of the salsiccia recipe (pages 27–28) to make one large sausage (you don't need to link the mortadella).
7. Hang the mortadella in the fridge overnight to let the ingredients meld and develop (put a bowl underneath to catch any drips).
8. The next day, preheat the oven to 80°C (175°F). Place the mortadella on a wire rack set over a baking tray and bake for approximately 7 hours or until a thermometer inserted into the centre reads 65°C (149°F).
9. Transfer the mortadella to iced water for 5–10 minutes, then drain and pat dry. Place in the fridge to cool completely. The mortadella will keep for up to 3 weeks in the fridge.

10. When you're ready to crack into the mortadella, cut it in half so you can see inside and admire your handiwork. Wrap one of the halves in plastic wrap and place it in the fridge. Peel the casing off the other half. Ideally, you'd have a gravity-feed slicer to shave it as thinly as possible. But I wouldn't expect you to have one at home – hell, I don't – so instead take your sharpest long knife and carefully shave off slices as thinly as you can. You can now make yourself a sandwich on a crisp soft bun with salsa verde (page 222), or simply fold those pink hankies over themselves on a plate with some pickles and good-quality bread and butter.

VARIATIONS

Blood bologna
For something a little different, and to raise a few pulses, you can substitute the crushed ice with frozen pig's blood. When sliced, blood bologna has a striking visual appeal and is very rich and tasty.

Kangaroo mortadella
We like to make a kangaroo mortadella as well. To do so, we follow the method above but substitute the lean pork mince with kangaroo mince. (You still have to use pork fat in the recipe as kangaroo meat is very lean.)

SERVING YOUR MORTADELLA

You can serve mortadella and any of these variations as part of a beautiful charcuterie plate or draped over pizza after it comes out of the oven. If you find yourself feeling poorly, or you're deathly hungover, you can always cut off a thick patty and fry it in a pan, then pop it on some bread with loads of butter and tomato sauce for a steadying fried bologna sandwich.

PEPPERONI

When we first started tinkering with this recipe, we couldn't believe how much it tasted just like… pepperoni! It's such a common flavour, but making it yourself really lets you pause and appreciate the complexity and deliciousness. Not only does this taste even better than the one you buy at the deli, it does all the aesthetic things, too – like curl up in the oven on top of a pizza to form those little pepperoni 'cups' (see page 45). We also love filling a large fibrous casing with this and using it sliced as a sandwich filling or as part of a charcuterie spread.

MAKES ABOUT 1 KG (2 LB 4 OZ)

700 g (1 lb 9 oz) skinless pork shoulder, minced with 5 mm (¼ in) plate
120 g (4.25 oz) crushed ice
22 g (0.8 oz) fine salt
1 g sodium nitrite – curing salt #1 (see page 15)
300 g (10.5 oz) pork fat, minced with 5 mm (¼ in) plate
1 metre (39½ in) of 34–36 mm (1¼ in) hog casing, rinsed of salt and soaked for at least 2 hours

SPICE KIT

40 g (1.5 oz) milk powder
10 g (0.4 oz) smoked paprika
6 g (0.2 oz) ground cayenne pepper
1 g (0.05 oz) ground allspice
1 g (0.05 oz) fennel seeds
2½ teaspoons white wine

1. Weigh out the spice kit and toss the ingredients together in a small bowl.
2. Prepare the sausage mix by following steps 5–7 of the basic salsiccia recipe (page 27), using the minced pork shoulder, crushed ice, fine salt and curing salt (add the curing salt along with the fine salt). Beat until tacky, then beat in the spice kit, followed by the minced pork fat.
3. Fill, link and hang the pepperoni following steps 10–15 of the salsiccia recipe (pages 27–28) and making the sausages around 250 g (9 oz) each.
4. Smoke the pepperoni (see page 30), then chill in iced water, drain and refrigerate. Pepperoni will keep for up to 2 weeks in the fridge or a month in the freezer.
5. The chilled pepperoni can be sliced with a sharp knife into discs about 2 mm (¹⁄₁₆ in) thick for pizza (page 44) or sandwiches.

PEPPERONI PIZZA

When my partner Tania was heavily pregnant with our son Frank she was constantly craving pizza, and I was more than happy to get on board with satisfying the urges. At the same time we were considering opening another business that LP's would be able to supply to make it all a tightly closed loop, and we had the lightbulb idea of opening a pizza place. We spoke with our business partners Joe Valore and Elvis Abrahanowicz of Porteño about the idea and – along with Frank – Bella Brutta was born.

You'll need to begin the dough 72 hours ahead. The dough has quite a low hydration, which makes it suitable for cooking at around 400°C (750°F). If you make a lot of pizza at home, I recommend getting a proper home pizza oven, such as a Gozney. If you're planning to bake this in a regular oven, turn it up as hot as it can go, add about 150 ml (5 fl oz) extra water to the dough, and increase the cooking time.

MAKES 6 x 30 CM (12 IN) PIZZAS

500 g (1 lb 2 oz) tinned San Marzano tomatoes
Caster (superfine) sugar, to taste
300 g (10.5 oz) fior di latte or mozzarella, cut into 2 cm (¾ in) cubes
100 g (3.5 oz) Parmigiano Reggiano
600 g (1 lb 5 oz) pepperoni (page 43), sliced into 2 mm (1/16 in) discs
Extra virgin olive oil, for drizzling
15 g (0.5 oz) toasted fennel seeds, lightly ground

PIZZA DOUGH

1½ teaspoons (2.5 g) dried yeast
600 ml (21 fl oz) chilled water
1 kg (2 lb 4 oz) tipo '00' flour
27 g (1 oz) fine salt
60 ml (2 fl oz) extra virgin olive oil

1. For the pizza dough, combine the yeast and chilled water in a bowl, cover and stand for 10 minutes or until frothy.
2. Combine the frothy yeast and flour in a stand mixer fitted with the dough hook attachment and mix until just shaggy. Leave the dough to stand for 15 minutes.
3. Add the salt and oil to the dough and mix until the dough is smooth and elastic, ensuring it doesn't reach a temperature above 24°C (75°F) – you can test it using a probe thermometer. Check that the dough is ready by performing a window-pane test: if you stretch it out thinly, you should be able to see the light through it. Transfer the dough to a lightly oiled bowl, cover the surface with plastic wrap and place in the fridge to ferment overnight.
4. The next day, divide the dough into six 280 g (10 oz) balls, place on a tray, cover and chill for 48 hours in the fridge.
5. Remove the dough from the fridge an hour before baking.
6. Push the tomatoes through a mouli or gently blend to a pulpy consistency in a food processor. Season with a pinch of sugar and salt.
7. Take one of the dough balls and stretch it out on a lightly floured bench to fit a pizza peel or tray. Ladle a spoonful of the tomato sauce onto the base and spread it out evenly, leaving a border of around 1.5 cm (⅝ in).
8. Distribute a handful of the diced fior di latte over the sauce and lightly grate some parmesan over the top. Arrange the pepperoni discs all over the pizza, but try not to have them overlapping.
9. Bake the pizza in a pizza oven for about 2 minutes or until the pizza is cooked and blistered.
10. Drizzle the pizza with olive oil and lightly season with the toasted fennel seeds. Repeat with the remaining dough balls to make six pizzas in total.

BOUDIN NOIR

The first time I was shown how to make boudin noir was at Blue Hill at Stone Barns in upstate New York. I've made countless variations since, following the traditions of Spain's morcilla and Italy's sanguinaccio.

This recipe is a mashup of my favourite things about all types of blood sausages. The boudin noir mix can be cooked in all kinds of ways – as breakfast sausages (pictured here), cocktail sausages, in rounds cut from a larger sausage (made with a 120 mm/4½ inch fibrous casing, perhaps) or even baked in terrine moulds in a water bath. The sausages here can be poached or smoked, following the directions on page 30.

Start this recipe a day ahead to prepare the rice and pork jowl.

MAKES 1 KG (2 LB 4 OZ)

100 g (3.5 oz) arborio rice
400 g (14 oz) skin-on pork jowl
200 g (7 oz) skinless pork shoulder, minced with 10 mm (½ in) plate
200 g (7 oz) pig's blood (ask your butcher)
50 g (1.75 oz) chopped walnuts
20 g (0.7 oz) currants
40 g (1.5 oz) caster (superfine) sugar
8 g (0.3 oz) fine salt
1 metre (39½ in) of 26–28 mm (1 in) hog casing, rinsed of salt and soaked for at least 2 hours

SPICE KIT

1 g (0.05 oz) finely grated garlic
1 g (0.05 oz) freshly grated nutmeg
1 g (0.05 oz) cocoa powder
1 g (0.05 oz) ground allspice
1 g (0.05 oz) ground cloves
1 g (0.05 oz) ground cinnamon
1 g (0.05 oz) chilli flakes

1. Put the rice in a small saucepan with 150 ml (5 fl oz) water. Bring to the boil, stir once, then cover, reduce the heat to low and gently cook for 10 minutes or until the water is fully absorbed. Fluff the rice with a fork, then spread it on a plate and refrigerate overnight, uncovered.
2. The same day, put the pork jowl in a large saucepan of water. Bring to a simmer, then cook for 45–60 minutes or until the jowl and skin are very tender. Refrigerate the jowl overnight in an uncovered dish.
3. The next day, chop the jowl, including the skin, into 1 cm (½ in) cubes.
4. Weigh out the spice kit and toss the ingredients together in a small bowl. Make sure all the other components are weighed and chilled.
5. Put the pork jowl cubes and rice in the chilled bowl of a stand mixer fitted with the chilled paddle attachment and add the pork shoulder, pig's blood, walnuts, currants, sugar, salt and spice kit. Mix slowly and gently until everything is thoroughly combined. You don't want to beat this too aggressively or the rice will break apart.
6. Fill, link and hang the sausages following steps 10–15 of the salsiccia recipe (pages 27–28). Hang the sausages over a bowl to catch any drips.
7. Chill the sausages until you're ready to cook them. They will keep for up to a week in the fridge or a month in the freezer.

BOUDIN NOIR WITH FRIED EGGS AND BROWN SAUCE

Heat two 80 g (2.75 oz) boudin noir in a saucepan of barely simmering water for 3–5 minutes. Meanwhile, fry 4 eggs in 3 teaspoons light olive oil over medium heat. As soon as the whites are cooked and crisp around the edges, remove the pan from the heat and add 15 g (0.5 oz) salted cultured butter. Slide the eggs onto warm plates. Give the sausages a sizzle in the buttery pan, then serve with the eggs and a dollop of brown sauce (page 221). Serves 2.

SCHINKENWURST

Schinkenwurst (or 'ham sausage' as it's known in English) is essentially a smooth, emulsified German sausage with pieces of cured ham suspended in it. When smoked and sliced, it has an incredible terrazzo-esque appeal. It's a very impressive product to make once you've familiarised yourself with the sausage-making and ham-brining methods in the book. I like saying 'schinkenwurst' almost as much as I like eating it.

MAKES 1.5 KG (3 LB 5 OZ)

730 g (1 lb 9 oz) skinless pork shoulder, minced with 3 mm (⅛ in) plate
250 g (9 oz) crushed ice
23 g (0.8 oz) fine salt
1.2 g sodium nitrite – curing salt #1 (see page 15)
260 g (9.25 oz) pork fat, minced with 3 mm (⅛ in) plate
500 g (1 lb 2 oz) raw brined ham (page 163), cut into 3 cm (1¼ in) cubes
1 metre (39½ in) of 120 mm (4½ in) fibrous casing, soaked in warm water for 20–30 minutes

SPICE KIT

12 g (0.4 oz) caster (superfine) sugar
4 g (0.1 oz) freshly ground black pepper
1 g (0.05 oz) ground coriander seeds
1 g (0.05 oz) freshly grated nutmeg
1 g (0.05 oz) ground cinnamon
6 g (0.2 oz) finely grated garlic

1. Weigh out the spice kit and toss the ingredients together in a small bowl.
2. Prepare the schinkenwurst mix by following steps 5–7 of the basic salsiccia recipe (page 27), using the minced pork shoulder, crushed ice, fine salt and curing salt (add the curing salt along with the fine salt). Beat until tacky, then beat in the spice kit, followed by the minced pork fat.
3. Working in small batches so as not to overload the machine, transfer the mix to a food processor and blend until smooth. It should take around 2–3 minutes to form a homogenous texture with no visible pieces of meat or fat. Monitor the temperature with a thermometer while processing to make sure the mix doesn't exceed 11°C (52°F). If it's getting close to that, pop the processor bowl in the freezer for 20–30 minutes, then keep going.
4. Transfer the smooth forcemeat to a large bowl and use a spatula to fold in the chunks of brined ham.
5. Fill the schinkenwurst following steps 10–13 of the salsiccia recipe (pages 27–28) to make one large sausage (you don't need to link the schinkenwurst).
6. Hang the schinkenwurst in the fridge overnight to let the ingredients meld and develop (put a bowl underneath to catch any drips).
7. The next day, preheat the oven to 80°C (175°F). Place the schinkenwurst on a wire rack set over a baking tray and bake for approximately 7 hours or until a thermometer inserted into the centre reads 65°C (149°F).
8. Transfer the schinkenwurst to a bowl of iced water for 5–10 minutes, then drain and pat dry. Refrigerate to cool completely. The schinkenwurst will keep for up to 2 weeks in the fridge.

SERVING YOUR SCHINKENWURST

Schinkenwurst is wonderful on a charcuterie plate or in any other scenario when you don't want to choose between ham and mortadella, such as on sandwiches, on pizza or as part of a ploughman's lunch.

FRANKFURTS

The burst and snap of a well-made frankfurt in a real lamb casing straight out of the smoker is unbeatable. I love seeing people crushing them when we serve them as hot dogs at our market stall on the weekends.

For the newly initiated, these can be slightly tricky to fill as the lamb casing is very thin and brittle. When it comes to twisting the links, if you do end up with a few that burst and pop, not to worry; just cut them open with a sharp knife, scoop the mix back into the filler and keep going.

If you're making hot dogs (pictured here), find a bakery that does a really soft roll – in Sydney, I like Organic Bread Bar in Darlinghurst. Andreas, the owner, makes an incredible long brioche roll. Make the franks slightly longer than your rolls so there's about an inch of overhang on each end. That first bite is the best.

MAKES 1 KG (2 LB 4 OZ)

500 g (1 lb 3 oz) skinless pork shoulder, minced with 3 mm (⅛ inch) plate
200 g (7 oz) crushed ice
11 g (0.4 oz) fine salt
1 g sodium nitrite – curing salt #1 (see page 15)
250 g (9 oz) pork fat, minced with 3 mm (⅛ in) plate
1 metre (39½ in) of 24–26 mm (1 in) lamb casing, rinsed of salt and soaked for at least 2 hours

SPICE KIT

30 g (1 oz) milk powder
5 g (0.2 oz) raw sugar
3 g (0.1 oz) ground white pepper
2.5 g (0.1 oz) sweet paprika
2.5 g (0.1 oz) ground coriander seeds
1.5 g (0.05 oz) mustard powder
1 g (0.05 oz) ground cayenne pepper
9 g (0.3 oz) finely grated garlic

1. Weigh out the spice kit and toss the ingredients together in a small bowl.
2. Prepare the frankfurt mix by following steps 5–7 of the basic salsiccia recipe (page 27), using the minced pork shoulder, crushed ice, fine salt and curing salt (add the curing salt along with the fine salt). Beat until tacky, then beat in the spice kit, followed by the minced pork fat.
3. Working in small batches so as not to overload the machine, transfer the mix to a food processor and blend until smooth. It should take around 2–3 minutes to form a homogenous texture with no visible pieces of meat or fat. Monitor the temperature with a thermometer while processing to make sure the mix doesn't exceed 11°C (52°F). If it's getting close to that, pop the processor bowl in the freezer for 20–30 minutes, then keep going.
4. Fill, link and hang the franks following steps 10–15 of the salsiccia recipe (pages 27–28). Use the small horn on the filler to accommodate the thin lamb casing and link the franks to your desired length.
5. Smoke the franks (see page 30) and serve them immediately or chill them in iced water, then drain and refrigerate. Franks will keep for up to 2 weeks in the fridge or a month in the freezer. They're best reheated by adding them to a large pot of water and bringing it to a gentle simmer, then cooking for about 5 minutes or until heated through.

HOT DOGS

Reheat the frankfurts as described in step 5. Drain the franks, then slot them into soft hot dog rolls. Spoon some mustard pickle relish (page 228) on top of the franks, followed by some finely diced white onion.

CHEESE KRANSKY

A smoked, cheese-filled sausage with Austrian roots and outsized popularity in Australia and New Zealand, cheese kransky have to be one of the most satisfying sausages to eat. Almost everywhere, they're a guilty pleasure – they feel naughty, maybe because they're so rich.

The sausage itself has a simple seasoning of garlic and black pepper, but it's the studs of cubed cheese that make it so exceptional – each bite reveals pockets of oozing molten cheese. Prepare yourself for scorched lips when you inevitably try to eat the kransky straight from the smoker, grill or poaching water.

MAKES ABOUT 1 KG (2 LB 4 OZ)

700 g (1 lb 9 oz) skinless pork shoulder, minced with 10 mm (½ in) plate
120 g (4.25 oz) crushed ice
20 g (0.7 oz) fine salt
1 g sodium nitrite – curing salt #1 (see page 15)
300 g (10.5 oz) pork fat, minced with 5 mm (¼ in) plate
230 g (8 oz) Swiss cheese, cut into 7.5 mm (¼ in) cubes
1 metre (39½ in) of 26–28 mm (1 in) hog casing, rinsed of salt and soaked for at least 2 hours

SPICE KIT

45 g (1.5 oz) milk powder
7 g (0.2 oz) freshly cracked black pepper
9 g (0.3 oz) finely grated garlic

1. Weigh out the spice kit and toss the ingredients together in a small bowl.
2. Prepare the kransky mix by following steps 5–7 of the basic salsiccia recipe (page 27), using the minced pork shoulder, crushed ice, fine salt and curing salt (add the curing salt along with the fine salt). Beat until tacky, then beat in the spice kit, followed by the minced pork fat.
3. Once the fat has been mixed in, add the diced cheese and mix slowly for a further 2 minutes or until thoroughly combined.
4. Fill, link and hang the kransky following steps 10–15 of the salsiccia recipe (pages 27–28) and making the kransky around 100 g (3.5 oz) each.
5. Smoke the kransky (see page 30), then sizzle them on a barbecue grill before serving. Alternatively, chill the smoked kransky in iced water, then drain and refrigerate. When you're ready to serve them, follow the reheating instructions on page 31. The kransky will keep for up to 2 weeks in the fridge or a month in the freezer.

SERVING YOUR KRANSKY

Cheese kransky are best served on bread – not only do you need the bread to insulate your hands from the looming heat within, it also makes a vehicle for different condiments and pickles to tag along. Try kransky straight up with my beer mustard (page 228), or add some sauerkraut or pickled cabbage (page 226), gherkins or relish, and enjoy with a cold beer.

PIG'S-HEAD SAUSAGES

This recipe uses fatty pork jowl as the fat component in the sausages, which gives them a wonderful gelatinous texture. The simple, subtle spices make these any-time-of-day all-rounder sausages, so it's worth having a try in a regular hog casing as well as the large-format fibrous casing. We use the fibrous casing when we're serving these on our breakfast sausage and egg muffins (see page 56).

MAKES ABOUT 1 KG (2 LB 4 OZ)

600 g (1 lb 5 oz) skinless pork shoulder, minced with 10 mm (½ in) plate
120 g (4.25 oz) crushed ice
16 g (0.6 oz) fine salt
1 g sodium nitrite — curing salt #1 (see page 15)
400 g (14 oz) trimmed pork jowl (no skin or glands), minced with 5 mm (¼ in) plate
1 metre (39½ in) of 26–28 mm (1 in) hog casing, rinsed of salt and soaked for at least 2 hours, or 110 mm (4¼ in) fibrous casing, soaked in warm water for 20–30 minutes

SPICE KIT

12 g (0.4 oz) milk powder
3 g (0.1 oz) ground white pepper
2 g (0.1 oz) ground ginger
5 g (0.2 oz) finely grated garlic

1. Weigh out the spice kit and toss the ingredients together in a small bowl.
2. Prepare the sausage mix by following steps 5–7 of the basic salsiccia recipe (page 27), using the minced pork shoulder, crushed ice, fine salt and curing salt (add the curing salt along with the fine salt). Beat until tacky, then beat in the spice kit, followed by the minced pork jowl.
3. Fill, link and hang the sausages following steps 10–15 of the salsiccia recipe (pages 27–28). You don't need to link the sausage if you are using the fibrous casing to make one large sausage.
4. Follow the poaching method if you are using the fibrous casing; follow either the poaching or smoking method if you are using the hog casing (see page 30).
5. Once the sausages reach 65°C (149°F), transfer them to a bowl of iced water for 5–10 minutes, then drain, pat dry and refrigerate to cool completely. Pig's head sausages will keep for up to a week in the fridge or a month in the freezer.

PIG'S-HEAD SAUSAGE MUFFIN

We make these over the weekends to serve at the markets for breakfast. They're the perfect one-handed brekkie to eat while perusing the organic vegetables.

Thanks on this one go to our ex-head chef Isobel Little – she concocted a genius way to cook the eggs so we weren't in the weeds frying hundreds of them to order. We coined it the 'aeroplane egg' for its convenience, not because it has the disappointing texture of the ones you might be served on a flight – far from it.

SERVES 4

6 free-range eggs
60 ml (2 fl oz) single (pure) cream
Oil spray, for greasing
Olive oil, for drizzling
4 pig's-head sausage patties (page 55), cut to 1 cm (½ in) thick
4 slices American 'burger' cheese
4 English muffins
Brown sauce (page 221)

1. Beat the eggs and cream in a bowl and season with salt.
2. Liberally spray a small, shallow non-stick baking tray with oil – it needs to be small enough that the egg will come approximately 1.5 cm (⅝ in) up the sides. Pour in the beaten egg mix, then tightly cover with plastic wrap and poke a couple of holes in the top. Place the baking tray in a steamer basket over simmering water and cook for 20 minutes or until the egg is set. Remove the baking tray from the steamer and refrigerate until completely cooled.
3. Remove the chilled egg from the tray and cut it into squares to fit the muffins.
4. Heat the barbecue or a couple of frying pans to medium–high heat, drizzle in a little olive oil, then add the sausage patties and fry until coloured on both sides. Remove from the heat and place a cheese slice atop each patty.
5. Split the muffins and place them in the toaster. Meanwhile, give the egg squares a quick fry in a lightly oiled pan over low heat just to heat through; you don't want too much colour.
6. Add a generous dollop of brown sauce to both of the muffin halves, place the cheesy sausages on the bases, then place the egg on top of that and close the lids. Once constructed, I like to wrap the muffins in greaseproof paper before eating; I find that the whole thing steams through in the residual heat and it all melds together.

CHAPTER .TWO.

CURING & FERMENTING

CONTENTS

INTRODUCTION	61
GUANCIALE	66
COPPA	69
BRESAOLA	70
BRESAOLA WITH PARMESAN CUSTARD	73
CURED SARDINES WITH PICKLED VEGETABLES	74
CURED SALMON (OR OTHER WILD-CAUGHT FISH)	75
PICKLED MUSSELS WITH CHILLI OIL	79
LEVEL UP: SALAMI	80
SAUCISSON	83
'NDUJA	89
TOAST WITH 'NDUJA, RICOTTA AND HONEY	90

Dry-cured meats are wonderful to eat. Sliced thinly, they're luxurious and special, akin to tasting an aged wine. And like wine, cured meat products have an air of mystery about them – how can a pig's leg rubbed with nothing more than salt be so overwhelmingly delicious?

I still recall trying jamón Ibérico for the first time. It blew my mind. Years later, while I was interning at restaurant Mugaritz and staying in the Basque Country, my affection for it was solidified.

It's fascinating that the combination of just meat, salt and time can create something so complex. But the truth is that exceptional jamón or coppa or salami doesn't just happen: someone has made this, watched it, paid close attention to it.

Dry-curing is considered the oldest form of preservation, and it's one of the simplest. In its purest form, it simply involves covering raw meat in salt for a number of days. The salt not only diffuses through the muscle, but slowly draws moisture to the surface, creating an environment that's inhospitable for pathogens and inhibits their growth.

It just so happens that this preservation process also intensifies the flavour and adds layers of depth and complexity. Apart from the protein and, in some cases, fat, cured meats have naturally high levels of glutamate and glutamic acid, the basis for MSG (almost pure umami), which goes some way towards explaining the moreish savouriness they offer.

Cured meats often carry a lot of tradition. Old World producers will bury pork legs in mountains of salt, knowing from generations of experience when they've taken on just the right amount. The way we do whole-muscle curing, however, is by percentage, using three per cent salt for the total weight of the meat. For example, if you are going to cure a piece of meat that weighs 2.75 kilograms, you'll need 82.5 g of salt. This salt is then distributed all over the muscle and rubbed into any nooks and crannies to make sure it's in contact with the whole surface.

The great thing about percentage curing is that the product cannot get overly salty from being left sitting in the cure. Also, it's more measurable and repeatable.

For whole muscles to cure effectively, they need to stay in the salt in the fridge for two days per kilogram (even if I'm working with smaller quantities, I don't leave them any less than two days to ensure they are properly cured). It's also good practice to flip the product over each day to redistribute the salt and the accumulated juices. In the curing world, this is called overhauling.

The meat is then hung up to dry in specific conditions while the salt continues to work its magic. When the meat has lost 30 per cent of its initial weight, it's ready to eat.

This preservation process can be applied to fish, too. Bacalao or salt cod, anchovies and gravlax are all examples of salting being used to halt or slow down degradation. Using varying levels of salt can also add complexity and transform the texture. We do this with salmon (see page 75), for example, while curing the likes of sardines or mussels in brine gives a quicker and altogether different result (see pages 74 and 79).

When we started looking at producing dry-cured products at LP's, it was to offer something more to the restaurant. We knew the rough theory of how to make the products, and were successfully making our own coppa, bresaola and guanciale in a temperature-controlled wine cellar rigged up with a domestic humidifier.

We also tried our hand at dry-cured hams, with varying results: some were fantastic, some not so good. The outlay of time with these large cuts is massive – to let a whole leg dry slowly can take up to a year – and when the time comes to cut the ham you might find it hasn't cured properly, it's gone rancid, or the bone hasn't been salted enough and has rotted through. The results can be extremely disappointing: a waste of time, precious space, and one or more beautiful pork legs.

It was for these reasons that we decided to stick to smaller cuts. Also, the relatively quick turnaround meant we could keep them rotating on the menu, and the results were consistent and good.

It wasn't until we decided to look at making salami that we realised there was a lot more to curing than just adding salt to meat and letting it happen. Because the meat for salami is minced, there's a risk that bacteria from the surface of the meat can be distributed throughout the sausage. Unlike with the dry-curing process, where the exterior comes into immediate contact with salt, the lower salt levels in salami recipes are sometimes not enough to deal with pathogens.

YOU CAN PUT A STICK OF SAUCISSON IN YOUR BAG WITH A SMALL KNIFE AND BE EQUALLY WELCOME AT A PICNIC OR A PARTY.

This is where fermentation begins to play its part, with the goal of helping to promote the growth of beneficial bacteria and prevent harmful pathogens taking hold. There are plenty of benefits to making your own fermented cured meats, but they come with risk, too, which is why we've gone into much more detail on pages 80–81, before the saucisson and 'nduja recipes – the only recipes in the book that use this method. Make sure you give it a read before you give either of those a crack.

Like many things in life, if you take your time and sink into the process, the doing can be just as satisfying as the results. And while there are certainly some specific matches that just seem to work (prosciutto – or coppa – and melon; bresaola and pear; salami and cheese on crackers... it's a long list), I think that when you've gone to the effort of making your own, it's best enjoyed on its own, pure and simple. You really want to taste it, analyse it and enjoy it, and experience the clarity of flavour. But go ahead and add some good bread, butter and pickles if you must.

If you do get to it, saucisson is my personal favourite. It's so funky and complex, not to mention portable. You can put a stick of saucisson in your bag with a small knife and be equally welcome at a picnic or a party. And it's also a meal on its own. A shopkeeper in Bordeaux once told me that a classic French dinner sometimes amounts to nothing more than a stick of saucisson and a bottle of wine. What a dream, especially if you've made it yourself.

CURING & FERMENTING

GUANCIALE

Guanciale is made from the jowl of the pig, which sits below the cheeks and adjoining the neck. Apart from being delicious, it's relatively easy to cure and doesn't take too long compared with some other preparations.

Guanciale is exceptional sliced thinly and served as it is, lending richness to a salad or else slipped on top of a hot pizza, where the fat becomes melty and translucent. It is also one of the key ingredients in carbonara.

This recipe is for one jowl, but if you're going to cure one you may as well cure two. Either way, you'll need a maturing chamber (see page 15) and some butcher's twine.

MAKES 1

1 skin-on pork jowl

CURE
Fine salt
Freshly ground black pepper

1. Begin by inspecting the pork jowl. Look carefully for any greyish glands that may be present on the meat (they can sometimes be a bit deceiving and look a little like the meat itself) – they aren't good to eat, so must be removed. Remove with a sharp knife, making long, clean cuts. You don't want to create any pockets in the meat where bacteria can hang out; also, holes don't look great in the finished product.

2. Weigh the jowl and write down this starting weight – you'll use it to determine when the jowl has lost enough moisture to be ready.

3. To prepare the cure, weigh out 3% of the weight of the jowl in salt, followed by 1.5% in freshly ground pepper. Mix the salt and pepper together in a container large enough to hold the jowl.

4. Take the jowl and rub the cure all over the skin and meat. Be careful to not lose any of the cure from the container. When the cure has been evenly distributed all over the jowl (you may have some excess), transfer the jowl to a resealable plastic bag along with any cure that's left in the container. Seal the bag, expelling as much air as you can.

5. Transfer the bag and its contents to a clean tray or bowl and put it in the fridge for the jowl to cure. As a rough rule, cure the jowl for 2 days per 1 kg (2 lb 4 oz); anything under this weight should still be cured for 2 days. Flip the bag each day to overhaul and redistribute the cure.

6. Remove the jowl from the bag and discard the remaining contents, then rinse the jowl under cold water and pat it dry with paper towel or a clean tea towel. Make a hole through the skin at one edge and tie a loop through it with some twine.

7. Hang the jowl up to dry in your maturing chamber with the setting between 10–16°C (50–61°F) and 70–80% humidity, until it has lost 30% of its initial weight. This should take about 3–4 weeks. Once dried, the guanciale will keep for at least 3 months in the fridge.

COPPA

Coppa, or capocollo, is made by dry-curing pork neck, a cut taken from the shoulder. It's a heavily marbled cut by nature, and as salumi it rivals dry-cured ham both in its intensity of flavour as well as its ease of curing.

Coppa is never more appealing than when it's thinly sliced and simply piled high, or draped over some freshly cut ripe fruit. Try rockmelon cut into cubes, or maybe some fancy wedges in a style reminiscent of the classic prosciutto and melon combination – it's even better with something sparkling in your glass.

You'll need a maturing chamber (see page 15) and some butcher's twine.

MAKES 1

1 pork neck
1 beef bung, rinsed of salt and soaked for at least 2 hours

CURE
Fine salt
Freshly ground black pepper
Fennel seeds
Chilli flakes

1. Inspect the pork neck and trim off any unsightly flaps of meat, using smooth strokes with a sharp knife. The neck needs to be a uniform shape and smooth all over with no nooks and crannies – they're ideal places for bacteria to hang out, and also don't look great in the finished product.
2. Weigh the pork neck and write down this starting weight – you'll use it to determine when the coppa has lost enough moisture to be ready.
3. To prepare the cure, weigh out 3% of the weight of the pork neck in salt, followed by 1% in freshly ground pepper, 1% in fennel seeds and 1% in chilli flakes. Mix these seasonings together in a container large enough to hold the neck.
4. Take the pork and rub the cure all over the meat. Be careful to not lose any of the cure from the container. When the cure has been evenly distributed all over the pork (you may have some excess), transfer the pork to a resealable plastic bag along with any remaining cure from the container. Seal the bag, expelling as much air as you can.
5. Transfer the bag and its contents to a clean tray or bowl and put it in the fridge for the pork to cure. As a rough rule, cure the pork for 2 days per 1 kg (2 lb 4 oz); anything under this weight should still be cured for 2 days. Flip the bag each day to overhaul and redistribute the cure.
6. Remove the pork from the bag and discard the remaining contents, then rinse the pork under cold water and pat it dry.
7. Stuff the pork neck into the soaked beef bung, taking care not to tear the casing. Working slowly, push the neck all the way into the end. Tie it off tightly with twine, then trim the excess casing. Make a loop with the twine, then prick the casing all over with the tip of a knife.
8. Hang the pork up to dry in your maturing chamber with the setting between 10–16°C (50–61°F) and 70–80% humidity, until it has lost 30% of its initial weight. This should take about 4–6 weeks. Once dried, the coppa will keep for at least 3 months in the fridge.

CURING & FERMENTING

BRESAOLA

Bresaola, referring to dry-cured beef, can be made from numerous cuts, but the most common is the eye round – in Italian called the girello – a perfectly round cylinder of marbled muscle that's ideal for this sort of treatment. We tend to use wagyu or a high-marble-score beef for the intense fatty marbling you get throughout. The result is such that when you hold thinly sliced pieces of the bresaola up to the light, they look like a stained-glass window.

You'll need a maturing chamber (see page 15), a netting sock (optional) and some butcher's twine.

MAKES 1

1 beef girello, ideally with a high marble score

CURE
Fine salt
Freshly ground black pepper

1. Inspect the beef and trim off any unsightly flaps of meat, using smooth strokes with a sharp knife. The beef needs to be a uniform shape and smooth all over with no nooks and crannies – they're ideal places for bacteria to hang out, and also don't look great in the finished product.
2. Weigh the beef and write down this starting weight – you'll use it to determine when the bresaola has lost enough moisture to be ready.
3. To prepare the cure, weigh out 3% of the weight of the beef in salt, followed by 1% in freshly ground pepper. Mix the salt and pepper together in a container large enough to hold the beef.
4. Take the beef and rub the cure all over the meat. Be careful to not lose any of the cure from the container. When the cure has been evenly distributed all over the beef (you may have some excess), transfer the beef to a resealable plastic bag along with any remaining cure from the container. Seal the bag, expelling as much air as you can.
5. Transfer the bag and its contents to a clean tray or bowl and put it in the fridge for the beef to cure. As a rough rule, cure the beef for 2 days per 1 kg (2 lb 4 oz); anything under this weight should still cure for 2 days. Flip the bag each day to overhaul and redistribute the cure.
6. Remove the beef from the bag and discard the remaining contents, then rinse the beef under cold water and pat it dry.
7. You can truss the beef as you would truss a roast in order to keep its shape even, or you can place it inside a netting sock. Either way, tie it off with a loop of twine.
8. Hang the beef up to dry in your maturing chamber with the setting between 10–16°C (50–61°F) and 70–80% humidity, until it has lost 30% of its initial weight. This should take about 4–6 weeks. Once dried, the bresaola will keep for at least 3 months in the fridge.

BRESAOLA WITH PARMESAN CUSTARD

This uses the bresaola from page 70 to make little canapés or snacks that go down very well with an aperitivo. You can use whatever vessel you wish for the custard and bresaola – crackers or small rounds of baguette would work well, but the gnocco fritto on page 236 would be my choice.

If you have any left-over parmesan custard, use it to fill gougères, or dollop it on a plate and top it with blanched green beans.

MAKES ABOUT 24 PIECES

Gnocco fritto (page 236), crackers or baguette rounds, to serve
Thinly sliced bresaola (page 70)

PARMESAN CUSTARD
150 g (5.5 oz) finely grated or blended Parmigiano Reggiano
100 ml (3.5 fl oz) milk, plus extra as needed
4 eggs

1. To make the parmesan custard, put the parmesan, milk and eggs in a saucepan and mix well.
2. Cook over low heat, stirring constantly, until the custard reaches 85°C (185°F) on a thermometer. It will be quite thick and look a little curdled.
3. Remove the pan from the heat and scrape the custard into a container. Cover and refrigerate until completely cool.
4. Put the chilled custard in a food processor and blend until there are no lumps (blending should bring the custard back to a homogenous consistency). If it is too thick and isn't blending easily, add a little more milk. The custard should be salty enough, but season it well with freshly ground black pepper.
5. Spoon the custard into a piping bag. Pipe a small dollop onto the gnocco fritto, crackers or baguette rounds. (You can also simply spoon it on.)
6. Lay a couple of bresaola slices on top of the custard. I like to scrunch them up slightly so they look wild and have a bit of shape.

CURING & FERMENTING

CURED SARDINES WITH PICKLED VEGETABLES

If you see sardines in immaculate condition at the fish markets, buy them. This recipe is a brilliant way to celebrate their freshness and, when served with smoked olive oil, capers and crème fraîche, cured sardines make for a truly delicious dish.

SERVES 4–6

12 whole sardines (or 24 fillets)
Fine salt
5 French shallots
2 garlic cloves
1 bunch baby carrots
½ bunch thyme leaves
5 fresh bay leaves
5 g (0.2 oz) black peppercorns
100 ml (3.5 fl oz) smoked olive oil
30 g (1 oz) salted capers, soaked for 20 minutes and rinsed
Crème fraîche, to serve

PICKLING LIQUID

250 ml (9 fl oz) cider vinegar
100 g (3.5 oz) caster (superfine) sugar
10 g (0.4 oz) salt

1. Clean and fillet the sardines and put them in a non-reactive container. Season heavily with fine salt – a good, generous sprinkle on both sides. Place in the fridge to cure for 30 minutes.
2. Meanwhile, prepare the vegetables. Peel the shallots and garlic and thinly slice them into rounds. Cut the carrots into 2 mm (1/16 in) rounds. Add the vegetables to another non-reactive container along with the thyme, bay leaves and peppercorns.
3. For the pickling liquid, combine the vinegar, sugar and salt in a saucepan. Bring to a simmer, swirling to dissolve the sugar and salt. Pour the hot liquid over the vegetable mixture and set aside at room temperature until just warm.
4. Rinse the sardines under cold water and pat them dry with paper towel or a clean tea towel. Once the picking liquid is just warm, pour it over the sardines. Cover and refrigerate for an hour to cure the sardines (the acidic vinegar will 'cook' the flesh).
5. Check if the sardines are ready by breaking open a fillet to see if the pickle has cured the fish; it should no longer look raw and be slightly opaque. If they're not ready, return them to the fridge for another 30 minutes. Once they're ready, the sardines are best served immediately, but they can also be covered with a layer of mild olive oil and refrigerated for a couple of days.
6. Remove the sardines from the pickle and arrange them on a large plate or individual plates. Dress with the vegetables and some of the pickling liquid. Pour the smoked olive oil over the top and sprinkle with the capers. Serve with a large spoonful of crème fraîche.

CURED SALMON (OR OTHER WILD-CAUGHT FISH)

I loved making and eating cured salmon. However, just as all animal farming has negative impacts, certain fish farming has been shown to be quite detrimental for oceans, waterways and underwater habitats. It's murky, quite literally. Because of this, I now try to avoid eating farmed salmon where possible. Fortunately, this cure works very well with wild-caught fatty white fish, such as kingfish or trevally. The result is a well-seasoned, firm fish that can be sliced very thinly for plates or bagels. If you must use salmon, approach it with caution and scepticism. Hopefully aquaculture can bring more positive changes to salmon farming in the future.

This cured fish is a delicious preparation for all times of the day – breakfast, lunch and dinner. I like to serve it by spreading crème fraîche over a serving dish and draping the sliced fish in layers over the top, then dotting it with salted capers, watercress sprigs and thinly sliced red onion. Finally, I season it well with freshly ground black pepper, lemon juice and extra virgin olive oil.

You can also cold-smoke the fish once it's been cured (see pages 153–154). This will also go well with sharp flavours, such as raw red or white onion, salted capers, watercress, dill and lemon juice. It will benefit from some relieving dairy components, too – think crème fraîche or a cream cheese schmear in a bagel.

SERVES 4–6

600 g (1 lb 5 oz) skin-on fillet of fish (see note on page 76), pin-boned

CURE

110 g (3.75 oz) fine salt
40 g (1.5 oz) brown sugar
85 g (3 oz) white (granulated) sugar
0.6 g sodium nitrite – curing salt #1 (see page 15)
3 fresh bay leaves
3 g (0.1 oz) freshly ground white pepper
3 g (0.1 oz) ground allspice
3 g (0.1 oz) ground cloves
3 g (0.1 oz) freshly grated nutmeg

1. For the cure, blend all of the ingredients in a food processor until well combined.
2. Put the fish in a non-reactive tray or dish and evenly coat it all over with the cure.
3. Cover the fish and place in the fridge for 48 hours to cure. It will be noticeably firmer to the touch, and the liquid will have leached out.
4. Rinse the fish under cold water to remove the cure, then pat it dry with paper towel or a clean tea towel.
5. Slice and serve the fish immediately (see below) or return it to the fridge, uncovered, to dry out overnight. The fish can then be cold-smoked (see pages 153–154).
6. To slice your fish, place the fillet on a cutting board, skin side down, with the tail to the left (if you're left-handed, have the tail on the right).
7. Take a long, sharp filleting knife and hold it at a 45° angle. Beginning at the tail end of the fillet, start at the hilt and pull long, steady strokes with the knife, cutting the fish as thinly as possible.

»

8. Once you get to the skin, don't cut through it, but change the angle to flatten the knife against the board, then continue cutting to release the fish from the skin. Carefully pick up the slice and lay it on a plate.
9. Extra cured or smoked fish can be wrapped in plastic wrap and kept refrigerated for up to 2 weeks.

Note

The quantities for the cure ingredients are calculated based on percentages of the total weight of the fish. If you're not using a 600 g (1 lb 5 oz) fish fillet, calculate the quantities based on the percentages listed below.

Salt: 18%
Brown sugar: 7%
White (granulated) sugar: 14%
Sodium nitrite – curing salt #1 (see page 15): 0.001%
   (1 g per 1 kg/2 lb 4 oz) of fish
Freshly ground white pepper: 0.5%
Ground allspice: 0.5%
Ground cloves: 0.5%
Freshly grated nutmeg: 0.5%
4 fresh bay leaves per 1 kg (2 lb 4 oz) of fish

PICKLED MUSSELS WITH CHILLI OIL

This makes a great snack at the start of a meal or dinner party as a do-it-yourself mussel-on-bread situation. Lightly pickling the mussels makes them plump and juicy, like the really good versions of the tinned Spanish conservas. Be sure to keep plenty of napkins handy – this chilli oil is not your laundry's friend.

SERVES 4–6

1 kg (2 lb 4 oz) mussels, cleaned and debearded
250 ml (9 fl oz) white wine
½ white onion, sliced
½ bunch dill, leaves picked
Fresh baguette and butter, to serve

CHILLI OIL

50 g (1.75 oz) chilli flakes
50 g (1.75 oz) smoked paprika
250 ml (9 fl oz) neutral oil, such as grapeseed or canola

PICKLING LIQUID

125 ml (4.5 fl oz) chardonnay vinegar
60 g (2.25 oz) caster (superfine) sugar
15 g (0.5 oz) salt
1 teaspoon soy sauce
3 fresh bay leaves
1 piece of kombu
3 garlic cloves, sliced

1. Discard any mussels that don't smell good or that don't readily close when you tap them on the bench.
2. For the chilli oil, put the chilli flakes and paprika in a heatproof bowl. Heat the oil in a saucepan until it reaches 160°C (320°F). Carefully pour the oil over the chilli and paprika – stand back as it will sizzle and froth. Allow to cool, then strain the oil into a jar through a coffee filter, muslin cloth or clean Chux cloth. The chilli oil can be stored for up to a month.
3. To cook the mussels, heat a large heavy-based pot over medium–high heat. Check that it's ready by dripping a drop of water into the pot; if it dances around, the pot is hot enough. Add the mussels and wine and cover the pot with a lid. Steam the mussels, swirling the pan a couple of times, for 1–2 minutes or until they have opened.
4. Remove the pot from the heat and transfer the mussels to a tray or dish to cool down.
5. While the mussels are cooling, make the pickling liquid. Pour 475 ml (16.5 fl oz) water into a saucepan and add the pickling ingredients. Gently heat the mixture (don't let it boil), stirring to infuse the liquid with the flavourings and dissolve the sugar. Remove from the heat.
6. Remove the cooled mussels from their shells and place them in a glass or plastic container. Pour the warm pickling liquid over the mussels, then refrigerate until chilled (ideally overnight). The mussels will keep in the liquid for up to a week.
7. To serve, arrange the mussels on a plate. Top with slices of white onion and dress with a small amount of the pickling liquid. Generously spoon the chilli oil over the mussels, then top with the dill and season with freshly ground black pepper. Serve with fresh baguette slices, spread with butter.

LEVEL UP

SALAMI

SALAMI MAKING IS AN INCREDIBLE PROCESS THAT PRODUCES TREMENDOUS RESULTS, BUT IT'S ALSO A PROCESS WITH DETAILED STEPS THAT MUST BE FOLLOWED TO THE LETTER TO PRODUCE A CONSISTENT AND SAFE PRODUCT. DO SO AND AN INCREDIBLE, DELICIOUS SAUSAGE LIES AT THE FINISH LINE.

Because the meat for salami is minced, there's a chance that bacteria from the surface can spread throughout the sausage, increasing the risk of food poisoning. Unlike with dry curing, where the exterior comes into direct contact with salt, the lower salt levels in salami are sometimes not enough to deal with pathogens. This risk is mitigated by fermentation.

Bacteria are everywhere, some good, some bad. With fermentation, we're promoting the growth of beneficial bacteria, and preventing the possibility of any harmful pathogens taking hold. We do this by inoculating the meat with lactic-acid producing bacteria, and adding sugars – most often in the form of dextrose – to feed them. The result is a drop in pH, which causes the environment to become acidic. Pathogens, particularly the high-risk bacterium *E. coli* (the presence of which is a risk factor in processing, and can lead to severe food poisoning, sickness and even death), cannot survive in this environment. Bacteria are not always detectable without lab testing, and it's a requirement for us that a sample from every batch of salami we make at LP's be tested for the presence of *E. coli* before release. Needless to say, if you're making salami yourself, the pH needs to be carefully monitored.

The other thing that's important to be aware of is the potential for salami to cultivate the botulism toxin, which is one of the deadliest toxins on earth. The *Clostridium botulinum* bacterium grows in anaerobic environments (that is, without oxygen), meaning that any air pockets in salami can create the perfect conditions for this bacterium to thrive. Just the fact that it takes its name from the Latin word *botulus*, the word for sausage, gives you some idea of how closely the two are linked.

Thankfully, the growth of these bacteria can be halted by the addition of nitrates. These naturally occurring chemicals are found in high levels in leafy green vegetables such as spinach, silverbeet and celery. Our bodies are designed to process these chemicals as they are broken down in our saliva and, as well as acting as powerful antibacterial agents that work within our digestive tract, nitrates are also believed to benefit our cardiovascular system.

Nitrates and nitrites (see page 15) have a rather bad reputation due to the concern of them being recognised as a carcinogen when consumed regularly and when cooked in particular ways.

Producing salami commercially in New South Wales legally requires nitrates to be added to products in specific amounts to safe guard against botulism. Studies have been undertaken to validate an alternative, but to date no effective single replacement material has been identified as an alternative to nitrite and nitrate to inhibit *Clostridium botulinum* growth and its toxin production. Some producers use organic nitrates derived from vegetables so they can clean label their products with statements like 'chemical nitrate-free', but the nitrates used in these products are chemically identical to all other nitrates and must be added in the same specific quantities required to make them safe.

In a 2011 Food Standards Australia and New Zealand food study, the major sources of estimated nitrate and nitrite exposure across different population groups were vegetables and fruits (including juices). Sodium nitrites from processed meats accounted for only a relatively small amount of total dietary exposure (between five and seven per cent). Of course, all foods should be eaten in moderation and the use of nitrates in food should be limited to the minimum requirement to keep them safe. The research is still evolving, but my opinion, the risk of not using nitrates in salami is too great.

Once you've made your salami to the letter, fermentation is the next step. This must be closely monitored in the first 48 hours, during which time the salami's pH must come down below 5.2. After fermentation, the salami is hung up to dry and mature in the same way as whole-muscle dry-cured meat. The moisture is drawn out of the salami, and the water content of the product comes down further, creating an inhospitable environment for bacteria. The active water levels must be below 0.85 per cent at the end of maturation, which accounts for about a 30 per cent loss in weight from drying.

As the salami hangs, mould can begin to flourish on the surface. It can be a bit confronting to see white, chalky or fine fluff bloom on your salami. However, just like bacteria, some moulds are bad and some are good. As a rough rule, white mould (even if it has a slight grey or green tinge) tends to be okay to eat. Any other colour – black, orange, yellow, green, whatever – is not safe to eat. If you notice mould of any of these colours developing on your salami, remove it by promptly wiping it off with a clean cloth and some vinegar. Left too long, it can burrow into the salami, making it dangerous to eat.

To avoid things turning too wild in these recipes, you'll notice that we inoculate our salamis with an isolated mould strain, which is applied straight after filling to give this desirable mould a headstart and leave no room for other strains to flourish. Mould contributes character, funk and flavour to the salami. It also shields the surface from light, which aids in preventing rancidity and in the proper drying of the salami.

Salt, nitrate, starter culture, dextrose, active water percentages, ratios and pH levels are non-negotiable for these recipes and cannot be changed. Any tweak could compromise the food safety of the product and potentially make it dangerous to consume.

Making salami safely can be tricky, and it doesn't always work out. Learn from the mistakes, discard a batch if you need to, and start again. There's no room for taking shortcuts and being careless with salami making. Follow the rules first, then enjoy the results.

SAUCISSON

This is a basic method for salami or, more accurately, mould-ripened saucisson, which is the style we prefer at LP's. Beneficial moulds can develop naturally, but we inoculate our saucisson with the isolated mould strain *Penicillium nalgiovense* – any specialty curing shop will sell this and the starter culture – which we like for its character and funk. Alternatively, a light cold-smoking (see page 153) will also inhibit surface mould growth.

It's vital that the ratios and method aren't altered (and please don't try to make this before carefully reading the notes on pages 80–81). That said, this recipe can be adapted to make all styles of saucisson or Italian-style salami (such as the saucisson sec variation on page 86, pictured opposite), and the flavours and seasonings can be tinkered with – different spices, wines and possibly even different types of meat. Generally, though, it pays to keep the flavours subtle.

As with sausages, this is a recipe for which you'll need to thoroughly clean all your equipment with hot soapy water, before sanitising it with spray. You'll also need a mincer and a sausage filler, a calibrated pH meter, a fermentation chamber, a maturing chamber (see page 15) and some butcher's twine.

MAKES ABOUT 1.3 KG (3 LB)

- 0.5 g salami starter culture
- 50 ml (1.5 fl oz) filtered water
- 2.5 g mould culture plus 1 litre (35 fl oz) filtered water (optional; follow manufacturer's instructions)
- 1.4 kg (2 lb 2 oz) skinless pork shoulder, coarsely minced with 10 mm (½ in) plate
- 600 g (1 lb 5 oz) pork fat, coarsely minced with 10 mm (½ in) plate
- 60 g (2.25 oz) fine salt
- 10 g (0.4 oz) freshly ground black pepper
- 9 g sodium nitrate – curing salt #2 (see page 15)
- 30 g (1 oz) dextrose
- 30 ml (1 fl oz) red wine
- 2 x 30 cm (12 in) lengths of beef middle casing, rinsed of salt and soaked for at least 2 hours

1. Put the salami starter culture in a small bowl and add the filtered water.
2. If you're also using mould culture, prepare this in a separate bowl in the same way. Set the mixtures aside at room temperature until needed.
3. Add the pork shoulder, pork fat, salt, pepper, curing salt and dextrose to a stand mixer fitted with the paddle attachment and mix on low speed for 1 minute.
4. With the motor running, slowly drizzle in the wine. Once it's well incorporated, add the salami starter culture slurry (reserve the mould culture for later). It's important that the starter culture is added after the other ingredients have been mixed thoroughly, because the culture is sensitive and can become inactive if it hits a patch where the salt concentration is too high. Stop the mixer while you set up for filling (unlike with raw sausages, the forcemeat can be left out of the fridge while you do this since the fermentation process has already begun).
5. Set up your sausage filler. Make sure the horn and seals are assembled correctly so there are no leaks. Taking note of how big the mouth of your filler is, use a wet hand to scoop up an appropriately sized ball of forcemeat and slam it back into the mixing bowl to remove any excess air. Then, as accurately as possible, slam the ball of forcemeat into the mouth of the filler. (Try to get it into the filler cleanly and tightly to push out any air pockets so that you don't end up with holes in the saucissons.) Repeat until you've used all the mix or the filler is full.
6. Prime the filler by cranking the handle until the mix pokes out the end of the horn. Use the pH meter to check the pH of the mix, noting it down.

»

7. Open one end of the casing and pour in some water, allowing it to run all the way through from end to end to get rid of any salt on the inside of the casing. Slide the casing onto the filler, bunching it up on the horn, and tie off the other end with a knot using twine. (You want most of the casing to be on the horn, with just a little overhang, so the sausage fills from the tied end first.)

8. Make sure the bench you're working on is wet – this will allow the sausage to slide around as it fills, mitigating the risk of the casing tearing. Begin to crank the handle on the filler, trying to be as steady and smooth as possible; it's best to use one hand to turn the filler and the other to gently hold the casing on the horn as it fills and gets pushed off. There needs to be a slight resistance to ensure the casing is even and you get a nice tight and full fill. Depending on the size of your maturing chamber, you can make the links whatever length you like, but I find around 250 g (9 oz) is a nice size for a finished saucisson: fill about 250 g (9 oz) of forcemeat into the casing and then, keeping some extra casing on the end, cut the casing from the filling horn. You can now slide your fingers down the casing to snugly push the meat into the casing to make it a tighter fill. Keeping the tension, tie a length of twine around the open end using a tight double knot to hold it securely, and then lock it with another double knot. Use the two pieces of twine to make a loop about 3 cm (1 ¼ in) long so the sausage can be hung up. Now keep filling the remaining casing.

9. Weigh the sausages and record the weight; this is the starting point to calculate moisture loss.

10. If you're using the mould culture, this is the time to spray the casings as per the supplier's instructions. I like to put the culture in a clean spray bottle (don't be looking at the neglected one in the shed!), but if you don't have a suitable spray bottle, you can dip the saucissons into the mould-inoculated water.

11. The saucissons now need to be incubated for 48 hours in a fermentation chamber set at 25°C (77°F) and 80–90% humidity. Check the pH reading at 24 hours by inserting the pH meter into the saucissons to see if the pH has lowered from what you noted down earlier, then check it again at 48 hours: it has to be below 5.2 at this point to ensure any pathogens are killed; if it's not, the only safe thing to do is to discard the saucissons.

12. If the saucissons are in the correct pH zone, hang them in your maturing chamber, ideally at 10–16°C (50–61°F) and 70–80% humidity. The saucissons are ready when they've lost 30% of their initial weight. This should take about 3–4 weeks.

»

CURING & FERMENTING

13. When the saucissons have lost the desired amount of weight and feel firm, cut into one to assess it. It should have a dark red colour throughout, with good definition between meat and fat. Most of all, it should smell good – salami-like, even, with a faint tang and sourness. If it has dried properly, it should be evenly coloured from edge to edge; if you notice a hard, dark ring around the outside, this means the humidity was not high enough during the maturing stage, leading to 'case hardening'. At worst, hardening can inhibit moisture loss, which can result in the inside rotting, but if the hardening is mild and the saucisson has still lost the correct weight and smells good, it's a green light – just make a note for next time to up the humidity slightly.
14. If your saucissons are ready, cut a plate of thin slices and crack open a bottle of wine. I love to eat saucisson with the rind on – I think the mould contributes amazing flavour. As for the left-over saucissons, if they haven't been cut into, they can be kept in a cool, dark place. Otherwise, wrap them in paper or stuff them into a paper bag and store them in the fridge for up to 4 months.

VARIATIONS

Saucisson sec
This is a simple but delicious saucisson (pictured on page 82). It's so good, in fact, that it's now the only salami we sell at LP's. Follow the method above, but replace the ground pepper with 10 g (0.4 oz) whole black peppercorns and add 18 g (0.6 oz) finely grated garlic.

Spiced saucisson
This is about as far as we go in terms of spicing things up with saucisson. The seasonings are subtle, but add a delicious fragrance and flavour, thanks in part to the fennel pollen, which is like gold dust. (Pick it yourself or look for it in gourmet food shops and online stores, or use fennel seeds instead.) Follow the method above, but replace the 10 g (0.4 oz) pepper with:

18 g (0.6 oz) finely grated garlic
12 g (0.4 oz) fennel pollen
4 g (0.1 oz) lightly ground aniseed
4 g (0.1 oz) chilli flakes
4 g (0.1 oz) freshly ground black pepper

'NDUJA

'Nduja is a salume from Calabria in southern Italy that's super fiery, complex and delicious. One of its most appealing features is its soft and spreadable texture, a result of its high fat content. This makes it useful for a number of applications – on toast, on pizza, with pasta, in a ragù, stirred through breadcrumbs to make a spicy, meaty pangrattato – and maybe goes some way to explaining its spike in popularity in the past few years.

Making 'nduja may be quicker than salami, but the process needs to be followed precisely, as do the safety notes on pages 80–81. And since 'nduja only loses about 10% of its weight during maturation, you'll need to pay close attention to the fermentation along with the water content. In this case, the requirement is that the pH drops below 4.4. To achieve this, we increase the amount of dextrose that goes into the mix, which gives more food to the lactic-acid-producing bacteria, resulting in a bigger drop in pH and a higher level of acidity. Technical? Yes. But making 'nduja doesn't take very long compared with other salami.

As with sausages, this is a recipe for which you'll need to thoroughly clean all your equipment with hot soapy water, before sanitising it with spray. You'll also need a mincer, a sausage filler, a calibrated pH meter, a fermentation chamber, a maturing chamber (see page 15) and some butcher's twine. Look for the salami starter culture in a specialty curing shop.

MAKES 1 KG (2 LB 4 OZ)

0.25 g salami starter culture
50 ml (1.5 fl oz) filtered water
300 g (10.5 oz) skinless pork shoulder, finely minced with 3 mm (⅛ in) plate
600 g (1 lb 5 oz) pork fat, finely minced with 3 mm (⅛ in) plate
150 g (5.5 oz) long red chillies, blended to a smooth paste
20 g (0.7 oz) chilli flakes
35 g (1.25 oz) smoked paprika
6 g (0.2 oz) freshly ground black pepper
6 g (0.2 oz) ground fennel seeds
40 g (1.5 oz) dextrose
27 g (1 oz) fine salt
4 g sodium nitrate – curing salt #2 (see page 15)
1 metre (39½ in) hog casing, rinsed and soaked for at least 2 hours

1. Put the salami starter culture in a small bowl and add the filtered water. Set aside at room temperature until needed.
2. Add the remaining ingredients (except the casing) to a stand mixer fitted with the paddle attachment and mix on medium speed for about 1 minute or until all the ingredients are thoroughly combined. With the mixer still running, slowly drizzle in the starter culture slurry.
3. Set up your sausage filler. Make sure the horn and seals are assembled correctly so there are no leaks. Taking note of how big the mouth of your filler is, use a wet hand to scoop up an appropriately sized ball of forcemeat and slam it back into the mixing bowl to remove any excess air. Then, as accurately as possible, slam the ball of forcemeat into the mouth of the filler. (Try to get it into the filler cleanly and tightly to push out any air pockets so that you don't end up with holes in the 'nduja.) Repeat until you've used all the mix or the filler is full.
4. Prime the filler by cranking the handle until the mix pokes out the end of the horn. Use the pH meter to check the pH of the mix, noting it down.
5. Open one end of the casing and pour in some water, allowing it to run all the way through from end to end to get rid of any salt on the inside of the casing. Slide the casing onto the filler, bunching it up on the horn, and tie off the other end with a knot using twine. (You want most of the casing to be on the horn, with just a little overhang, so the sausage fills from the tied end first.)

»

6. Begin to crank the handle on the filler, trying to be as steady and smooth as possible; it's best to use one hand to turn the filler and the other to gently hold the casing on the horn as it fills and gets pushed off. There needs to be a slight resistance to ensure the casing is even and you get a nice tight and full fill. Depending on the size of your maturing chamber, you can make the links whatever length you like, but I do find that 'nduja works well in pairs, using around 250 g (9 oz) of forcemeat for each. Fill 250 g (9 oz) of the forcemeat into the casing and then, keeping some extra casing on the end, cut the casing from the filling horn. You can now slide your fingers down the casing to snugly push the meat into the casing to make it a tighter fill. Keeping the tension, tie a length of twine around the open end using a tight double knot to hold it securely, and then lock it with another knot. Use the two pieces of twine to make a loop about 3 cm (1¼ in) long so the 'nduja can be hung up. Now keep filling the remaining casing.
7. Weigh the 'nduja and record the weight; this is the starting point to calculate moisture loss.
8. The 'nduja now needs to be incubated for 48 hours in a fermentation chamber set at 25°C (77°F) and 80–90% humidity. Check the pH reading at 24 hours by inserting the pH meter into the 'nduja to see if the pH has lowered from what you noted down earlier, then check it again at 48 hours: it has to be below 4.4 at this point to ensure any pathogens are killed; if it's not, the only safe thing to do is to discard the 'nduja.
9. If the 'nduja is in the correct pH zone, hang it in a maturing chamber set at 12–16°C (54–61°F) and 75–85% humidity. The 'nduja is ready when it has lost 10% of its initial weight. This should take about 2 weeks. The 'nduja can then be stored in the fridge for up to 3 months.

TOAST WITH 'NDUJA, RICOTTA AND HONEY

This makes a simple yet delicious snack. It has never been on our menu, but is a regular treat for the kitchen team when the bread comes out of the oven in the afternoon. Liberally spread a slice of toasted sourdough with 'nduja. Spoon some ricotta on top, drizzle with honey and finish with freshly cracked black pepper. These ingredients also work very well together on a pizza.

CHAPTER .THREE.
TERRINES & PÂTÉS

CONTENTS

INTRODUCTION   95

CHICKEN LIVER PÂTÉ   99
PORK AND CHICKEN LIVER TERRINE   103
COPPA DI TESTA   107
   PIG'S-HEAD CROQUETTES   111
DUCK GALANTINE   112

I wasn't taught how to make terrines in my early days as a chef, and I never spent much time thinking about them. In fact, it wasn't until we started to make duck galantine (page 112) at LP's that my interest was sparked. Once I realised that terrine making was much like sausage making, in that a terrine is an assortment of ingredients that come together to form a single item with complex layers of flavour, I was hooked.

Once we added terrines to the menu at LP's they never came off and we loved serving them to guests at the start of a meal. For us, the satisfaction came from meticulously preparing a product that seemed rustic, but a cross-section revealed the level of skill and finesse that went into it. Pâté is much the same, with the texture being the key indicator of quality. Plenty of people have fond memories of sitting at the LP's bar and kicking off with a slice of our pâté before letting the evening unfold.

A slice of pâté or terrine makes a wonderful snack with some good bread, mustard and a nice glass of something. It's also perfect to share – a brilliant addition to your picnic spread on a blanket in the park, and also right at home on the kitchen bench occupying friends while you get the rest of dinner sorted.

While pâtés and terrines are similar, there are some differences. Terrines can be made with all kinds of meat, including rabbit or birds such as quail and pheasant, and may even contain a mix of various meats. They're typically eaten cold, so include quite a high ratio of fat (normally pork fat) – not only because it's delicious, but also because it helps them stay soft and creamy at cool temperatures. Livers are often added for depth and richness, along with a whole array of spices, nuts, vegetables and fruit.

Terrines usually have a coarse texture, which is what makes them so appealing to the eye when you cut a slice. Since the name comes from the vessel they're cooked in, the style can also vary – flip to the coppa di testa on page 106, and you'll see a terrine that's set in gelatine rather than made with forcemeat, for example. To me, terrines have an Old World, almost medieval appeal, and at their most refined resemble a piece of art.

Pâté, on the other hand, can mean a lot of things, ranging from coarse, rustic, terrine-like preparations to something set inside a pastry shell – such as pâté en croûte, where pâté is baked in a highly decorated pastry case. Typically, however, pâté is a smoother preparation of liver enriched with eggs and butter, flavoured with a reduction of alcohol, then gently cooked until set. The result is usually spreadable, and is incredibly rich and full bodied, and might well be served on bread along with something refreshing such as a pickle, chutney or jelly.

The type of liver used to make the pâté will determine the appropriate accompaniment. Pâtés made from pork liver, for example, are robust and full of depth, so need something bold like red onion pickle (page 232). Pâtés made from goose livers are incredibly fatty and smooth, providing a luxurious mouthfeel that suits buttery brioche. Finally, pâtés made from duck or chicken livers, which are the style I usually go for, can be very smooth, enriched with butter and rendered duck fat to make them velvety and decadent. These tend to go well with sweeter garnishes, such as pickled currants or prunes (page 232) or candied cumquats (page 233).

The basic chicken liver pâté (page 99) and pork and chicken liver terrine (page 103) recipes are the starting blocks for anyone new to this world. Once you've mastered them, the coppa di testa (page 107) and duck galantine (page 112) are your next steps. If you do give these a crack, the key is to be patient and not to rush. You'll be rewarded with a beautifully finished terrine that's sure to impress.

TERRINES HAVE AN OLD WORLD, ALMOST MEDIEVAL APPEAL, AND AT THEIR MOST REFINED RESEMBLE A PIECE OF ART.

CHICKEN LIVER PÂTÉ

This pâté, which we served for a long time at LP's during its restaurant days, is a relatively easy one. It goes in a smooth, rather than coarse, direction, with a texture almost like parfait that's easily spreadable, which is probably why we almost always served it with a hunk of sourdough bread.

The port reduction is the opportunity to add flavour to your pâté. You can use a mixture of different alcohols, including sweet sherry or even sweetened red wine.

This pâté might be relatively simple to make, but it does pay to be organised and weigh out your ingredients before starting. It's important that they're all of a similar temperature when you're ready to mix. You can cook the pâté in a 1 litre (35 fl oz) terrine mould or in several smaller ramekins or jars, depending on the occasion. You'll also need a baking dish deep enough to hold the mould or ramekins.

MAKES 500 G (1 LB 2 OZ)

150 g (5.5 oz) salted butter
30 g (1 oz) duck fat
230 g (8 oz) trimmed chicken livers (no sinew or blemishes)
2 eggs, plus 1 egg yolk
8 g (0.3 oz) fine salt
0.5 g sodium nitrite — curing salt #1 (see page 15)
1 tablespoon maple syrup

PORT REDUCTION

100 ml (3.5 fl oz) port
100 ml (3.5 fl oz) cognac
100 ml (3.5 fl oz) Madeira
1 French shallot, sliced
1 garlic clove, sliced
5 black peppercorns
2 fresh bay leaves
1 small sprig of thyme

1. Make the port reduction by combining all the ingredients in a small saucepan and bringing to a simmer. Reduce the heat and simmer very gently until you have about 50 ml (1.5 fl oz) of liquid left. Strain the reduction through a fine sieve, discarding the solids.

2. Gently heat the butter and duck fat in a small saucepan until just melted. Remove from the heat and leave to cool while you prepare the remaining ingredients. Set everything aside for about an hour to come to room temperature.

3. Preheat the oven to 100°C (200°F). Fill and boil the kettle. If you plan to serve the pâté in its mould or ramekins (see above), you don't need to do anything to prepare them. If you plan to turn the pâté out of the mould once it's cooked, you'll need to line the mould: pour in a little water to wet the mould, rubbing it all over the inside, then tip out the excess. Tear off two pieces of plastic wrap large enough to line the mould and extend well over the edges, then lay them on top of each other. Drape the double layer of plastic over the mould, then gently push it down into the mould, making sure it sits tightly in the corners. Try to avoid trapping air between the plastic and the mould.

4. Put the livers, eggs, egg yolk, salt, curing salt, maple syrup and 30 ml (1 fl oz) of the port reduction in a food processor and blend until very smooth, about 3 minutes. With the motor still running, slowly drizzle in the butter and duck fat, blending until emulsified.

5. Pour the mixture into the mould or ramekins, then give it a firm tap on a chopping board to knock out any air bubbles. If you've lined your mould, gently fold in the excess plastic on all sides so the top of the pâté

»

6. is covered; if you haven't lined your mould or are using ramekins, tightly cover the pâté with plastic wrap. Finally, tightly cover with foil, folding down the edges to seal.

6. Gently lift the mould or ramekins into a baking dish. Pour in enough hot water from the kettle to come halfway up the sides of the mould or ramekins. Carefully place the dish in the oven and bake for about an hour or until a probe thermometer inserted into the centre of the pâté reads 70°C (158°F). Remove the mould or ramekins from the water bath and transfer to the fridge to chill.

7. When the pâté is fridge-cold, it's ready to serve. Remove the foil and gently peel the plastic from the top of the pâté. If you've lined your mould, gently ease the plastic in from the edges to create some space between the pâté and the mould. Invert the mould onto a serving plate; it may need a light tug to release it. Discard the plastic wrap.

8. Serve the pâté with your favourite condiments, or try some of the ones in the Sauces & Staples chapter (I prefer it with sweeter condiments, such as the pickled currants on page 232 or candied cumquats on page 233). If you don't finish all of the pâté in one sitting, it will need to be covered thoroughly to prevent it discolouring. Lay a sheet of plastic wrap directly on the surface, gently pressing it onto all sides. The pâté should then keep for up to a week in the fridge.

TERRINES & PÂTÉS

PORK AND CHICKEN LIVER TERRINE

This recipe is a window into all sorts of terrines that follow the same general method but have different flavourings. The base is pork shoulder and jowl, with options that then extend to the type of liver – usually chicken or duck – and the seasonings you include. Terrines are a wonderful vehicle for a wide range of flavours, and the variations I've suggested on page 104 – one with parsley and green peppercorns (pictured here), the other with orange and pistachio – are just the beginning.

Experiment, and see what takes your fancy. Just keep in mind that the ratios in this recipe result in a great finished texture, so try to keep within these parameters. The pork shoulder and jowl – in equal quantities – determine the ratio. Set their total at 100%, then calculate the other inclusions around that: liver can range from 10–20% of that total; the port (or any other wine) makes up 5%; and the egg white and shallots another 10% each. This recipe uses 10% livers to the total amount of meat, but it can be scaled up to 20% for a richer terrine. You can also substitute the pork shoulder with another meat, such as venison or chicken, but keep the pork jowl in there as it adds just the right amount of fat.

You'll need a 1 litre (35 fl oz) terrine mould and a baking dish deep enough to hold the mould.

Start this recipe 2 days ahead.

MAKES 1 KG (2 LB 4 OZ)

- 500 g (1 lb 2 oz) skinless pork shoulder, coarsely minced with 10 mm (½ in) plate
- 500 g (1 lb 2 oz) skinless pork jowl, coarsely minced with 10 mm (½ in) plate
- 16.5 g (0.6 oz) fine salt
- 1 g sodium nitrite – curing salt #1 (see page 15)
- 3 g (0.1 oz) freshly ground black pepper
- 100 g (3.5 oz) trimmed chicken livers (no sinew or blemishes), cut into 2 cm (¾ inch) cubes
- 100 g (3.5 oz) finely diced French shallot
- 50 ml (1.5 fl oz) port
- 100 g (3.5 oz) egg white (from about 3 eggs), beaten
- Oil spray, for greasing

1. Weigh out and prepare all the ingredients, then refrigerate them for at least an hour; it's important that everything is at 4°C (39.2°F) before mixing.
2. Line the base of the terrine mould with baking paper, then lightly spray the inside of the mould with oil.
3. Put the minced pork shoulder and pork jowl into the bowl of a stand mixer fitted with the paddle attachment. Combine the salt, curing salt and pepper, then sprinkle them over the pork and mix slowly until homogenous, with a slightly tacky texture. Add the liver, shallot and port and gently mix until incorporated. With the motor running, slowly drizzle in the egg white and mix until thoroughly combined.
4. Use a wet hand to scoop up a handful of the terrine mix, dragging it up against the side of the bowl. Shape it into a rough ball, then – and this can be slightly tricky, so try to be careful and accurate – throw the ball into the mould with a firm slap (this expels any air pockets, resulting in a uniform texture in the finished terrine). Continue until all the terrine mix is used, then run a wet hand over the surface to smooth the top and ensure there are no gaps.
5. Cover the surface of the terrine with plastic wrap, then place it in the fridge overnight to cure and allow the flavours to develop.

»

6. The next day, preheat the oven to 180°C (350°F). Uncover the terrine, then place the mould in a deep baking dish and bake until the top is a nice golden brown, about 30 minutes.
7. Reduce the heat to 100°C (200°F). Boil the kettle, then pour hot water into the baking dish to come halfway up the sides of the mould. Keep baking the terrine until a probe thermometer inserted into the centre reaches 75°C (167°F).
8. Remove the terrine from the baking dish. Let it cool for an hour before covering it and placing it in the fridge overnight to cool and set.
9. The next day, run a knife around the inside of the terrine mould, then carefully turn out the terrine. It will have accumulated some juices that will have turned to jelly, which can be gently scraped off or served with the terrine – it can be a bit messy, but it tastes delicious.
10. Take a sharp knife and cut a thick slice of terrine. Serve it with a big spoonful of mustard, cornichons and crusty bread. Any left-over terrine can be refrigerated for up to a week.

VARIATIONS

Parsley and green peppercorn terrine
Fold 50 g (1.75 oz) chopped flat-leaf parsley leaves (5% of the total weight of meat) and 150 g (5.5 oz) drained green peppercorns in brine (15% of the meat weight) through the terrine mix along with the liver and shallot. Use a good brand of peppercorns so they aren't too soft; inferior peppercorns can be disappointingly mushy in the finished terrine.

Orange and pistachio terrine
Finely grate in the zest from 1 orange and fold in 150 g (5.5 oz) pistachios (15% of the total weight of meat) along with the liver and shallot. You can swap the chicken livers for duck livers, which are a classic pairing with orange.

TERRINES & PÂTÉS

COPPA DI TESTA

This can be a bit of a wild thing to make… if you're squeamish, perhaps turn the page. Or, pour yourself a wine and forge ahead.

Coppa di testa is the Italian version of England's brawn, France's fromage de tête and Germany's presswurst. In many ways, they're all variations on the same thing, which is a pig's head simmered with aromatics until exquisitely soft, then picked from the bone, seasoned, formed into a mould and set with its own gelatine. Despite the gnarly aspect, coppa di testa is delicious and truly honours the pig by delighting in every aspect of what it offers. Let's just not call it head cheese.

Talk to your butcher ahead of time about sourcing a pig's head, to make sure you get all the bits – the last thing you want is the head turning up with no ears or tongue (it happens). If you have enough fridge space, I would recommend brining the head for 3 days in ham brine (see page 163) before cooking to give it a well-seasoned flavour and an attractive pink hue. If you're not brining the head, you'll only need to start this recipe a day ahead. You'll also need a disposable razor and a very large pot. You can either set the coppa di testa in a 2 litre (70 fl oz) terrine mould or use the mixture to fill a 120 mm (4½ in) fibrous casing, as we've done here.

MAKES 1.5 KG (3 LB 5 OZ)

1 pig's head
Ham brine (page 163, optional)
2 pig's trotters
2 onions, cut in half
2 long red chillies, cut in half lengthways
10 fresh bay leaves
6 garlic cloves
1 tablespoon red wine vinegar
1 tablespoon Dijon mustard
½ teaspoon chilli flakes
½ nutmeg, freshly grated
Pinch of ground cinnamon
Pinch of ground cloves
Flaky salt
1 metre (39½ in) of 120 mm (4½ in) fibrous casing (optional), soaked in warm water for 20–30 minutes

1. Use a razor to shave off any hair that hasn't been removed from the pig's head. Cut off the pig's ears and remove its tongue. (If this feels too visceral, ask your butcher to kindly help you out.)
2. If you are brining the meat, submerge the head, ears and tongue in the ham brine and refrigerate for 3 days (be sure to clear some room first). Otherwise, proceed to the next step.
3. Put the pig's head in a very large pot (drain and rinse it first if it's been brined), add the trotters and cover with water. Add the onion and chilli halves, bay leaves and garlic. Bring to the boil over high heat.
4. Reduce the heat to a gentle simmer and simmer for 30 minutes, then add the ears and tongue. Skim off any foamy impurities that float to the surface as it's simmering – this will help keep the stock clear.
5. Simmer for 2–3 hours, checking regularly with a pair of tongs – you want the meat to be very tender and easy to pull away. Keep checking the ears and tongue as these may cook relatively quickly – remove them from the pot once they're ready and leave them to cool. Once the tongue is cool enough to handle, peel off the outer skin. Once the head is tender, gently lift it out of the pot and leave it to cool for 30 minutes.
6. In the meantime, put a saucer in the freezer (you'll use this to check that the stock is ready). Strain 2 litres (70 fl oz) of the stock from the pot into

»

a clean saucepan. Bring it to the boil, then reduce to a simmer and cook, skimming occasionally, until it's reduced by half. This intensifies the gelatine that has accumulated in the stock, which will act like a glue to bind the terrine. Once the stock has reduced, check if it's ready by tasting a little: it should feel slightly sticky on your lips. To make sure, spoon a little of the stock onto the cold saucer and chill it in the fridge for a couple of minutes. If the stock wrinkles when you push it with your finger and is set and jelly like, it's done. If not, keep simmering. When it's ready, season the stock with the red wine vinegar and mustard and set it aside.

7. Once the head is cool enough to handle, use your hands to pick through the meat and remove it from the bones, placing it in a large bowl. This can be a bit grim, but be brave! Discard any tendons, brains, eyes or gland-looking things, and be careful not to include any small bones or teeth. It should come apart very easily, but the meat needs to be in small chunks rather than strands, so be very gentle while handling. Find the cheeks and jowls and cut any large pieces into 1 cm (½ in) cubes. Cut the ears into very thin slices and chop up the snout. You can also include some of the skin, if you like. Add all of the meats to the bowl.

8. Add all of the spices, then pour in the reduced stock and gently fold everything together. Check the seasoning and adjust if necessary, seasoning it a bit harder than you think, since the flavours will be a little muted once it cools; it should be very hard to stop tasting!

9. Line a 2 litre (70 fl oz) terrine mould with plastic wrap and spoon in the meat mix. Give the mould a good tap on the bench to eliminate any air pockets, cover the surface with plastic wrap and place in the fridge overnight to set. Alternatively, fill a 120 mm (4½ in) fibrous casing with the meat mixture, following steps 10–13 of the salsiccia recipe (pages 27–28) to make one large sausage (as shown on page 106). Set in the fridge.

10. Remove the coppa di testa from the fridge. Invert the terrine onto a chopping board and use a sharp knife to cut it into 1.5 cm (⅝ in) slices. Alternatively, slice the sausage into thin slices. It's best to let the coppa di testa temper for 10 minutes so it's not fridge-cold and can soften slightly. Serve with mustard or other sharp condiments, such as red onion pickle (page 232), and some bread.

PIG'S-HEAD CROQUETTES

The coppa di testa mix from page 107 can also be formed into brilliant two-bite croquettes to serve as canapés or snacks. You can follow this recipe from the beginning (starting a day ahead) or, if you cook the mix in a terrine mould and find you can't eat the whole thing, you can cut it into pieces, bread it and fry it to make croquettes. These are fantastic with hot sauce (page 220) or sauce gribiche (page 221).

Scale the amounts of flour, egg wash and breadcrumbs according to how many croquettes you're making.

Coppa di testa mix (page 107)
Vegetable oil, for deep-frying
Plain (all-purpose) flour
Eggs
Milk
Panko breadcrumbs
Flaky salt

1. Make the coppa di testa up to the end of step 8. Press the mixture into a deep baking tray lined with plastic wrap, flattening it so it's around 2–3 cm (1 in) thick. Cover and refrigerate overnight to set.
2. The next day, invert the tray onto a cutting board and cut the set coppa di testa into squares or rectangles (or triangles, if you must). Half-fill a large saucepan or a deep-fryer with oil and heat it to 170°C (338°F).
3. While the oil is heating, put the flour in a bowl. Crack the eggs into another bowl and whisk in a splash of milk to loosen them. Put the breadcrumbs in a third bowl. Crumbing can get messy, so using your best coordination – one wet hand, one dry hand – toss the coppa di testa pieces into the flour, dust off the excess, then dip them in the egg and drop them into the breadcrumbs, tossing to coat. Some cooks opt to double-crumb by running the pieces through the sequence again. I find this is good if you've missed a spot, but usually once is enough. Lay the crumbed croquettes on a tray.
4. Gently lower the croquettes into the hot oil and cook in small batches until golden brown and heated through, about 3–4 minutes.
5. Drain the croquettes on paper towel, then lightly season with flaky salt. Serve hot with your sauce of choice.

DUCK GALANTINE

A galantine is a party piece, something big and bold to present proudly to the table. This recipe can be quite tricky, and starts with carefully removing the duck's skin before boning the bird. The meat is then seasoned, turned into a farce and rolled back up into the skin, before the entire duck is set and cooked, then cooled, fried and sliced.

Serve the sliced galantine cold, as you would a terrine. Alternatively, you can adapt it for a main course by reducing the seasonings and serving it hot. Those who have precise fine-motor skills can also use this recipe as a springboard for a chicken or even quail galantine.

It can take a while to skin a duck meticulously without piercing the skin; at LP's, we used to tag-team on this job. Take your time with it – you don't want any holes in the duck skin or you risk the farce bursting out during cooking.

You'll need to start this recipe 2 days ahead.

SERVES 6–8

1 whole duck (2.2 kg/5 lb)
Vegetable oil, for deep-frying

GALANTINE FARCE

300 g (10.5 oz) pork mince, approximately
30 g (1 oz) fine salt
1.7 g sodium nitrite – curing salt #1 (see page 15)
6 g (0.2 oz) freshly grated nutmeg
6 g (0.2 oz) ground cinnamon
6 g (0.2 oz) ground allspice
6 g (0.2 oz) ground cloves
7 g (0.2 oz) freshly ground black pepper
70 g (2.5 oz) pistachios
100 ml (3.5 fl oz) port
15 g (0.5 oz) honey
15 g (0.5 oz) white (shiro) miso paste
Finely grated zest of 1 orange
100 g (3.5 oz) egg white (from about 3 eggs), beaten

1. Start by skinning the duck. Put the bird on a chopping board, breast side down, and give it a pat with paper towel to make sure it's dry.
2. Referring to the images on page 114, use a small, sharp boning knife to cut through the skin from the top of the duck's neck all the way down its spine to the parson's nose. It's important to make long, clean, careful cuts to avoid making holes in the skin as you separate it from the meat; in some parts you'll have to use your fingers.
3. Adjust the angle of the knife and carefully release the skin from the spine, slowly following the seam around each side of the duck until you reach the middle of the breast. When you get to the thigh bone joints, release them from the frame by cutting through the joint. Do the same with the wing joints. Leaving the legs and wings for now, continue to work around the frame until you can remove it completely.
4. With a heavy chef's knife, chop off the ends of the drumsticks, then chop off the wings at the elbow. Discard the knobbly knees and wing tips, or keep them in the freezer for making stock or soup.
5. Starting with the legs, fold the skin back, pulling the bone through from the drumstick end to expose the meat, almost as if you're turning the leg inside out. With the tip of your knife, very carefully cut the leg and thigh away from the skin. Do the same with the other leg and the wings (the skin will now have four holes where the legs and wings were attached). Put the skin in the fridge until needed.
6. Thoroughly work through the duck frame by cutting off the breast meat and any other meat you can without putting your hands in risky positions. Remove all the leg meat that's still attached to the skin.

»

114 QUALITY MEATS

7. Dice the breast meat into 1 cm (½ in) cubes. Coarsely mince the leg meat and trimmings using a mincer fitted with the 10 mm (½ in) plate. If you don't have a mincer, dice the leg meat into 1 cm (½ in) cubes. Combine the breast meat with the leg meat and trimmings and weigh the meat (it should be around 1.5 kg/3 lb 5 oz). To make the farce, add enough of the pork mince to bring the total up to 1.75 kg (3 lb 14 oz), then put it in the bowl of a stand mixer fitted with the paddle attachment.
8. Mix the salt, curing salt and dry spices together, then add them to the farce along with the pistachios, port, honey, miso paste and orange zest. Mix on low speed until everything is incorporated. With the motor running, slowly add the egg white and mix until thoroughly combined.
9. Lay two large pieces of plastic wrap, one on top of the other, on the bench (I like to dampen the bench with a wet cloth first so the wrap sticks to the bench). Lay the duck skin out flat on the plastic wrap. Pull the skin from the wings and legs through to the inside so they're not flapping on the outside (as if you're pulling a sleeve inside a jacket).
10. Wet your hands, then scoop up the duck and pork mixture and place it along one side of the duck skin, shaping it with your hands into a long, even log just inside the border of one half of the skin. Fold the remaining skin over the top, tucking it in underneath the mixture on the opposite side.
11. Keeping the plastic wrap taut, roll up the galantine to seal it, then take the two ends of the plastic wrap in your hands and roll the whole thing on the bench so that the plastic tightens around the galantine and makes a tight cylinder. Transfer to the fridge and leave overnight to set and allow the flavour to develop.
12. The next day, preheat the oven to 80°C (175°F). Unwrap the duck and place it on a wire rack set over a baking tray. Bake until a probe thermometer inserted into the centre of the galantine reaches 65°C (149°F). This may take as long as 3–4 hours. Remove the galantine from the oven and let it cool at room temperature for an hour, then place it in the fridge, uncovered, to cool overnight.
13. The next day, half-fill a deep-fryer or a large saucepan with oil and heat it to 170°C (338°F). Remove the galantine from the fridge and carefully immerse it in the hot oil; you only want to quickly colour the skin, not heat the meat – this should only take about 1 minute. Carefully remove the galantine from the oil and place it back on the rack to drain and cool. Refrigerate until ready to serve. It will keep for up to a week.
14. When you're ready to serve, cut one end off the galantine, then carve a few slices and lay them on a plate. Let the galantine temper slightly, then serve with mustard and condiments, such as pickled currants (page 232) or candied cumquats (page 233).

CHAPTER .FOUR.
RAW, GRILLED & ROASTED

CONTENTS

INTRODUCTION	119
MEAT COOKERY	122
BEEF TARTARE	128
GRILLED FISH	130
PIL PIL	133
GRILLED OCTOPUS	134
PORCHETTA	136
GRILLED PORK CHOP	140
SWEET-AND-SOUR GRILLED ONIONS	141
GRILLED STEAK	142
CHEESEBURGERS	144

For something as elemental as meat, there's a surprising amount of thought and attention that goes into making it as good as it possibly can be. Fernand Point described perfection as 'lots of little things done well', and when it comes to meat, it really is the little things that make a difference.

Whether it's sourcing, handling, ageing, preparing or carving, each step along the way contributes to the outcome, and each requires care, focus and attention.

In many ways, these recipes start well before you even think about picking up a knife or firing up the grill, going all the way back to when you visited the butcher. The importance of a good butcher cannot be overstated. Whatever you're cooking, getting the best outcome on the plate starts with sourcing the best meat possible. Butchery is one of the oldest professions in the world, and a noble trade; when you find a good butcher, it pays dividends to develop a relationship with them.

I've forged relationships with a whole range of meat purveyors over the years. Most recently, we have begun sourcing our meat for the restaurant from butchers who are in direct contact with the farm where the animals are raised. When possible, we choose pasture-raised and grass-fed animals; not only does the meat taste better, these methods are better for the animals and the environment.

Butchers provide the connection to farmers and act as translators for the customer. A passionate butcher is inspiring, and will often help you decide what you'll be having for your next meal – I get excited looking at all the possibilities, and often walk out the door with much more than I came for. Look for a butcher who knows as much about their produce as possible, who sources free-range, grass-fed animals and who – this is a bonus – has a dry-ageing program.

Dry-ageing meat results in a wonderful transformation. After the animal has been dispatched, rigor mortis occurs, which causes the muscles in the carcass to tense up and stiffen. The enzymes present then begin to work their magic by breaking down the muscle fibres and undoing the rigor. Typically this process is allowed to run for up to 28 days, with the enzymes disrupting the protein and tough collagen, which can then dissolve into delicious gelatine during cooking, as well as converting proteins into savoury amino acids and glycogen into glucose.

The result of these miraculous changes is meat that's more tender and flavourful. A lot of meat tends to be briefly aged before sale, but taking

> **NOT ONLY DOES SEASONING EARLY ALLOW THE SALT TO BETTER PENETRATE THE MEAT, I THINK IT HELPS DEVELOP A BETTER CRUST, WHICH IS THE KEY TO FLAVOUR.**

things a step further and pushing the length of time can further develop the texture and flavour. In the best cases, this results in meat with an intense savouriness, and length and depth on the palate.

Dry-ageing often occurs once the carcass is broken down into cuts, and is done under specific conditions that allow the meat to age slowly, usually with humidity levels around 70–80 per cent and a temperature around 1–4°C (33.8–39.2°F). The low temperature slows down microbiological growth but doesn't completely stop it, meaning that the longer the meat is dry-aged, the more funky and nutty flavours tend to develop. Since the meat loses moisture as it ages, the flavour also naturally intensifies over time.

Seeking dry-aged meat isn't an imperative, but splashing out on it for something like beef tartare (page 128) or a steak grilled over charcoal (page 142) can be illuminating, the result being meat with an incredibly profound flavour and a succulent texture.

There are a couple more things to think about before you start cooking. The first is to allow time to temper your meat. Tempering is simply the process of allowing the raw meat to come to room temperature. Whether it's meat, fish or birds, the benefit is that before you even add any heat to the equation, it's closer to the final target temperature (see page 124). Cooking meat cold from the fridge, on the other hand, can result in a finished product that has a tough, dry exterior, but is undercooked or even raw on the inside. Tempering therefore contributes to a more even result, as well as reducing the overall cooking time. As a general rule, I try to temper meat for at least one to two hours before cooking.

The other important thing to consider is seasoning. Whether you're grilling or roasting, season hard with salt. After all, the exterior is only a small portion of the whole, so usually the flesh can take a little more than you think. If you're grilling, you'll lose a lot of salt during the cooking process, so you may also need to season again after carving. I like to season early and heavily – you can even season during tempering (keeping in mind that fish doesn't need nearly as much time or seasoning as meat).

Not only does seasoning early allow the salt to better penetrate the meat, I think it helps develop a better crust, which is the key to flavour: as meat browns at high temperatures, it undergoes a process called the Maillard reaction, an interaction between amino acids and sugars that results in a caramelised exterior with a wonderfully savoury, complex flavour. This is what really gets your mouth watering, and the reason that those gnarled edges or crisp pieces of skin are usually the first to get picked off, sometimes before carving even begins.

RAW, GRILLED & ROASTED

MEAT COOKERY

In restaurants, young chefs often view the meat section – that is, the hot section – as a place of high energy, extreme heat and excitement. It certainly can be all these things, but what's often missed is the level of nuance that goes with it, all the way through to resting and carving.

GRILLING

When it comes to grilling meat, nothing beats cooking over charcoal. Even the scent and glow of charcoal as it's heating up is appealing, but it's when the fat renders and drips onto the coals, the flames leap and wisps of smoke curl and linger, that the smell becomes truly intoxicating. Meat cooked over coals is just better, lending an inimitable flavour to food. But just because it's as primal and pure as it gets, that doesn't mean it needs to be imprecise.

Almost invariably, the grill section in restaurants is seen as macho – the more flames, bravado, poking and prodding, the better. It doesn't help that it's also one of the busiest sections, where chefs get stacked with rows of orders all at once, and the stress and pressure is high. As intense as it is, though, a grill is at its best when it's approached with lightness and a deft touch.

I first witnessed this at Mugaritz, where we'd grill pieces of veal ever so gently over the fire, placing handfuls of grape-vine cuttings directly onto the coals to create light plumes of smoke that would flavour the meat while its internal temperature slowly rose.

I saw it again when Isobel Little came to work with us at LP's. She'd just returned from a stint overseas and had brought with her a cooking style that embraced a slowed-down version of grill cookery.

Until then, we'd used a charcoal oven that, with the door closed, would create a contained but wild and fierce heat – we'd needed this early on as we did massive sittings and had to get the orders out quickly. By the time

Izzy started, we'd reduced the capacity in the restaurant, so we had a little more time, and she would keep the oven door open during service. Initially this seemed counterintuitive, but the cooking on the proteins was better, with the degree of doneness more consistent from edge to edge. By slowing down, she achieved a slower heat transfer, meaning more even cooking, with time to monitor and adjust the temperature if needed. Nowadays, this is the only way I do it.

As for other tricks? Grilling meat or fish on fine-mesh wire cake racks or similar is very handy, because they're light, extremely mobile and don't hold a huge amount of heat, meaning they're easy to pick up and move. I also like the fact that they can be gripped with a tea towel and lifted to eye level to peek underneath and see how well the crust is progressing or the skin is crisping, without having to turn anything. They work particularly well with fish, and you can flip a fillet or a whole fish by inverting the rack onto a board and giving it a stiff bang, then sliding the fish back onto the rack to cook the other side, rather than shovelling a scraper underneath, which nearly always results in lost skin.

There seems to be a belief that meat should only be flipped a certain number of times (even as little as once) while grilling. I am, however, an advocate for lots of flipping, which allows all sides to get an even amount of heat and encourages an even result. When I'm grilling, I like to think of myself as a human rotisserie, making sure no one area is favoured over any other. Then, towards the end of the cooking process, I might lower the grill or increase the heat to get the desired colouring and crust, keeping in mind that the hotter the temperature, the more residual heat there'll be as the meat rests.

Another piece of dubious grill lore is the poking and prodding that goes on to determine doneness, with different hand configurations meant to correspond to rare, medium–rare and so on. It's not the worst guide, and I do believe you can develop a sixth sense around doneness that's honed through touch, intuition and experience, but there's no better tool in your arsenal than a thermometer. It's like X-ray vision. And why ruin a beautiful piece of meat just because you're determined to prove you're some kind of clairvoyant? I like to use intuition as a guide, then validate it with a thermometer. You can't argue with fact.

Degrees of doneness
for beef, lamb and pork

Bleu: 45°C (113°F)
Rare: 50°C (122°F)
Medium–rare: 55°C (131°F)
Medium: 60°C (140°F)
Medium-well: 65°C (149°F)
Well-done: 70°C (158°F)

Keep in mind that when you're grilling or roasting, the residual heat continues to cook the item even after it's taken off the heat. This means you'll need to pull it off when it's a few degrees shy of where you want it to be. You can always cook something more if it's under, but you can't go back if it's over.

ROASTING

Roasting is often associated with using as high a heat as possible to create a wonderful dark crust. But while this works very well with some cuts, roasting can also be broken down into different controlled stages to achieve the desired results, which in most cases is a crisp skin or a dark brown exterior, and a tender, juicy interior. It can be hard to nail both.

Before you even start cooking, however, there are a few things you can do to encourage the skin (if the cut you're cooking has any) to turn a beautiful burnished colour and go extra crisp. Skin is made up of water, fat and tough connective tissue. During cooking, the tough connective tissue needs to be dissolved into gelatine, the fat needs to render and the water needs to be removed. This can be encouraged by drying out the skin beforehand, cooking at high heat, and rubbing oil on the surface, which promotes fast heat transfer.

Meats that are to be roasted benefit enormously from sitting in the fridge, uncovered, for a couple of days before cooking, which dries out the surface or skin.

When it comes to chickens and particularly ducks, you can take the extra step of scalding the skin with boiling water before you leave them to dry, which tightens the skin and starts to break it down just a little. This is best done at least a day before cooking, and makes for a crisp, glassy result after roasting.

With larger cuts, my friend and business partner Elvis Abrahanowicz, of Bodega and Porteño fame, blew my mind a few years ago by describing a method where the process of roasting could be divided into two stages. The first is where the meat is roasted at a relatively low heat and taken close to the final degree of doneness, almost in slow motion, with a huge margin for error on timing. This low temperature denatures the proteins slowly, tenderising the meat and helping it retain its juices. Then, after the meat has reached the desired doneness, it's removed from the oven and the temperature is turned up. The meat is then returned to the oven and the intense blast of high heat rapidly gives it a dark crust and crisp exterior without affecting all the work you've done on the inside.

As with grilling, a thermometer is your friend here.

RESTING

Resting is a step that's sometimes overlooked, but it allows the cooked meat to relax and the juices to be distributed evenly throughout the muscles. This means that when you carve, all that precious juiciness stays in the meat, rather than spilling over the sides of your chopping board.

How long you should rest meat after cooking is up for debate, but what's not is the fact that everything tends to continue cooking after you remove it from the heat. It pays to remove the meat when it's a little underdone, then watch the temperature rise to the correct doneness as it rests, rather than settle for meat that's overcooked. The rise can be significant, depending on the temperature at which the meat was cooked.

Resting should happen uncovered, so that you retain that beautiful exterior you worked so hard to achieve. Rather than guessing at how long to rest something (although half the cooking time is a good rule), I like to wait until the internal temperature comes down to around 50°C (122°F) before serving.

CARVING

There isn't too much to be said about carving, but it can make the difference between good and great. Carve across the grain, which increases the sensation of tenderness, or you risk serving meat that's chewy or even ropey.

A very sharp knife also means you don't need to use as much force when you're slicing, so you won't push out any of the juices through added pressure.

Finally, you might like to season the meat again after you've carved it, since this will be the first time the interior has been salted. Flaky salt adds a little extra texture and helps bring out the natural flavour of the meat. It's a small thing, but it takes you one step closer to perfection.

BEEF TARTARE

A good beef tartare is a simple, delicious classic, and one of the finest ways to eat raw beef. It can be served as a canapé, a starter or a main course, along with all kinds of vehicles to scoop it up or spoon it onto: vegetables, robust leaves, crackers, crisps and even French fries or gnocco fritto (page 236).

There are a couple of things that turn a mound of raw meat into something truly elegant. The beef should always be cut, by hand, at the very last minute. And while seasoning is down to personal preference, and you can go classic or not-so-classic, striking a balance is always the key. Find what you like by adding a small amount of each seasoning, then taste and adjust until you hit the sweet spot for balance and mouthfeel.

SERVES 4

400 g (14 oz) dry-aged beef, such as rump, topside or tri-tip
1 tablespoon smoked olive oil
2 egg yolks
1 tablespoon Dijon mustard
1 tablespoon hot sauce (page 220)
1 tablespoon fish sauce
2 tablespoons finely diced French shallot
1 tablespoon rinsed and chopped salted capers
1 teaspoon freshly chopped tarragon (optional)
1 bunch of chives (optional), finely chopped

1. Trim the beef of any sinew and cut it into 5 mm (¼ in) cubes. Put the beef cubes in a bowl and dress with the smoked olive oil. I like to do this to coat the beef first and keep the other acidic ingredients from discolouring the meat (this may be a placebo, but I do feel it offers some waterproofing attributes).

2. Add the remaining ingredients and gently fold them together, taking care not to mix too vigorously as it can cause the mix to turn cloudy. This doesn't affect the taste but can ruin the aesthetics of a bright and defined tartare.

3. Taste the mix and assess what it needs. If you think it needs a bit more heat, add a small amount of hot sauce. If it needs more piquancy, add a tad more mustard. More umami or savouriness? Add a splash more fish sauce. Throughout, adjust the seasoning with salt and freshly ground black pepper to your taste. Be careful to not overload the tartare and make it so you can only endure one mouthful. It should be balanced, nuanced and delicious. Serve with your favourite vessel, such as the gnocco fritto (page 236) and thinly sliced radishes pictured here.

GRILLED FISH

Freshly grilled fish (pictured overleaf) is delicious, but cooking it can be a tricky task when the fish misbehaves by sticking or tearing. Grilling fish well requires focus and patience.

For me, it doesn't get better than cooking a whole flat fish; the skin, bones and cartilage all offer attributes that make it wonderfully succulent and delicious, and the cooked flesh easily peels away from the bones. All species of flounder and sole have high amounts of collagen that, when cooked, turns into gelatine, giving a luxurious mouthfeel; they're fantastic when offset by lemon juice or a sharp dressing.

When I was working at Mugaritz in the Basque region of Spain, I was taught a recipe for a vinaigrette called 'refrito', which means re-fry. It was dressed onto turbot during the cooking process, adding an incredibly clean flavour and balance to the fish. When served, the dressing and gelatine from the fish combine to make a loose sauce in the bottom of the dish to be mopped up with bread.

Any other fish can be cooked in this way – and if you're more comfortable cooking boneless fillets, this is also fine.

SERVES 2

1 large flounder, about 600–700 g (1 lb 5 oz–1 lb 9 oz)
Flaky salt
Pil pil (page 133) or pistachio, caper and lemon sauce (page 222), to serve (optional)

REFRITO

75 ml (2.25 fl oz) good-quality cider vinegar
30 g (1 oz) peeled garlic cloves
8 g (0.3 oz) fine salt
150 ml (5 fl oz) extra virgin olive oil

1. Light a charcoal grill or barbecue and let the charcoal burn down to a solid bed of glowing coals; it doesn't need to be a huge fire but the coals should spread out underneath the entire fish and be at least 5 cm (2 in) deep. When the coals are ready, you should be able to hold your hand above them for just a couple of seconds before you need to pull it away.
2. While the coals are heating, remove the fish from the fridge and let it temper.
3. Make the refrito by blending the vinegar, garlic and salt with a stick blender or in a food processor until very smooth. Pour the mixture into a bowl, add the olive oil and lightly mix to combine; it's not an emulsification, just a loose dressing. You can use a spoon to apply the refrito over the fish while it's cooking, or you can go one step further and use a clean, food-safe spray bottle.
4. Put a wire cake rack over the coals and let it heat up. Spoon or spray a small amount of the refrito all over the fish and lay it gently onto the rack, top side down (since this is the thicker side). You may need to play with heights and positioning of the rack; you want the fish close enough to the heat to caramelise and cook, but not so close that it burns.

5. Cook the fish for 5–10 minutes, checking the underside often: grip the cake rack with a tea towel and lift the rack above your eye level to peek underneath and check on the progress. When you start to see gentle browning and bubbling on the skin, add some more refrito (be careful as the oil can drip and flare up).
6. Take a plate or tray large enough to hold the fish, then grab one end of the rack with a tea towel and lift it away from the coals. In one motion, flip the rack over and give the other end a sturdy tap to release the fish onto the plate.
7. Return the rack to the coals, then slide the fish onto it (with the uncooked side down). Apply some more refrito to the fish and cook for another 5 minutes.
8. Check the internal temperature of the fish in the thickest part. Once it reaches 50–55°C (122–131°F), use the same sturdy tapping technique to transfer the fish to a warm serving dish. If you are unsure if the fish is cooked, make a cut in the thickest part with a small knife and look inside – the flesh should be white and some juices should flow out. If it looks slightly raw on the bone, cook it a little longer.
9. Dress the fish with a bit more refrito and let it rest for a few minutes – during this time, its internal temperature should rise to around 58°C (32°F), which is perfect for serving. Season the fish with flaky salt and serve it as is, or try it with pil pil or pistachio, caper and lemon sauce.

RAW, GRILLED & ROASTED

PIL PIL

Here's a sauce that utilises the gelatine from fish skins to create an emulsion similar to pil pil. This classic fish and sauce preparation from the Basque region of Spain is made when cooking the local delicacy of kokotxas. Small pieces of highly prized meat from the throat of cod are cooked in olive oil in an earthenware dish, releasing gelatine as they cook. The shaking of the dish – an action known as 'pil pil' – causes the gelatine to emulsify with the olive oil.

The recipe might sound odd, but it's delicious and makes for a brilliant condiment to accompany your fish. You can adjust the recipe according to how thick you want the sauce to be. For a thinner sauce, reduce the olive oil by 1 or 2 tablespoons.

Unless you can accumulate a lot of fish skins, you'll need to ask your fishmonger to save them for you. They need to be scaled and all the flesh and blood lines must be removed to prevent a cloudy stock.

MAKES 250 ML (9 FL OZ)

500 g (1 lb 2 oz) clean, scaled fish skin
20 g (0.7 oz) honey
1 tablespoon cider vinegar, plus extra to taste
225 ml (7.5 fl oz) olive oil

1. Start by making a stock from the fish skin. Put the skin in a large saucepan and cover with 750 ml (26 fl oz) water. Bring to a simmer over medium heat, then turn the heat down so the water is just below simmering point and cook for 2–3 hours. This gentle heat will break down the fish skin; if the heat is too high, the gelatine can stick to the bottom of the pan. It also needs to cook very slowly so the liquid doesn't evaporate.
2. Check if the stock is ready by tasting a small amount of the liquid – it should be very sticky on your lips.
3. Gently strain the stock through a sieve into a container and discard the fish skin. Put the stock in the fridge (it will set like a jelly). It will keep for a week and can also be frozen.
4. To make the pil pil, spoon 75 g (2.5 oz) of the set fish-skin stock into a heatproof bowl set over a saucepan of gently simmering water. Add the honey, vinegar and a pinch of salt. Stir until the stock has just melted and the salt has dissolved, then remove the bowl from the heat and set aside to cool to lukewarm.
5. Whisk the olive oil into the stock mixture, adding the oil drop by drop at first and then in a slow drizzle, whisking the whole time as if you were making a mayonnaise. The sauce will gradually thicken and turn pale.
6. Once all the oil has been added, check the seasoning and adjust with salt, pepper and cider vinegar to taste. Similar to a hollandaise, the pil pil sauce must be kept at room temperature and used on the day it's made. If it goes in the fridge, the stock will set to a jelly again and split from the oil.

GRILLED OCTOPUS

I've made this many times, both in the restaurants and at home. This dish is full of brilliant flavours and textures: charred, tender octopus, plus fresh, aromatic salsa verde and salty, earthy potatoes.

My preferred octopus here are the large, frozen octopus hands. The freezing process helps tenderise the flesh and the tentacles, when cooked, have a soft, pork-like texture.

Start this recipe 2 days ahead so the octopus is thawed, cooked and chilled, ready for grilling.

SERVES 4–6

1 kg (2 lb 4 oz) frozen octopus hands, thawed in the fridge overnight
500 g (1 lb 2 oz) small potatoes, such as Nicola or kipfler (fingerling)
Olive oil, for drizzling
1 lemon
Salsa verde (page 222), to serve

1. Take a pot large enough to comfortably hold the octopus and fill it with water. Bring to a rolling boil, then carefully add the octopus and turn the heat down so the temperature sits below a simmer – you're looking for it to hover around 80°C (176°F).
2. Cook the octopus for 45 minutes or until tender. This can be tested by cutting a small slice off the thickest part of the octopus and tasting it. If it's not tender, keep cooking, checking it every 10 minutes. When it's ready, remove the pot from the heat and drain off most of the water until the octopus is just covered. Leave the octopus to cool in the remaining liquid to room temperature, then drain, place it on a tray, cover and refrigerate overnight to chill and set.
3. Light a charcoal grill or barbecue and let the coals burn down until white and glowing. While you're waiting, remove the octopus from the fridge and let it temper. If the tentacles are connected, cut them into individual tentacles to ensure you get an even colour all over while cooking.
4. Meanwhile, put the potatoes in a large saucepan and cover them with cold water. I like to season the water with what seems like an absurd amount of salt: 250 g (9 oz) to every 1 litre (35 fl oz) of water. This results in potatoes with a fine, powdery coating on their surface when they dry, and a deep flavour. Season your water, then bring the potatoes to a gentle boil and cook until tender – the tip of a knife should slide in and out easily.
5. Gently tip the potatoes into a colander or sieve to drain; don't rinse them, or you'll wash off the salty exterior. Transfer the potatoes to a plate and leave them to dry and cool. (Potatoes cooked like this are delicious on their own, but are also wonderful on a crudité platter or with a ramekin of aïoli – see page 223.)
6. If you don't already have some salsa verde handy, make it now.

7. Lightly oil the octopus and place it on a preheated wire cake rack set over the hot grill (ensuring the rack is really hot when you add the octopus helps reduce sticking). Grill the octopus hot and fast (it's already cooked through) until it colours nicely and starts to char a little – check the underside by lifting the rack and peeking underneath. When it's nicely coloured with an attractive crust, flip it over to colour the other side and warm it through (you can check this with a metal skewer or the tip of a knife). When it's done, flip the octopus onto a chopping board.

8. Put the potatoes on a large platter, cutting any larger ones into halves or quarters, then chop the octopus to roughly the same size and add it to the platter. Dress with enough salsa verde to coat the octopus and potatoes. Use a microplane to grate the lemon zest over the top, then cut the lemon in half and squeeze the juice over as well, catching any seeds with your fingers. Season generously with salt and pepper.

PORCHETTA

In traditional terms, porchetta (pictured overleaf) refers to a whole deboned pig that's been rolled, stuffed, trussed and roasted. Since you'd need an army to get through the thing, a few variations have been popularised, the goal being to make it much more manageable, if a little less impressive.

The most common, or at least classic, variation consists of half a deboned middle of the pig (the belly and the loin cuts) rolled up and trussed to form a large cylinder. I have, however, always found this a tricky cut to cook – while the belly is forgiving, the loin can be temperamental and often ends up dry. Making a porchetta with the belly only gives a more consistent and, to my mind, better result.

Start this recipe a day ahead so the skin has time to dry out, then you'll need to start cooking about 10 hours before you want to eat. You'll need some butcher's twine for trussing.

SERVES 8–10

1 boneless, skin-on pork belly, about 3 kg (6 lb 12 oz)
35 g (1.25 oz) fine salt
Olive oil, for drizzling
Extra virgin olive oil, to serve

PORCHETTA SEASONING

1 head of garlic, cloves separated and peeled
5 fresh bay leaves
1 handful of picked rosemary leaves
3 tablespoons toasted fennel seeds
1 tablespoon chilli flakes
1 tablespoon freshly cracked black pepper
2 tablespoons flaky salt
200 ml (7 fl oz) olive oil

1. For the porchetta seasoning, blend or crush all the ingredients with a mortar and pestle to form a rustic paste.
2. Put the pork belly on a large chopping board, skin side down, with one of the long edges facing you. Taking extreme care, and using a sharp knife held parallel to the bench, score the entire length of the side of the belly that's facing you from end to end, trying to keep the incision in the centre of the flesh. The idea is create a flap that you will open out. Deepen the cut in long, even strokes to open up the piece of meat, stopping just before you get to the other side. Open out the cut flap like a book.
3. Rub the garlic and herb paste all over the exposed meat, then roll up the belly like a Swiss roll, starting from the section you opened out and continuing until the skin is all on the outside.
4. Truss the pork, starting from the middle of the roll and using individual loops. I use a simple butcher's knot, which acts like a slipknot and holds its place once it's tightened. Make sure the knots are sturdy to prevent the pork unravelling during cooking. Rub the porchetta all over with the salt and refrigerate overnight, uncovered, to dry out.
5. The next day, preheat the oven to 70°C (160°F). Brush the excess salt from the porchetta, then place it on a wire rack over a shallow roasting tin. Gently roast the pork for 10 hours. When you take it out of the oven it will look dry and dusty on the skin and the ends will look slightly jerky-like; do not fear, the inside will be juicy and tender.

6. Remove the porchetta from the oven and increase the temperature to 220°C (425°F). (If you're not ready to serve, you can keep the pork at room temperature for up to 4 hours before you finish roasting it at the higher temperature.) Rub olive oil all over the skin, then return the porchetta to the oven and roast until the skin is puffed and crisp, about 30 minutes. The beauty of this method is that the pork will definitely be cooked on the inside, so this stage is entirely about crisping the skin. If the skin isn't crisp and hasn't coloured sufficiently after 30 minutes, roast the porchetta for a further 10 minutes, keeping a close eye on it.
7. Remove the porchetta from the oven, taking extreme care since hot rendered fat may have accumulated in the roasting tin. Let the pork rest for 30 minutes.
8. With a sharp knife or scissors, cut the twine and gently remove it. Cut the porchetta into rounds using a serrated knife. (If the scraggly ends are too dry to eat, trim off and discard them.) Taste a slice to check the seasoning and season with salt if needed. Arrange the slices on a hot dish or plate. Drizzle with some good-quality extra virgin olive oil right before serving.

GRILLED PORK CHOP

It's hard to beat a good pork chop (pictured on the previous page). It has all the best things about pork: a salty, golden crust, a juicy interior, a bone to chew on and, if you play it right, delicious salty crackling.

Make sure the chop is of a decent thickness, otherwise it will cook too quickly without developing those lovely characteristics we want to achieve. It's best to use pork that's been dry-aged for a minimum of a week so the skin has had time to dry thoroughly; if you're cooking pork that's been packed in a plastic vacuum bag or wrapped in plastic, there's a high chance it won't reach its full potential.

Grilling pork chops over coals can be a wild experience because pork is incredibly fatty; as the fat renders onto the coals, it can cause uncontrollable flare-ups. You can limit this by paying attention to how you position your chop, and ensuring the area beneath it (where it might drip) is free of coals. Or you can follow the method I use here and start cooking the pork in a cast-iron frying pan over the coals; it'll help the flesh achieve a great crust while also rendering out some excess fat.

SERVES 2–4

1 pork loin chop, about 500 g–1 kg (1 lb 2 oz–1 lb 4 oz)
Mild olive oil, for drizzling
Flaky salt

1. Remove the pork chop from the fridge and leave it to temper for at least an hour before cooking.
2. Light a charcoal grill or barbecue and let it burn down to a steady bed of white, glowing coals, then place a cast-iron frying pan on a wire rack set above the coals to get very hot.
3. Rub a little olive oil all over the chop to coat, then season it liberally with flaky salt. Place the chop in the pan and let it cook undisturbed for 3–4 minutes or until it colours and develops a crust. Flip the chop over and let it colour and develop a crust on the other side.
4. The pan should have accumulated some fat from the chop, which is great for crisping the skin. Using a pair of tongs, carefully balance the chop upright in the pan, skin side down, and cook for about 5 minutes or until the fat has rendered, and the skin is golden and starting to crackle nicely. Due to the shape of the chop, you may need to roll it backwards and forwards as it cooks to get an even result.
5. Set the pan aside, reserving the rendered fat, and transfer the chop onto the wire rack set over the coals. Let the chop gently cook through, flipping it occasionally and monitoring the internal temperature with a probe thermometer. You're looking for a final temperature of 57–60°C (135–140°F), so remove it from the heat when it's around 55°C (131°F) and let it creep up to temperature as it rests. The meat will be around medium; you can cook it longer, but you don't do the pig justice by doing so – cooking your pork slightly pinker results in a far superior, juicier chop. I then like to put the chop back into the rendered fat in the pan to chill out until it cools to around 50°C (122°F).

6. To carve the pork chop, stand it on a chopping board with the rib bone pointing up, and run a sharp knife between the bone and meat. Once you get to the bottom, you'll need to change the angle of the knife to horizontal to follow the bone around and release the meat. Lay the meat flat on the board, taking care not to let the crackling come into contact with any juices, which will make it soggy and undo all your hard work. With your knife at a 45-degree angle, cut the meat into 1 cm (½ in) slices, then arrange it on a warm plate and gently season with salt between each slice. Lay the bone alongside and pour any extra juices over the meat.

Sweet-and-sour grilled onions

Charred, sweet onions and a sharp, sweet dressing make a brilliant garnish for your grilled pork chop, as on page 139.

SERVES 2–4

1 white onion, skin on
1 red onion, skin on
2 spring onions (scallions), greens and roots attached
Olive oil, for drizzling
2 tablespoons palm-sugar vinegar (page 209)
80 ml (2.5 fl oz) extra virgin olive oil
Juice of ½ lemon
250 g (9 oz) red mustard leaves (optional)
Flaky salt

1. Add the whole white and red onions to a large saucepan of boiling water. Cook at a gentle boil for 25 minutes or until tender, then plunge them into a bowl of iced water to cool them. Blanch the whole spring onions in the same pan of water for 1 minute, then add them to the iced water to cool. Transfer all the onions to a clean tea towel to dry.
2. Meanwhile, light a charcoal grill or barbecue and let it burn down to glowing coals. (If you're cooking the pork chop first, just keep the grill going after you take off the pork to let it rest.)
3. Cut the white and red onions in half, then cut one of each of the halves in half again. Peel off the skin, then separate the layers. Cut the roots from the spring onions, but otherwise leave them whole.
4. Lightly drizzle all of the onions with olive oil, then season with salt. Place them on a rack set over the coals and cook, tossing occasionally, for 2–3 minutes or until the onions are charred around the edges.
5. Transfer the onions to a bowl and dress them with the palm-sugar vinegar. Add the extra virgin olive oil and lemon juice – and the mustard leaves, if using. Season with flaky salt and pepper and gently toss it all together with your hands. Pile the onions on top of the pork chop.

GRILLED STEAK

Good steak is a luxury. I much prefer to cook steak only occasionally, sourcing the finest I can from the butcher. That way, it keeps its value as a cut built around excitement and anticipation.

My absolute favourite steak is rib-eye. If you're more of a fillet or sirloin person, you may find this cut tastes fattier due to its high level of intramuscular fat, but I prefer it – it adds juiciness and brings different textures. You can cook sirloin following the same method, although I recommend trying to get it on the bone: cooking steak on the bone adds flavour, and it just looks better on the plate.

It pays to get a fairly large piece of steak, as I've suggested here. Anything less, and it's hard to develop a nice crust before the inside begins to overcook. Plan to cook your steak gently and slowly, and you'll be rewarded.

SERVES 2–4

1 kg (2 lb 4 oz) rib-eye steak
Olive oil, for drizzling
Flaky salt

1. Remove the steak from the fridge and leave it to temper for at least an hour before cooking.
2. Light a charcoal grill or barbecue and let it burn down to a steady bed of white, glowing coals, hot enough that you can only hold your hand close for a couple of seconds. It would also be good to have one area with less embers and another with no coals so that you can slow things down or move the steak away from the flames if things get out of hand. Set a wire rack above the coals.
3. Rub a little olive oil all over the steak to coat, then season it liberally with flaky salt. Season harder than you think, because a lot of salt will fall off during cooking and with meat this thick, you won't risk overseasoning.
4. Place the steak on the rack above the coals. Rearrange the coals if needed, positioning the meat so it can cook slowly. Gently cook the steak, flipping it every few minutes to evenly distribute the heat, and monitoring the temperature with a probe thermometer.
5. When the steak is around 10–12°C (20°F) below your desired doneness (see page 124), start working on developing the crust: lower the rack closer to the coals and rearrange the coals to form more of a hot zone. Continue to turn the steak occasionally, allowing a nice crust to form. When the steak is 5°C (10°F) below your desired doneness, remove it from the heat and leave it to rest. The residual heat will continue to cook the meat as it rests and carry it to the desired temperature.
6. To carve the steak, stand it on a chopping board with the bone pointing up, then carefully run a knife between the bone and the meat. Lay the meat flat on the board and, with your knife at a 45-degree angle, cut the steak into 1 cm (½ in) slices. Try to keep the slices in formation for serving by sliding the knife underneath the whole lot and transferring them to a warm plate. Gently season with salt between each slice.

CHEESEBURGERS

My opinion on burgers is that it's the synergy between all the components that makes them undeniably delicious, so I'm pretty specific about ratios, buns, sauces and the rest. If you can find it, I recommend Golden State mustard. I steer clear of mayonnaise, but a proper tomato sauce (I like Heinz Tomato Ketchup) is a must. Gherkins, white onion and a sweet bun are essential.

For the beef patty, I like to use equal parts brisket and chuck, which I dice and salt at a ratio of 12 grams of salt per kilogram of meat before passing it through a mincer. You can form this into patties by doing the whole patty-cake, back-and-forth thing between your hands, but I like to use a technique adopted from an old Heston Blumenthal *In Search of Perfection* episode, where he keeps the strands of minced meat aligned as they come out of the mincer, creating a log with a distinct grain. This log gets wrapped and chilled, then you cut it into patties across the grain, giving you a better texture.

You'll need four sheets of greaseproof paper for wrapping your burgers.

MAKES 4

350 g (12 oz) beef brisket
350 g (12 oz) beef chuck
9 g (0.3 oz) fine salt
40 g (1.5 oz) butter
4 burger buns, cut in half – use milk buns (see page 237) or brioche buns
2 tablespoons olive oil
8 slices American cheese
4 tablespoons American mustard
4 tablespoons tomato sauce
½ white onion, finely diced
8 slices gherkin

1. Dice the brisket and chuck to fit into the mouth of your mincer. Place the diced beef in a large bowl and toss with the salt to coat.
2. Lay two 40–50 cm (16–20 in) square layers of plastic wrap on the bench (moisten the bench first with a damp cloth to help the plastic stay put).
3. This next step is easier with two people – one operating the mincer, one catching. Place the beef into a mincer fitted with a 5 mm (¼ in) plate, and turn it on. If you're the catcher, hold the mince as it comes out, using some slight resistance towards the mincer so the meat doesn't just fall out – you want it to come out in one long log if possible. Lay the mince (hopefully with the strands all aligned) on the plastic wrap, then roll it up to create a log slightly smaller in diameter than the buns. Holding each end of the plastic, roll the log on the bench a few times to tighten it. Knot each end, then place the log in the fridge for 2–3 hours to firm up.
4. Slice the wrapped log into eight patties, around 80 g (2.75 oz) each, then carefully peel off the plastic. Gently press the patties so they are slightly wider than your burger buns, as they'll shrink during cooking. Return the patties to the fridge if you're not cooking them straight away.
5. You're going to toast the buns and grill the patties at the same time, so set everything up for cooking: bring all of the ingredients to room temperature; place a wire cake rack over a tray, ready for constructing burgers; heat your barbecue flatplate to high, leaving a section on low to toast the buns; and have everything else close at hand.
6. Melt the butter on the flatplate over low heat, then place the buns, cut sides down, on top, using the first few to spread the butter around. After 2 minutes, check your buns to see how they're toasting, moving

them around and changing spots if some are toasting quicker than others. After a couple more minutes, check the buns again – if they're golden brown, transfer them to the cake rack in pairs, toasted sides up.

7. While the buns are cooking, drizzle the oil onto the hotter zone of the barbecue, then lay the patties on top – they should sizzle with the heat. Grill for 2–3 minutes or until they are starting to develop a good crust and have blood coming through the top, then flip them over and place a slice of cheese on each. Cook for another 2–3 minutes to finish them off.

8. Lay four sheets of greaseproof paper on the bench. Spoon the mustard and tomato sauce onto the bun lids, then top each one with a spoonful of chopped onion and two gherkin slices. Using a spatula or grill scraper, stack two patties together and lift them onto the bun bases. Quickly place the lid on each burger.

9. Wrap each cheeseburger snugly in greaseproof paper and let them rest for a minute or two – this allows the bun to steam through and the whole burger to amalgamate and fuse together. Now it's time to unwrap and eat.

RAW, GRILLED & ROASTED

CHAPTER

.FIVE.

SMOKING

CONTENTS

INTRODUCTION	149
SMOKING 101	152
BACON	158
DRY-CURING	158
WET-CURING	159
SMOKING	159
BACON CHOPS	160
SMOKED HAM	163
MAPLE AND MUSTARD GLAZED CHRISTMAS HAM	164
SMOKED SAUSAGES	165
SMOKED MACKEREL	166
SMOKED MACKEREL NACH HAUSFRAUENART	169
SMOKED CHICKEN	170
SMOKED DUCK	172
CARVING POULTRY	173
SMOKED DUCK À LA CUMQUAT	175
SMOKED BEEF TONGUE	176
LEVEL UP: SMOKED BRISKET	178
SMOKED BRISKET SANDWICH	183
SMOKED BEEF SHORT RIBS	184
SMOKED PRIME RIB	187
CREAMED SPINACH	188
YORKSHIRE PUDDINGS	189

Smoked meat is the best meat. When LP's first opened in 2014, it was in the midst of the hipster movement. In hospitality, guys with beards, moustaches and tattoos obsessing over coffee, craft beer and barbecue were in. I'm proud to say that I never grew a moustache, and at LP's we tried hard to establish an identity that existed outside of trends – one that, as meaty as it was, steered away from 'dude food' and towards something more refined.

Yes, you could order smoked beef short rib or smoked lamb belly stuffed with merguez, but we weren't doing brisket or sliders or slaw. And we definitely weren't serving our meats with crinkle-cut chips in red plastic baskets. We might have had ZZ Top on the speakers, but on the plate LP's had more to do with my fine-dining roots than with clichés of the barbecue genre.

We imported two Southern Pride smokers from Tennessee – barbecue country. Our large smoker is a gas-assisted rotisserie smoker that we fuel with logs of apple and ironbark wood sourced from the Blue Mountains here in New South Wales. It weighs half a tonne and can smoke 70 chickens at once. And it provides us with a unique flavour as the burning logs flicker with flames, as opposed to just smouldering away like most chip smokers. It's built specifically for American barbecue, which means that at times it's totally impractical for our purposes, but we do love the end results. And once we started using it for brisket, we were really pleased with the outcome.

Our other smoker is a small electric smoker that features a chip box set over a heating element, which gives it the ability to burn woodchips while running at a lower temperature. We use this smoker for fish and when we want to impart a smoky flavour to something without cooking it, such as for cheese – typically what you'd call cold-smoking.

Our smokers have defined the menu at LP's more than anything else, and have remained a standby as we've transitioned more to wholesale. The flavours and textures smoking draws out are special: at once totally unique and insanely addictive.

Smoke is primal and elemental. Smoking may not be a preservative on its own, but the drying effect it has, combined with the coating of antibacterial phenols and other chemicals that are a result of the process, serve to inhibit microbiological growth. Combined with curing, it's a very effective method of preservation, which goes some way to explaining its popularity around the world and throughout history, and its importance in many food cultures.

Think of smoked haddock in Scotland, the Romanian–Jewish tradition of pastrami that then made its way to the US, Japan's katsuobushi, and the integral part smoking plays in Japanese cuisine as a core component of dashi. Then there's bacon in its many forms throughout Europe, including speck in Germany and pancetta in Italy. Follow the path north in Europe and things get even smokier, with people in colder areas relying even more on the process, often hanging fish or meats in their chimneys to cure and dry.

Today, smoking is done primarily to make food taste good. But those traditions endure, with smoking usually coupled with curing or heavy salting, less for preservation these days than for deliciousness.

At its most simple, there are two main ways to smoke food: cold-smoking and hot-smoking. The former is performed by salting and curing a product, then smoking it at a low temperature, generally below 35°C (95°F). This doesn't cook the product, but allows the smoke flavour to penetrate it. It's usually used for smoked salmon, and with salami and air-dried hams.

Hot-smoking, on the other hand, is typically done with products that have been salted or cured more gently, at a temperature high enough to cook the product, usually above 60°C (140°F), breaking down proteins as it does so. Lengthy hot-smoking can tenderise hard-working muscles such as pork shoulder and beef brisket, melting tough collagen fibres and rendering them super tender while adding a signature savoury smoked flavour.

The significant difference between cold-smoking and hot-smoking is that with the former, it's purely about flavour. Everything is kept cool and the end result is a product that seems closer to raw than cooked – compare translucent, sliceable smoked trout or salmon with the hot-smoked kind, which you can flake into pieces. Hot-smoking has a similar impact on flavour (although usually it's less subtle), but the key difference is that you're cooking at the same time. Often this still happens at a low temperature, hence why it's used with tougher cuts of meat that benefit from slow cooking, breaking down to become tender under prolonged heat.

Whatever path you choose, there's one step that will make a significant difference to the overall result: drying your fish or meat well after it's been brined or cured. This took us a while to appreciate at LP's. When you let your brined or cured protein dry properly – often in the fridge, uncovered,

SMOKING IS A MEDITATIVE PROCESS, AND IT CAN BE SOME OF THE MOST SATISFYING COOKING YOU'LL DO.

overnight – a fine, tacky coating forms on the surface, called a pellicle. This coating is crucial for smoking, as it allows the smoke to adhere, giving a more even result and creating that inviting mahogany or golden colour so often associated with smoked foods. Dry things well, and the results will speak for themselves.

When it comes to equipment, there's an enormous variety of options. I've seen huge machines featuring automated drying stages, smoking stages and even cold-showering stages designed to cool everything down rapidly after cooking, and I've also cold-smoked bacon in a (clean!) trash can.

For simple, quick smokes done for flavour, you can get away with using some woodchips, a perforated tray and some foil in a hooded barbecue. The biggest hurdle to overcome when you're taking things a little more seriously is temperature control. You might be able to get away with using a Weber for smoking something relatively fast like sausages, but for a ham, where you might need to smoke it for 10 hours, maintaining the right conditions (not to mention the focus) becomes increasingly difficult.

Thankfully, small automatic smokers with thermostats that can maintain a consistent temperature are available from most hardware stores. They have a hopper that holds woodchips or pellets, and they allow you to walk away without having to monitor things the whole time. There are also all sorts of makeshift smokers you can rig up – a quick Google search will throw up loads of ideas.

No matter what route you take, a thermometer is your friend. Using it can be as simple as sticking a probe into a piece of meat every now and then, or as high-tech as having a thermometer wirelessly connected to your phone, which will send you an alert when something is within range or close to being cooked.

You can get as technical as you want, but the key is to start small and to be open to experimentation and, most of all, to enjoy the process. Smoking is a meditative process, and it can be some of the most satisfying cooking you'll do, with results that far exceed the effort you put into it.

SMOKING 101

Smoking isn't complicated, but there is a bit of method and planning behind it, and it pays to understand the principles before you light a fire. Understanding how and when to brine, drying things out, then how you set up – noting the difference between hot and cold methods – are crucial steps. Start here, then you'll be primed to take a swing at the recipes that follow.

BRINING

You'll notice throughout this chapter that plenty of the things we smoke are brined first. Brining isn't intrinsically tied to smoking – it can do plenty for a chicken or a lamb shoulder before it's roasted, for example – but they do often go hand in hand.

Even if brining's historical roots are largely about preservation, the benefits run far deeper. When you soak meat in a brine, according to food-science sage Harold McGee, the salt first works to partially dissolve the protein structure and disrupt the muscle fibres. The salt and meat then interact in a way that allows the meat to hold more water in its cells, meaning it absorbs the brine. The result is well-seasoned meat, with a structure that holds onto its juices when cooked, resulting in an increased sensation of tenderness when you eat it. When you smoke meat, a process that adds flavour but encourages dryness, brining is the backstop that helps keep it juicy.

Knowing that there's a flow of brine into the muscle means you can take advantage of the brining process by flavouring the brine with herbs and spices. As the meat brines, the flavours move through the cell walls and deep into the flesh. This is why a brined ham can taste of cloves and cinnamon, or why pastrami might taste of coriander, garlic and pepper.

There are a few different brining methods you can employ. The method we favour at LP's is called equilibrium brining. It works by placing a cut of meat into a brine with four to seven per cent salt, which is less than you might see with other methods (such as gradient brining, where the salt can be as high as 10 per cent). The lower salt percentage means you need to brine for longer, sometimes up to two weeks, so the salt can slowly work its way to the centre of the meat. After a sufficient amount of time, the salt levels in the brine and the meat itself will effectively become equal.

Not only does this method prevent your meat from becoming overly salty, but it also gives a more even and predictable result. This is particularly important for cuts that use curing salt, such as hams or pastramis; if the curing salt doesn't spread evenly through the meat, you'll see it in the final result, which can be streaky or unevenly coloured.

The efficiency of this method can be increased with the help of injection brining. At an industrial scale, you'll see injecting machines and vacuum tumblers used to minimise the amount of time a product takes to cure. At home, it can be as simple as using a small brining needle, which you'll find in most homeware and kitchen stores. Suck up the brine with the needle, then gently inject it into the meat following an even grid pattern: you'll notice the meat start to swell as the fibres stretch and the brine works its way in. More often than not, some brine will spray out of a random hole, but just keep going.

You can see how much brine the piece of meat has taken on by weighing it before and after brining. A good rule of thumb is to inject enough brine that the meat increases from its original weight by about 10 per cent. Once you're finished, submerge the meat in additional brine in a container large enough to hold both the meat and brine (but that will also fit in your fridge).

One final note: in the recipes in this chapter, the brine is generally suitable for 1 kg (2 lb 4 oz) of meat. If you scale the quantity of meat up or down, scale the brine to match. This should ensure that the salinity level is correct, as well as giving you enough brine to fully submerge the meat.

SMOKING AT HOME: DOS, DON'TS AND WORK-AROUNDS

The simplest way to tackle smoking is with professional equipment, but that shouldn't stop you from giving it a crack – there are many alternatives and options that will still give a good result. Whatever method and whatever set-up you're using, you do need to pay attention to a few things, and it pays to be across the principles of both cold- and hot-smoking. Use these pages as a reference throughout this chapter, and as a fallback when you don't have access to the precise equipment.

COLD-SMOKING

Cold-smoking can be achieved with very basic equipment, mainly because you're really only using smoke as a flavouring, rather than cooking at the same time. At its most simple, you can do this by placing a piece of fish or meat in a lidded or hooded barbecue, then heating a cast-iron pan filled with woodchips on the stove until the pan is screaming hot and the woodchips ignite (you may still need to use a lighter or blowtorch to light them up; it pays to have an extraction fan on high and the windows open when you're doing this). Take the pan outside, extinguish the flames by covering the fire (briefly placing another pan on top works well), then place the pan in the barbecue and close the lid, letting the woodchips smoulder and the smoke swirl all around. You can repeat this a few times using fresh woodchips to get a smokier flavour.

While this method works, it can be quite labour-intensive. If you want to get a little more serious, look into cold-smoke generators, made by brands such as Smoke Daddy or Smokai. These are very effective at producing a consistent flow of smoke, and can be easily MacGyvered into all kinds of vessels that can act as smoking chambers: barbecues, old wardrobes, trash cans, old fridges or even purpose-built, handmade cedar boxes all work well.

Cold-smoke generators have a steel hopper that's filled with woodchips and then lit. A pipe connects the hopper to a chamber, with a small pump supplying a steady flow of oxygen to keep the chips smouldering. These are great as you can light them and walk away for up to an hour, before reloading the chips if you want more smoke.

It's important to make sure there's a damper or chimney on your chamber to allow smoke to escape; as much as you might think flooding the chamber with smoke is desirable, if it accumulates in large volumes it can produce very acrid, stale and bitter flavours.

If you buy a cold-smoke generator, you'll typically need to attach it to your barbecue by drilling a hole in the side. They usually come with instructions for doing this, and for making sure you've got adequate ventilation to let the smoke flow through. These are handy because you can rig them up to most barbecues without affecting the function at all.

Here's a basic method for cold-smoking a fish, such as kingfish or trout, that has been sufficiently cured and dried, and has a well-developed pellice to which the smoke can adhere. If you're cold-smoking anything else, the method is much the same, with time being the biggest variable.

1. Insert the pipe from your smoking device into a lidded barbecue with a small hole made in the side to accommodate the smoke generator.
2. Load the smoke generator with applewood chips and light it. Get the chips burning with a good steady flow of smoke, then lay the fish on the rack in the barbecue.
3. Cover the barbecue with the lid, leaving the damper open, and let the fish smoke for about an hour, topping up the smoker if needed.
4. Remove the fish from the smoker; it should have a golden hue from the smoke that has adhered to the surface.

HOT-SMOKING

Hot-smoking is a very similar process to cold-smoking, except that there has to be a heat source that can cook the food as well as smoke it. Visit your local barbecue shop or hardware store, and you're likely to find plenty of options, including electric, pellet and Texas-style offset smokers, plus others that might work with the barbecue you already have. A simple kettle barbecue modified to hold a smoke generator will allow you to cook most of the recipes in this book.

Each smoker will produce a slightly different result, but for most recipes the biggest consideration is temperature control. You either need a smoker that's accurate and that can hold a steady temperature, or one that's simple enough that you can manipulate the temperature as needed.

The more you get into smoking, the more you'll notice how seemingly small things can affect the final outcome. When you're burning wood, every degree of heat makes a difference, resulting in different chemicals being released and shifting flavour profiles and nuances in the finished product. If you're hot-smoking meat for a long period of time, particularly beef, you'll often also see a smoke ring develop, where the outside takes on a deep hue but the interior remains rose-coloured. This is certainly attractive, and is often used as a measure of quality, but it doesn't actually bring anything to the table in terms of flavour; in fact, we rarely see it in our products because we cook them at such low temperatures.

Short of using any specialist equipment, you can do a cheat's version of hot-smoking by cold-smoking a product for flavour (see the woodchip method, left), then finishing it in the oven. The result won't be the same, but it's worth a go in a pinch.

Here's a basic method for hot-smoking a piece of bacon, using a kettle barbecue that's been modified to hold a smoke generator (for more detail, see the recipe on pages 158–159). Before you start, make sure your pork has been sufficiently cured and dried and has a well-developed pellice to which the smoke can adhere. If you're hot-smoking anything else, the method is much the same, with time being the biggest variable.

1. Light a small fire in the bottom of your barbecue. I recommend using charcoal and getting a small, solid bed of coals going, but you could also use wood if you're feeling confident. Let the coals really burn down, then push them to one side of the barbecue; you don't want the bacon sitting right above the coals, which are there to heat the barbecue rather than grill the bacon.
2. Close the lid and monitor the temperature until the barbecue is running at a steady 95°C (203°F); this may take some tweaking, like adding or removing a piece of charcoal here and there to keep it consistent.
3. Set up the smoke generator with applewood chips and get a steady flow of smoke going. Put the bacon on the rack, skin side up, on the opposite side to the coals so it's cooking indirectly. Replace the lid and open the damper to allow the smoke to flow through, then cook until the bacon's internal temperature reads 65°C (149°F) on a probe thermometer, adjusting the heat as needed.
4. Remove the bacon from the grill. Let it cool at room temperature for an hour before transferring it to the fridge.

If you don't have a smoker, you can also use a regular lidded barbecue and a cast-iron pan (or a pan with foil covering the base). Put the pan on the heat with woodchips in the base and get it smoky, then light the chips using a blowtorch or barbecue lighter. Let the chips burn down a little, then extinguish them by placing another pan on top. Remove the top pan, place the pan of woodchips in the barbecue, then close the lid and let the smoke flow. You might do this a few times throughout a cook. Alternatively, you could put the woodchips in a pan or a pouch of foil on the hot barbecue flatplate and let it smoke away; or, if you're using a charcoal or briquette barbecue, just add some chips to the fire occasionally.

BACON

Bacon needs no introduction. One of the world's most delicious pork products, it's almost universally loved, and the smell of bacon cooking in the morning is enough to raise even the most lethargic soul. Making your own bacon can be immensely satisfying, and it's also really achievable at home.

There are a couple of different cuts that are used for bacon: the loin and the belly. In Australia and New Zealand, you typically see belly bacon with the loin attached, but you can also find streaky bacon, which is just the belly. I prefer to use the belly only, which has wonderful fat streaking through the muscle that renders out as it cooks to make the bacon extra crisp and delicious.

There are two schools of thought when it comes to curing bacon. Wet-curing is done by immersing the pork in brine to cure, which results in bacon that stays juicy and doesn't taste overly salty. Dry-curing is done by rubbing the pork with a blend of salt and sometimes sugar, and letting this draw out moisture and cure the meat. Dry-cured bacon is a saltier, drier style with a concentrated flavour. In either case, the cured pork is hot-smoked to finish it off, and is usually cooled and sliced before cooking.

I prefer to brine (or wet-cure) my bacon, but I've provided instructions for wet- and dry-curing. Give both methods a try and decide which you like best.

Dry-curing

Like the recipes in the Curing & Fermenting chapter (page 58), the quantities for dry-cured bacon are based on percentages, with the pork as the reference point. This makes it easy to scale the recipe up or down.

You'll need to start this recipe 6 days ahead.

1 skin-on boneless pork belly

DRY CURE
For every 1 kg (2 lb 4 oz) of pork, use:
25 g (1 oz) fine salt (2.5%)
13 g (0.5 oz) brown sugar (1.3%)
1 g sodium nitrite – curing salt #1 (0.1%) (see page 15)

1. Weigh the pork and calculate the quantities for the dry cure based on the percentages listed above. For example, if your pork weighs 2 kg (4 lb 8 oz), use 50 g (1.75 oz) salt, 26 g (1 oz) brown sugar and 2 g curing salt.
2. Weigh out the dry cure ingredients and combine well in a bowl.
3. Put the pork into a snug vessel, such as a roasting tin, and rub the cure all over the pork, distributing the cure as evenly as possible.
4. Cover and refrigerate the pork for 5 days, flipping the meat each day to redistribute the cure.
5. Briefly rinse the pork under cold water to wash off any excess cure. Pat the pork dry with paper towel or a clean tea towel. Hang up the pork (from a meat hook or similar), or sit it on a wire rack, and set it over a tray. Refrigerate the pork overnight to allow it to dry and develop a pellicle.
6. Follow the instructions opposite to smoke the bacon.

Wet-curing

Wet-cured bacon uses a percentage method to determine the concentration of salt in the brine. The pork can be of any size, as long as there's enough brine to comfortably cover it. A good rule of thumb is to have the same weight of brine as meat. Regardless of how much meat you're curing, the percentages in the brine don't change.

You'll need to start this recipe 6 days ahead.

1 skin-on boneless pork belly

BACON BRINE
For every 1 kg (2 lb 4 oz) of pork, use:
1 litre (35 fl oz) water (100%)
85 g (3 oz) fine salt (8.5%)
75 g (2.5 oz) brown sugar (7.5%)
15 g (0.5 oz) black peppercorns (1.5%)
5 fresh bay leaves
3.7 g sodium nitrite – curing salt #1 (0.37%) (see page 15)

1. For the brine, combine the water, fine salt, brown sugar, peppercorns and bay leaves in a large pot (it's good if your pot fits in the fridge; clear some room). Bring to a simmer, stirring until all of the salt and sugar have dissolved. Turn off the heat and leave to cool to room temperature.
2. Add the curing salt to the brine and whisk to dissolve.
3. Add the pork to the pot, cover and refrigerate for 5 days.
4. Rinse the pork under cold water, then pat it dry with paper towel or a clean tea towel. Hang the pork (from a meat hook or similar), or sit it on a wire rack, and set it over a tray. Refrigerate the pork overnight to allow it to dry and develop a pellicle.
5. Follow the instructions below to smoke the bacon.

Smoking

Whether you've chosen to dry-cure or wet-cure your pork, the smoking process is the same.

1. Start your smoker for hot-smoking (see page 154), aiming to achieve a consistent temperature of around 95°C (203°F).
2. Place the cured pork in the smoker, skin side up, and smoke until a thermometer inserted into the centre reads 65°C (149°F). This can take 2–3 hours. Be sure to keep adding fresh wood or woodchips so the bacon takes on a dark mahogany colour. Remove the bacon from the smoker and let it cool for an hour.
3. Hang the bacon from a meat hook, or sit it on a wire rack, and set it over a tray, then place it in the fridge to cool completely.
4. Once chilled, the bacon can be left whole, to be sliced whenever you have a hankering. Try cutting it to different thicknesses, but always cut it against the grain. The bacon will keep for up to 2 weeks in the fridge or 3 months in the freezer.

BACON CHOPS

Now that you've delved into the world of bacon, why not go one step further and make bacon chops, which uses the same brining technique but with bone-in, skin-on pork loin. You can do it with just a few bones – I'd say a minimum of three is good – or even a whole rack (pictured on page 151).

You'll need to start this recipe 6 days ahead.

1 bone-in, skin-on rack of pork
1 tablespoon lard
Quince mustard (page 229), to serve

BACON BRINE
For every 1 kg (2 lb 4 oz) of pork, use:
1 litre (35 fl oz) water (100%)
85 g (3 oz) fine salt (8.5%)
75 g (2.5 oz) brown sugar (7.5%)
15 g (0.5 oz) black peppercorns (1.5%)
5 fresh bay leaves
3.7 g sodium nitrite – curing salt #1 (0.37%) (see page 15)

1. Brine the pork following the method on page 159, giving the pork a few injections of bacon brine in a grid pattern using a brining needle (see page 14) before you refrigerate it in the remaining brine for 5 days.
2. After 5 days, remove the pork from the brine and follow the method for drying on page 159 (step 4).
3. Smoke the pork following the method on page 159 (steps 1–2), making sure that when you test the temperature of the pork, you do so in the centre, which is the thickest part.
4. Remove the pork from the smoker and let it cool to room temperature, then place it in an airtight container or wrap it in plastic wrap and refrigerate until completely cold.
5. When you are ready to eat your bacon chops, cut the pork rack into individual chops by slicing in between the bones to separate them. Leave them to temper at room temperature for an hour.
6. Heat a large cast-iron frying pan or a barbecue flatplate to medium heat and add the lard, swirling it to melt. Add the chops and quickly colour each side, making sure they're warmed through. Keep in mind that the chops have already been cooked in the smoker so they won't need a lot of cooking, around 3–4 minutes. Remove the chops from the heat and leave to rest for a few minutes.
7. Place the chops on warm plates and serve with quince mustard.

SMOKED HAM

At its most simple, smoked ham is a sandwich staple, best enjoyed with plenty of butter and even more Dijon mustard. But once you've made your own, you can take it in any direction: slice it and serve it as part of a ploughman's lunch with good bread, cheese and pickles; glaze it for Christmas, then make croque madame for breakfast; put it in quiches; use the bone for pea and ham soup. The list goes on...

Brining and smoking ham might feel intimidating, but it's definitely achievable in a home kitchen. Size makes a difference, though: a monster Christmas leg ham, for example, can take up to 16 hours to smoke, so maybe start small – you can still glaze a small ham, after all – and build from there. I like having the entire trotter on the leg as I think it looks striking; ask your butcher to keep the trotter on if you wish.

Although this recipe uses a suckling pig leg (which is more petite and manageable), don't feel restricted to legs. This brine works just as well with hocks or jowls, as long as you scale the ingredients accordingly.

You'll need to start this recipe 11 days ahead.

MAKES 1

1 suckling pig leg

HAM BRINE

For every 1 kg (2 lb 4 oz) of pork, use:
1 litre (35 fl oz) water (100%)
75 g (2.5 oz) fine salt (7.5%)
75 g (2.5 oz) brown sugar (7.5%)
2 cinnamon sticks
5 cloves
5 fresh bay leaves
5 g (0.2 oz) coriander seeds (0.5%)
3.7 g sodium nitrite – curing salt #1 (0.37%) (see page 15)

1. Combine all of the brine ingredients except the curing salt in a large pot (it's good if your pot fits in the fridge; clear some room). Bring to a simmer, stirring until all of the salt and sugar have dissolved. Turn off the heat and leave to cool to room temperature.
2. Add the curing salt to the brine and whisk to dissolve.
3. Note the weight of the suckling pig leg. Use a brining needle (see page 14) to inject brine into the leg in a grid pattern. Weigh the ham after brining to ensure it takes on a minimum of 10% in weight and a maximum of 20%. (You don't want to pump the leg with too much brine as it can cause the muscles and membranes to blow out and leave unsightly pockets of jelly once cooked and sliced.) Submerge the leg in the remaining brine, cover and refrigerate for 10 days, agitating the leg after 5 days so the salt doesn't settle.
4. Rinse the leg under cold water. Pat it dry with paper towel or a clean tea towel, then sit it on a wire rack over a tray, or hang it up. Refrigerate the leg overnight to allow it to dry and develop a pellicle.
5. Remove the leg from the fridge and start your smoker for hot-smoking (see page 154), aiming to achieve a consistent temperature of around 80°C (176°F) and a steady flow of smoke.
6. Place the cured leg on a rack in the smoker, skin side up, and smoke until a thermometer inserted into the leg reads 65°C (149°F); take multiple measurements around the thickest part of the leg to ensure there are no hidden cold spots. The ham can take up to 8 hours to smoke. Keep adding woodchips until the desired smokiness is achieved.

»

7. Remove the ham from the smoker and immerse it completely in iced water for 10 minutes to cool it down quickly. (Just as it's important to heat food above certain temperatures to keep it safe, it's also important to cool the ham as quickly as possible to minimise the time it spends in the danger zone where pathogens can thrive.) Remove the ham from the iced water and pat it dry, then lay it on a wire rack set over a tray and leave in the fridge, uncovered, to cool completely.
8. Once the ham is chilled, it's ready to eat. The skin can be peeled off, and the ham sliced. Store any left-over ham in the fridge for 2–3 weeks.

Maple and mustard glazed Christmas ham

I like to mix maple syrup and Dijon mustard with cinnamon, cloves and orange peel to create a glazed ham with a festive flavour. Smoke your own ham, then glaze it following this method and you've got one seriously impressive centrepiece to build Christmas lunch around.

MAKES 1

1 smoked ham (page 163)

MAPLE AND MUSTARD GLAZE
1 orange
500 ml (17 fl oz) maple syrup
30 g (1 oz) Dijon mustard
2 cinnamon sticks
4 fresh bay leaves
5 g (0.2 oz) cloves

1. For the glaze, use a sharp knife or peeler to remove all of the peel from the orange, avoiding the bitter white pith. Put the peel in a saucepan with the remaining ingredients and bring to the boil. Remove from the heat and set the glaze aside to steep and infuse for 30 minutes.
2. Meanwhile, preheat the oven to 170°C (325°F).
3. Strain the glaze through a sieve to remove the orange peel, cinnamon, bay leaves and cloves.
4. Carefully remove the skin from the ham. Score the fat in a diamond pattern, taking care to not cut into the meat.
5. Put the ham in a baking dish and bake for 15–20 minutes to get the fat slightly sizzling. Remove the ham from the oven and pour the glaze over the top, then season well with freshly cracked black pepper.
6. Return the ham to the oven and bake for 45–60 minutes, removing it every 15 minutes and spooning the glaze from the dish over the top. The ham is ready when the glaze has reduced and clings to the surface, creating a sticky, glistening beauty.
7. Let the ham cool for 30 minutes before slicing.

SMOKED SAUSAGES

Nothing beats a homemade sausage hot from the smoker.

If you've had a go at any of the sausages in this book, you'll have noticed that they typically need to be hung up to dry after they've been linked. This lets the flavours develop, but it also allows the casings to dry out a little, giving a more attractive finish and resulting in a surface that allows smoke to adhere nicely. The more you can let air flow between the sausages as they hang, the better the result.

Salsiccia (page 26), cotechino (page 35), pepperoni (page 43), frankfurts (page 51), cheese kransky (page 52) or pig's-head sausages (page 55), dried (see step 15 of the basic salsiccia recipe on page 28)

1. Start your smoker for hot-smoking (see page 154), aiming to achieve a consistent temperature of around 80°C (176°F) and a steady flow of smoke.
2. Hang or place the sausages in the smoker, ensuring they're spread out so the smoke is able to flow freely around them. Smoke the sausages for about 1–1½ hours or until a thermometer inserted into the centre of a sausage reads 65°C (149°F). Insert the thermometer from the end of the sausage, rather than through the side, for added accuracy.
3. Remove the sausages from the smoker. You can either serve them immediately, or immerse them in iced water – this ice-shocking cools the sausages rapidly, ensuring they're safe to store, and helping to keep them nice and plump. If you don't shock some types of sausage, the skin can shrink and wrinkle, becoming leathery. Leave the sausages in the iced water for no more than 10 minutes, then either hang them or lay them on a wire rack set over a tray in the fridge to dry.
4. Depending on your recipe, the sausages should keep for up to a week in the fridge. Reheat them according to one of the methods on page 31.

SMOKED MACKEREL

Smoking is a delicious way to prepare oily fish, such as mackerel. It goes without saying that using fresh fish is ideal, but with mackerel, it's essential – anything except the freshest mackerel tends to turn soft, with the final product likely to be mushy and completely underwhelming.

Since mackerel are only small, the fish is smoked at a very low temperature and with plenty of smoke to start with, which helps develop the flavour and an appealing golden colour. The heat is then dialled up to cook the fish through. For the best results, it's important to let the fish dry thoroughly after brining to develop a tacky exterior for the smoke to adhere to. Serve the mackerel in a bagel with crème fraîche and red onion pickle (page 232), flake it through a niçoise salad or use it in the smoked mackerel nach hausfrauenart on page 169.

You'll need to start this recipe 2 days ahead.

SERVES 1–2

1 whole blue mackerel, cleaned

MACKEREL BRINE

For each mackerel, use:
1 litre (35 fl oz) water
40 g (1.5 oz) fine salt
10 g (0.4 oz) brown sugar
2 fresh bay leaves
3 g (0.1 oz) black peppercorns

1. Combine all of the brine ingredients in a large pot. Bring to a simmer, stirring until all of the salt and sugar have dissolved. Turn off the heat and leave to cool to room temperature.
2. Place the mackerel in a non-reactive bowl or roasting tin and cover with the brine, then place in the fridge for 12 hours.
3. Remove the mackerel from the fridge and discard the brine. Use a couple of toothpicks to hold the cavity open and then either hang the mackerel or place it on a wire rack set over a tray and refrigerate overnight, uncovered, to dry and form a pellicle.
4. Remove the mackerel from the fridge. It should be dry enough that the surface feels slightly tacky to the touch.
5. Start your smoker for hot-smoking (see page 154), aiming to achieve a consistent temperature of around 50°C (122°F) and a steady flow of smoke.
6. Place the fish in the smoker for around 2 hours or until it has developed a nice golden hue.
7. Increase the temperature of the smoker to 90°C (194°F) and continue to smoke until a thermometer inserted into the thickest part of the fish reads around 60°C (140°F). Remove the mackerel from the smoker and let it cool to room temperature before placing it in the fridge, where it will keep for up to 3 days. Serve chilled.

SMOKED MACKEREL NACH HAUSFRAUENART

This dish is a twist on a traditional preparation I first encountered at the legendary Rogacki delicatessen in Berlin. The German name translates directly as 'housewife style', which I like to think indicates something made by people who really know what they're doing. It's unfussy, but the combination is excellent.

In Germany, this is typically made with pickled herring, but I've always enjoyed smoked mackerel with potatoes and a creamy sauce – the textures go so well together – so adapting this recipe felt like a natural fit.

Depending on how big your mackerel are, one fillet makes a brilliant starter, and a whole fish a sturdy lunch. Take the care to source waxy potatoes and their texture will add yet another dimension to the dish.

SERVES 2 AS A LIGHT MEAL, OR 4 AS A STARTER

8 small waxy potatoes, such as Nicola
1 bunch of flat-leaf parsley, finely chopped
2 whole smoked mackerel (page 166)

DRESSING
150 g (5.5 oz) natural yoghurt
100 g (3.5 oz) sour cream
½ bunch of dill (with stalks), roughly chopped
1 green apple, peeled and cut into julienne strips
1 small white onion, thinly sliced
2 gherkins, finely diced, plus 2 tablespoons gherkin pickling liquid

1. To make the dressing, spoon the yoghurt and sour cream into a bowl, stir to combine well, then add the dill, apple, onion, gherkins and pickling liquid and toss to coat. Check the seasoning and adjust to taste – be generous with the pepper, but keep in mind that the fish is salty so go easy on the salt. Put the dressing in the fridge until you're ready to serve.
2. Put the potatoes in a large saucepan, cover with water and season generously with salt. Bring to a simmer and cook until the potatoes are tender. Drain, then gently scrape off the skin with a knife while the potatoes are still hot. Cut them in half, season with salt and toss with the parsley.
3. Remove the smoked mackerel fillets from the bones, trying to keep the fillets whole and keeping an eye out for rogue bones.
4. Arrange the mackerel fillets on plates, add some boiled potatoes for company and generously spoon the dressing over the fish. Try to get a bit of everything in each mouthful.

SMOKED CHICKEN

Roast chicken is already undeniably delicious, but with the additional layer of mouth-watering complexity that smoking brings, it's on a whole new level.

This is one to share with family or friends. Just make sure you sneak some salty, smoky tidbits while you're carving and no-one is looking. Smoked chicken goes very well with the mash and gravy on page 206. I've even seen people (possibly including me) dip their chicken in the mash and gravy: beautiful.

You'll need to start this recipe 2 days ahead.

SERVES 4

1 whole chicken, about 1 kg
 (2 lb 4 oz)
50 g (1.75 oz) softened butter

CHICKEN BRINE

1 litre (35 fl oz) water
5 g (0.2 oz) fine salt
10 g (0.4 oz) black peppercorns
1 head of garlic, halved crossways
5 fresh bay leaves
1 bunch of thyme

1. Combine all of the brine ingredients in a large pot (it's good if your pot fits in the fridge; clear some room). Bring to a simmer, stirring until all of the salt has dissolved. Turn off the heat and leave to cool to room temperature.
2. Submerge the chicken in the brine, cover and refrigerate overnight.
3. Remove the chicken from the brine and place it on a wire rack set over a tray. Return the chicken to the fridge overnight, uncovered, for the skin to dry and form a pellicle.
4. Remove the chicken from the fridge to temper. Start your smoker for hot-smoking (see page 154), aiming to achieve a consistent temperature of around 160–170°C (320–338°F) and a steady flow of smoke.
5. Rub the chicken all over with the softened butter and liberally sprinkle it with freshly cracked black pepper and a small amount of salt (it will already be salty from the brine). As for trussing, I'm undecided: it makes sense that trussing a bird creates a tighter package that cooks more evenly, but on the other hand I like the idea of the cavity being open so the smoke can swirl around it, and the untrussed legs being exposed to more heat so their fat renders and they cook through before the breast has a chance to dry out. See what you prefer. (You could even stuff some thyme and half a lemon into the cavity, then make a couple of incisions in the loose skin around the cavity and cross the legs over, tucking the drumsticks into the incisions to hold them in place.)
6. Place the chicken in the smoker on a rack and keep the temperature and smoke steady for 60–70 minutes or until the juices run clear when you insert a small knife into the thickest part of the thigh and the breast. Remove the chicken from the smoker and let it rest until the internal temperature is around 50°C (122°F). It's now ready to carve – refer to 'Carving poultry' on page 173 for some tips.

SMOKED DUCK

This is a play on Chinese roasted duck, with the extra step of smoking thrown in. The smoking process doesn't cook the duck, but instead adds a fragrant savouriness that goes well with the traditional accompaniments. You can bust out the duck pancakes and hoisin sauce or follow the recipe on page 175 for a spin on duck à l'orange, made with candied cumquats.

I always used to think of cooking duck and getting a nice crisp skin on it as an intimidating process that's hard to nail, but it's actually quite simple. Scalding the duck's skin before cooking makes it taut and helps dry it out, giving a glass-like result.

You can scald the skin up to 3 days ahead of roasting, but do it at least a day ahead. After you've cooked and rested the duck, your most important task is keeping the skin crisp by minimising the time the skin comes into contact with the chopping board. Once you've carved the primary pieces, lay them with the meat side down so the skin doesn't become soggy from the accumulated juices.

You'll need a metal 'S' hook to hang the duck while you scald the skin.

SERVES 4–6

1 whole duck, wing tips removed
200 g (7 oz) honey
50 ml (1.5 fl oz) cider vinegar
100 g (3.5 oz) fine salt
Vegetable oil, for drizzling

1. To scald the duck, pour 5 litres (175 fl oz) water into a large pot and add the honey, vinegar and salt. Bring to a rolling boil.
2. Meanwhile, check the duck cavity and clean it out if necessary, then rinse the duck with cold water and pat it dry. Place a metal 'S' hook through the top of the duck's neck so you can safely hold it above the pot of boiling water. Very carefully, ladle boiling water over the duck's skin until you can see the skin tighten and turn pale in colour.
3. If you have room in your fridge, hang the duck up from the hook; otherwise, lay it on a wire rack set over a tray. Refrigerate overnight, or for up to 3 days, to allow the skin to dry and form a pellicle.
4. Start your smoker for cold-smoking (see page 153) and maintain a steady flow of smoke. Try to keep the heat as low as possible and not exceeding 40°C (104°F) – the smoker doesn't need to get too hot as you're only using the smoke to flavour the duck.
5. Place the duck in the smoker for an hour or until the skin takes on a golden hue.
6. Meanwhile, preheat the oven to 225°C (435°F). Lightly rub the entire duck with vegetable oil, then place it on a wire rack set over a baking tray. Roast the duck for 40–50 minutes or until the juices run clear when you insert a small knife into the thickest part of the thigh and the breast. Remove the duck from the oven and let it rest for 30 minutes.
7. Carve the duck following the instructions for carving poultry, opposite. When you're assembling the carved pieces, place the duck neck back in place as well.

Carving poultry

This poultry carving technique has stuck with me from when I worked at Longrain with Martin Boetz (although it's exceedingly common throughout Asia). I've used it ever since – it's much more satisfying to eat duck on the bone than off it. Same goes for chicken, for which I use the same method on page 170.

1. Place the bird on a chopping board with the legs facing away from you and take out a large, sharp knife. If you're carving a duck, cut off the whole neck, close to the breast.
2. Place the knife blade in the middle of the breast, resting it against the tip of the sternum. Cut through to the backbone and then cut all the way through the spine (this may require a stiff push on the back of the knife with your other hand). Be sure to keep the skin side up so it doesn't come into contact with any accumulated juices on the board and go soggy.
3. Now that you have two halves, place the knife in between the thigh and the breast and cut through the hip joint to separate the two. Do this for both halves.
4. Remove the wings from the breasts by cutting through the joints, then slice the breasts, starting from the bottom. You'll have to use steady downward crunching cuts to get through the bones. Keep the slices together and lay them in formation on a warm plate, with the two breasts laying flat and back to back, with the skin facing up.
5. Take the legs and separate the thighs and drumsticks through the joint. Cut the thighs in half through the bone, then lean them, along with the drumsticks (and the duck neck, if using), up against the breasts in formation.

SMOKED DUCK À LA CUMQUAT

A riff on the classic duck à l'orange, I like to make this during cumquat season, using the candied cumquats on page 233. Make the sauce while the duck is resting and serve it mostly underneath the duck, so as to not saturate and soften the skin.

SERVES 4–6

40 g (1½ oz) caster (superfine) sugar
250 ml (9 fl oz) chicken stock (page 234)
100 g (3.5 oz) candied cumquats (page 233)
3 fresh bay leaves
50 g (1.75 oz) chilled butter, diced
3 teaspoons chardonnay vinegar
1 smoked duck (page 172)

1. Put the sugar in a stainless steel saucepan with enough water to just moisten the sugar. Cook over medium–high heat, swirling the pan occasionally, until the sugar is a dark caramel (pay close attention here, because the caramel can quickly burn if you take your eye off it). Remove the pan from the heat and, working quickly and very carefully, add the chicken stock – be careful as it will spit and splatter.
2. Add the candied cumquats and the bay leaves, return the pan to the heat and simmer until the liquid has reduced by half.
3. Reduce the heat to very low so the pan just stays warm. Add the butter, one cube at a time, swirling the pan after each addition to emulsify the butter into the sauce. When all the butter has been incorporated, season with the vinegar, and salt and freshly ground black pepper to taste.
4. Pour the sauce around the carved duck (see page 173), trying to avoid getting too much on the crisp skin.

SMOKED BEEF TONGUE

Beef tongue is one of the most delicious cuts of beef. Not only is it incredibly marbled, but when it's gently cooked it has an amazingly soft and unctuous texture. Plus, there's only one per cow, so it pays to appreciate it.

Start this recipe a week ahead to allow time for the tongue to brine.

SERVES 6–8

1 beef tongue (you may need to order this from your butcher)
Salsa verde (page 222), to serve

TONGUE BRINE

2 litres (70 fl oz) water
80 g (2.75 oz) fine salt
25 g (1 oz) brown sugar
4 fresh bay leaves
10 g (0.4 oz) black peppercorns
4 g (0.1 oz) coriander seeds
7.2 g sodium nitrite – curing salt #1 (see page 15)

1. Combine all of the brine ingredients except the curing salt in a large pot (it's good if your pot fits in the fridge; clear some room). Bring to a simmer, stirring until all of the salt and sugar have dissolved. Turn off the heat and leave to cool to room temperature.
2. Add the curing salt to the brine and whisk to dissolve.
3. Use a brining needle (see page 14) to inject a few syringes' worth of brine into the tongue in a loose grid pattern, approximately every 2 cm (¾ in). Take care to not pump so hard as to swell and burst any membranes – you'll know this has happened if a clear, balloon-like projection bursts out of the side of the tongue (it can cause holes or pockets in the finished product). Submerge the tongue in the remaining brine, cover and refrigerate for 7 days, agitating the tongue after 5 days so the salt doesn't settle.
4. Start your smoker for hot-smoking (see page 154), aiming to achieve a consistent temperature of around 77°C (171°F) and a steady flow of smoke.
5. Rinse the tongue under cold water, then pat it dry with paper towel and place in the smoker for 4 hours to develop a light, tanned hue.
6. Transfer the tongue to a large pot and cover it with cold water. Bring to a gentle simmer (be careful not to let it boil; it can overcook quickly), then cook for 45 minutes or until it offers no resistance when you poke it with a paring knife (you can also tug at the skin and the underside with tongs to double-check it's tender). Remove the pot from the heat and set aside until the tongue is just cool enough to handle.
7. Gently peel off the outer skin (you should be able to use your hands, but a paring knife can help), taking care not to tear the meat.
8. Return the peeled tongue to the cooking liquid and transfer it to the fridge to cool completely. Once it's cool, drain it, wrap it in plastic wrap or greaseproof paper, and store it in the fridge for up to 2 weeks.
9. To serve the tongue, either cut it lengthways into 1 cm (½ in) slices and chargrill or fry them hard in a pan for a few minutes on each side, or thinly slice it across the length, spread out the slices on a baking tray and flash it in a 180°C (350°F) oven for no more than a minute. Spoon some salsa verde over the top and serve with some good sourdough.

LEVEL UP

SMOKED BRISKET

EVEN THOUGH WE RARELY SERVED SMOKED BRISKET AT LP'S – WE FELT IT WOULD BE A SURE-FIRE WAY TO BE PIGEONHOLED AS AN AMERICAN BARBECUE JOINT – WHEN WE DID SERVE IT, WE WANTED TO DO IT WELL, AND ALWAYS GAVE IT SERIOUS ATTENTION. BRISKET IS SPECIAL: A CELEBRATION, AN EVENT. TAKE THINGS SLOWLY AND DO IT THE RIGHT WAY, AND THE RESULT WILL ALWAYS BE A MEAL TO REMEMBER.

The fact is, brisket is a delicious cut, one that lends itself well to a long, slow cooking process, particularly smoking, where it can take on all those wonderful flavours.

The difficulty with brisket is that it's made up of two pectoral muscles, colloquially known as the 'point' and the 'flat', that seem to cook at different rates. Therein lies the balancing act of trying to cook them both properly: the point (the larger end), has incredible amounts of both fat and intramuscular fat, and can be quite forgiving; on the other hand, the flat, which is the flat muscle underneath, can be quite lean. I find the flat to be the Achilles heel of brisket cookery. If you don't cook a brisket correctly, it'll be the flat that suffers and comes up dry.

This risk can be mitigated by using beef with a really high marble score, such as wagyu, so the flat itself has intense marbling, which helps keep

it moist. I do find, however, that when the marble score is high, the finished product tends to be far too rich and even a bit sickly to eat.

To aid in our quest for good brisket cookery, we turn again to our much-loved technique of brining, which helps the brisket retain moisture while cooking. We're heading in the direction of American-style barbecue, but when you brine a brisket, you're only a step away from pastrami, the likes of which you might find at a Jewish deli in New York. If, on the other hand, you dry-cure your brisket, you'll be headed in the direction of equally delicious Montreal-style smoked meat.

Whatever the name, it's pretty hard to beat a hot smoked brisket sandwich, complete with plenty of mustard (see page 183). But this brined and smoked brisket can go in several directions, aided the whole way by being well-seasoned throughout, flavourful from the spices and its coating of black pepper, as well as deliciously succulent from the brine.

A big shout-out here to Matty Matheson, too, who gave us many pointers with our brisket when we were lost in the hills of despair during Covid lockdowns and trying to get our take-away offerings sorted. Matty's advice on temperature and timing really gave us some consistency in the final product – thank you, Matty!

You'll need some of that quintessential pink- or peach-coloured butcher's paper that's made specifically to wrap meat, creating a nice steamy environment that helps render it even more tender. Find it through barbecue shops.

It's worth noting that the brisket takes about 11 hours in the smoker. If that's too long for you, you could start the brisket in the smoker until it hits the first temperature checkpoint, then transfer it to the oven to finish cooking while you sleep.

Start this recipe 11 days ahead to brine and then dry the brisket. You'll need to scale up the brine if you're using a whole brisket – remember to use the equivalent amount of brine to meat.

SMOKING

SERVES 10–12

5 kg (11 lb 4 oz) grass-fed beef brisket (marble score 2–4)
Vegetable oil, for drizzling
25 g (1 oz) freshly cracked black pepper

BRISKET BRINE

For every 1 kg (2 lb 4 oz) of brisket, use:
1 litre (35 fl oz) water
45 g (1.5 oz) fine salt
15 g (0.5 oz) brown sugar
5 g (0.2 oz) star anise
10 g (0.4 oz) cinnamon sticks
2 g (0.1 oz) cloves
8 g (0.3 oz) fresh bay leaves
20 g (0.7 oz) garlic cloves
5 g (0.2 oz) black peppercorns
5 g (0.2 oz) coriander seeds
3.7 g sodium nitrite – curing salt #1 (see page 15)

1. Combine all of the brine ingredients except the curing salt in a large pot (it's good if your pot fits in the fridge; clear some room). Bring to a simmer, stirring until all of the salt and sugar have dissolved. Turn off the heat and leave to cool to room temperature.
2. Add the curing salt and whisk to dissolve.
3. Note the weight of the brisket. Use a brining needle (see page 14) to inject brine into the brisket in a tight grid pattern, approximately every 2 cm (¾ in), refilling the needle each time and being generous with the brine. Weigh the brisket after brining to ensure it takes on approximately 10% in weight. Submerge the brisket in the remaining brine, cover and refrigerate for 10 days, agitating the brisket after 5 days so the salt doesn't settle.
4. Rinse the brisket under cold water. Pat it dry with paper towel or a clean towel, then place it on a wire rack set over a tray. Refrigerate the brisket overnight to dry and develop a pellicle.
5. Start your smoker for hot-smoking (see page 154), aiming to achieve a consistent temperature of around 100°C (212°F) and a steady flow of smoke.
6. Remove the brisket from the fridge, lightly rub it all over with oil (just enough so the pepper will stick), then sprinkle the pepper all over the brisket, making sure you get it into all the nooks and crannies; as the brisket cooks, the meat will shrink, exposing other areas that can end up under-seasoned if you aren't attentive early on.
7. Place the brisket in the smoker, flat side down, and keep a steady heat and smoke going for around 7–8 hours. Monitor the temperature of the brisket with a probe thermometer; the point end needs to be around 80°C (176°F).
8. Remove the brisket from the smoker and wrap it snugly in butcher's paper. Keep track of which side was facing up, as you want to put the brisket back into the smoker facing the same way. Return the brisket to the smoker and try to maintain a steady 110°C (230°F) temperature (the smoke isn't as important now, since the brisket is wrapped, so focus on the heat).
9. Continue cooking until the flat of the brisket reaches 90–95°C (194–203°F); it's getting close when, if you try to push your finger through the flat, it gives way but still has a slight resistance. The goal is tender meat without any dry fibres. Remove the brisket from the smoker and let it rest in the paper until the internal temperature comes down to 60°C (140°F).

10. The brisket is now ready to slice. Since there are two muscles, they need to be carved in different ways. The flat needs to be cut horizontally, against the grain, starting from the end and working your way up to the point. Once you reach the point, you need to turn the point and cut it vertically.
11. You can serve the brisket in slices as part of a barbecue spread along with some pickles and barbecue sauce (page 220). The brisket can also be wrapped in plastic wrap and chilled to serve another time. Reheat it by putting an unwrapped piece of brisket in a steamer and gently heating until it is soft and heated through. Brisket can also be sliced when it's cold and served on a toasted sandwich as on page 183, with the gradual heat of the sandwich press warming it through.

 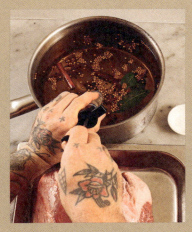 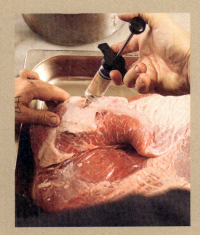

SMOKING

SMOKED BRISKET SANDWICH

Here's a classic way to serve brisket that riffs on all the marvellous smoked meat sandwiches, Reubens and salt-beef bagels of the world. I like the fact that it has all the balance and relief systems in place so that, as rich as it is, you can feel like you're having a good time without needing a lie-down afterwards.

There are a few components here that I encourage you to make yourself, especially the pickled cabbage and the milk bread (you should have plenty of time while the brisket is cooking!) – but, of course, you can always use good-quality, store-bought alternatives. Making these yourself does give an excellent result, though, and really leans into the special-occasion energy that cooking a whole brisket inevitably brings.

Eat this with your hands.

MAKES 1 SANDWICH

100 g (3.5 oz) smoked brisket (pages 178–181), sliced
2 slices of milk bread (page 237)
Soft butter, for spreading
15 g (0.5 oz) American mustard (I like Golden State)
15 g (0.5 oz) mayonnaise
2 slices of Swiss cheese
50 g (1.75 oz) drained pickled cabbage (page 226)

1. Remove the brisket from the fridge to temper. Heat a sandwich press to medium heat.
2. Lightly butter one side of the bread slices and lay them on a board, buttered side down. Spread one slice of bread with mustard and the other with mayonnaise. Place the cheese slices on the mayo side and the cabbage on the mustard side, followed by the brisket, then flip the cheese and mayo side on top of the brisket.
3. Carefully pick up the sandwich and place it in the sandwich press. Grill until the outside is golden brown and the inside is hot. Let the sandwich cool, just a little, before jumping in.

SMOKED BEEF SHORT RIBS

Beef short ribs are another delicious cut of beef. Raw, they're tough and full of collagen, with quite intense marbling, but when they're cooked low and slow, this collagen and fat breaks down and renders, making them rich and decadent. They're also super simple, requiring no special treatment other than a generous coating of salt and freshly cracked pepper before they're carefully smoked into submission.

You'll need some of the pink- or peach-coloured butcher's paper that's designed for wrapping meat to create a steamy environment and make it even more tender. Find it through barbecue shops.

These take about 9 hours to cook, and need a long rest, so start them nice and early.

SERVES 4–6

1 x 5-bone plate of beef short ribs
Olive oil, for drizzling
25 g (1 oz) fine salt
25 g (1 oz) freshly cracked black pepper

1. Remove the ribs from the fridge to come to room temperature at least an hour before cooking.
2. Start your smoker for hot-smoking (see page 154), aiming to achieve a consistent temperature of around 110°C (230°F) and a steady flow of smoke.
3. Lightly coat the ribs all over with olive oil (just enough so the salt and pepper will stick).
4. Mix the salt and pepper together in a bowl. Hold the ribs over the bowl and generously and evenly sprinkle them with the salt and pepper mixture (you may not need all of it; you just want to coat the ribs).
5. Put the ribs in the smoker, bone down, and keep a steady heat and flow of smoke going for around 9 hours or until the meat feels incredibly tender and giving when you poke it. You can also check them with a probe thermometer; the reading should be 95°C (203°F).
6. Remove the ribs from the smoker and wrap them snugly in butcher's paper. Rest them in a 50°C (120°F) oven, or even in a sealed insulated cooler box, until their internal temperature reaches about 60°C (140°F).
7. Unwrap the rested plate of ribs and cut them into individual ribs, following the bones. Serve on a barbecue platter with bread, pickles and barbecue sauce (page 220).

SMOKED PRIME RIB

This is one of my favourite ways to cook beef, and is an absolute show stopper. The beef becomes incredibly soft, smoky and meltingly tender due to the long, slow smoke at a temperature of around 70°C (158°F), which allows the beef to cook while also retaining a blushing-pink rareness.

The cut normally used for prime rib is a whole rib set, which can be quite a large piece of meat to cook at home (and, with the bones involved, is also tricky to portion nicely). I usually opt for cube roll, which is the boneless rib-eye. It's easy to carve, opening up traditional steakhouse cuts, such as English thin-cut or American thick-cut. You can also experiment with different beef cuts for this technique – this recipe works very well with sirloin, for instance.

Whatever cut you use, it's worth using a substantial piece of beef – you want it to be large enough that it doesn't cook too quickly and has time to develop a nice smoky crust. I recommend 2 kg (4 lb 8 oz) minimum, keeping in mind that any leftovers make a brilliant smoked beef sandwich, especially with plenty of horseradish in the picture.

Be sure to serve your smoked prime rib with all the mustards and condiments you have. If you're going to go all out, it makes sense to serve it with creamed spinach (page 188) and Yorkshire puddings (page 189), too.

SERVES 8–10

2 kg (4 lb 8 oz) piece beef cube roll
100 g (3.5 oz) Dijon mustard
Flaky salt
Vegetable oil, for drizzling
Beef jus (page 235)
Creamed spinach (page 188) and Yorkshire puddings (page 189), to serve
Condiments, such as beer mustard (page 228) or hot English mustard and horseradish sauce, to serve

1. Remove the beef from the fridge to come to room temperature at least an hour before cooking. Truss the beef with butcher's twine to create a uniform cylindrical shape, then rub the entire piece of beef with the Dijon mustard and generously season with freshly cracked black pepper and flaky salt.
2. Start your smoker for hot-smoking (see page 154), aiming to achieve a consistent temperature of around 70°C (158°F) and a steady flow of smoke.
3. Place the beef in the smoker until a thermometer inserted into the meat reads just below 50°C (122°F), around 4–5 hours. Now monitor it closely and, once the internal temperature reaches 52°C (126°F), remove the beef from the smoker and let it rest on a wire rack for 20 minutes. (If you're not ready to finish cooking the beef now, you can wrap it in plastic wrap and place it in a sealed insulated cooler box, wrapped in towels, for up to 2 hours before you finish it off.)
4. Preheat the oven to 230°C (450°F). Drizzle the beef with oil and rub it all over to lightly coat; this will help develop the crust. Place the beef on a wire rack set over a baking tray and roast for 10 minutes to give it a lovely caramelised crust.
5. Let the beef rest for 10 minutes. Remove the twine and carve the beef into thick slices. Arrange the slices on hot plates, season each slice with salt, then sauce with beef jus, creamed spinach and Yorkshire puddings, and serve with your condiments of choice.

CREAMED SPINACH

Spinach lends itself so well to a dish like this, which makes the most of the fact that it wilts down to almost nothing by folding it through a creamy sauce. The anchovies and garlic – two best friends that I turn to again and again in different guises (see the puntarelle recipe on page 208, for example) – add some edge here. Spinach is the most classic leaf to make this with, but you can use any leafy green – try kale, cavolo nero or silverbeet (Swiss chard).

SERVES 4

500 ml (17 fl oz) single (pure) cream
15 g (0.5 oz) garlic cloves, chopped
15 g (0.5 oz) drained anchovies in oil
1 sprig of rosemary
1 kg (2 lb 4 oz) English spinach leaves
Flaky salt
Fresh nutmeg, to serve

1. Pour the cream into a large saucepan, add the garlic, anchovies and rosemary and season with a couple of turns of freshly ground black pepper. Gently simmer over low heat until the mixture has reduced by half. Discard the rosemary sprig.
2. Blanch the spinach leaves in a large pot of boiling salted water for 10 seconds until just wilted, then drain and plunge into iced water to cool. Drain well, giving the spinach a good squeeze to remove excess water, then roughly chop it.
3. Return the cream mixture to medium heat and bring to a simmer, then add the spinach and fold it through. Season to taste with flaky salt and freshly ground black pepper. Spoon the creamed spinach into a serving bowl and finish with a little grating of nutmeg.

YORKSHIRE PUDDINGS

Yorkshire puddings are a magical preparation that turn any roast into a celebration. We've tried many recipes and methods at LP's over the years and at times they've not ended the way we'd hoped, but this method has always produced the best results. I'm the first person to admit that I prefer to measure everything in grams, especially when it comes to baking, so a recipe that does things by volume and ratio doesn't sit well with me, but you can't argue with the results.

The batter is typically cooked in beef dripping in the oven; by using smoked beef fat, there's an added layer of flavour, immediately evident in the mouthwatering scent that spills from the oven while they're baking.

You'll need an 8-hole metal muffin tray. Begin this recipe a day ahead to allow the batter to rest overnight.

MAKES 8

3 eggs, beaten
125 ml (4 fl oz) milk, approximately
75 g (2.5 oz) plain (all-purpose) flour, approximately
320 g (11.25 oz) smoked beef fat (page 212)

1. Pour the beaten eggs into a measuring jug, note the volume, then pour the eggs into a bowl. Measure out the same volume of milk and add it to the bowl with the eggs, then do the same with the flour.
2. Whisk thoroughly to ensure there are no lumps in the batter. Cover the bowl and refrigerate overnight to allow the batter to rest.
3. When you're ready to cook, remove the batter from the fridge and preheat the oven to 220°C (425°F). Scoop 2 tablespoons of the beef fat into 8 holes of a metal muffin tray. Place the tray on a baking tray, then put it in the oven until the fat is smoking hot.
4. With a ladle or a jug, carefully but confidently pour about 60 ml (2 fl oz) of the batter into each muffin hole. Carefully return the tray to the oven and reduce the heat to 200°C (400°F). Bake for 20–25 minutes or until the puddings are golden brown and puffed. Remove from the oven and flip them over to check the bases. If they need a little more colour, put them back in the oven, upside down, for another 2–3 minutes.
5. Season the puddings well with fine salt, then let them cool slightly on a wire rack before serving.

CHAPTER .SIX. VEGETABLES

CONTENTS

INTRODUCTION	193
SHAVED ZUCCHINI WITH HAZELNUTS AND MINT	196
TOMATO SALAD WITH HANDMADE STRACCIATELLA	198
STRACCIATELLA	199
ROASTED PUMPKIN WITH CHESTNUTS, SAGE AND BROWN BUTTER	203
BRAISED GREEN BEANS	204
MASH AND GRAVY	206
PUNTARELLE WITH ANCHOVIES AND GARLIC	208
LEAF SALAD WITH PALM-SUGAR VINAIGRETTE	209
CUCUMBERS AND MELON WITH HONEY AND RICOTTA	211
SMOKED BEEF-FAT ROAST POTATOES	212
CITRUS SALAD WITH BURNT HONEY AND PISTACHIOS	215

Despite this book being meat-driven, I absolutely love cooking and eating fresh seasonal fruit and vegetables. It may be true that in its days as a restaurant the lead story of LP's was largely about meat, but I always made it my mission to give vegetables their due. Many people with preconceived ideas about what we offered walked away pleasantly surprised at how much lightness there was alongside all the heaviness. Likewise, at Bella Brutta, there's plenty more going on than pizza, including a lot of vegetables.

The recipes in this chapter are a selection of classics from both restaurants, as well as dishes that my partner Tania and I make at home. I'm going to borrow a quote from Richard Purdue, head chef at Margaret in Sydney and longtime collaborator with Neil Perry, by saying that 'Good cooking is good shopping.' With fruit and vegetables, it couldn't be more true: if a tomato or a peach is fresh, ripe and full of flavour, it needs very little coaxing or messing around with.

Seasonality is an imperative. Australia can be a funny place – because of its sheer size, some products seem like they grow year round. However, since LP's set up a stall at Carriageworks Farmers Market in Sydney, I've tried to do my fruit and vegetable shopping there. The stallholders are only selling what they're growing, so the produce is always seasonal. If you've got access to a local farmers' market, that's the best way to buy in season.

In every case, produce from small growers tastes better – there isn't anyone more invested in it tasting good, and they'll make sure it's picked at its peak, when it's ripe and sweet and delicious. It's about taste, not shelf life.

While I love vegetables served raw, or blanched ever so briefly to retain their crisp and crunchy qualities, sometimes the pendulum can swing the other way, with long, slow cooking drawing out deeper flavours, such as green beans simmered with garlic until they almost break down (see page 204).

If we're talking fruit, ripeness is obviously ideal. That extends to tomatoes as well as melons, which both feature in this chapter. If there's a general rule, it's that if it doesn't look and smell good, it probably isn't going to taste good. Pick up your fruit, note its weight, smell it – use your senses. When you store it, try to keep it out of the fridge (especially tomatoes) otherwise the cold will mute the flavour.

There are a few recipes here, such as the mashed potatoes on page 206, that require a little more elbow grease than others. Whatever the dish, they can all find multiple partners throughout this book, adding lightness to the heaviness, brightness to the depth.

A note on seasoning: I love salt and acid. I tend to season most dishes hard, but with vegetables and salads I really go for it, leaning on salt, lemon, vinegar and olive oil. Lemon and vinegar? I think this brings the best of both worlds: the deep, rounded, sweet flavours of vinegar and the fresh spark of lemon, combined with salt, are both mouth-watering and addictive. I really like the Forvm Spanish cabernet sauvignon and chardonnay vinegars. For olive oil, I prefer buttery styles over anything too green or peppery, and when using it for dressing I really get my Jamie Oliver on and drizzle generously.

Pick the best seasonal produce, treat it well and dress it judiciously, and you'll find that these dishes are as much the star of the show as their meaty counterparts.

SHAVED ZUCCHINI WITH HAZELNUTS AND MINT

An ultra-refreshing salad that's a celebration of spring and summer, when zucchini are at their best and their flowers are in bloom. This combination creates great variation in texture, with hazelnuts adding crunch and fragrance, and a sharp dressing brightening it all.

With any watery vegetables, adding salt can draw out the liquid, so it's best to make this salad right before serving or you risk diluting the flavours. Try it with any variety of zucchini or squash you can get your hands on, basing your choice on seasonality and freshness. As you can probably imagine, this dish pairs very well with roasted and grilled meats.

This is one of those recipes where using a Japanese mandolin pays dividends; they're one of the best things for cutting thin, even slices of vegetables. They are, however, probably the most dangerous items in any kitchen, and make my skin crawl. Exercise caution, or feel free to use a very sharp knife instead.

SERVES 4–6

1 handful of roasted peeled hazelnuts
3 zucchini (courgette) flowers, with baby zucchini attached
1 large zucchini
2 yellow pattypan squash
½ bunch of mint, leaves picked
2 tablespoons olive oil
1 tablespoon hazelnut oil (or olive oil)
1 tablespoon chardonnay vinegar
Juice of 1 lemon
100 g (3.5 oz) thick yoghurt (preferably buffalo or sheep's)

1. Scatter the hazelnuts in a roasting tin and squash them with the base of a small saucepan (this draws out the fragrant oil from the nuts and gives them an interesting texture). Set aside.
2. Pick and set aside the zucchini flowers. Slice the baby zucchini, large zucchini and squash into thin rounds with a mandolin and combine them in a large bowl.
3. Tear the mint leaves into the bowl, then scatter in the hazelnuts. Dress the salad with the oils, vinegar and lemon juice, seasoning generously with salt and freshly ground black pepper. Gently fold the ingredients together with your hands. Check the seasoning and adjust if necessary.
4. Spoon the yoghurt into the centre of a serving dish, then gently layer the salad on top. As you get to the bottom of the bowl, there'll be some dressing and rubbly hazelnut stragglers – leave these in the bowl. Carefully tear the zucchini flowers into individual petals, removing the pistils, and toss them with the remaining dressing and hazelnuts. Pour this mixture over the salad and serve immediately.

TOMATO SALAD WITH HANDMADE STRACCIATELLA

Tomatoes are one of my favourite ingredients. I love them and look forward to eating and serving them at their peak every year. When they're 'on' – meaning super ripe, flavourful and delicious – there isn't a huge amount you need to do to them other than hit them with a simple dressing of vinegar and plenty of olive oil, followed by a generous seasoning of salt and pepper. There are a few extra moves that will make a big difference, though: cut them into variously sized slices and chunks to make each mouthful that little bit different from the last; I also dress them early, so that the salt can draw out the juices, which then mingle with the vinegar and oil, almost marinating the tomatoes.

You can call this a Caprese, if you want. Even if it's a salad that's become clichéd, the synergy between tomatoes, basil and mozzarella is undeniable. Ripe, sweet tomatoes; deep, flavourful vinegar; good-quality, buttery olive oil; fragrant basil; and rich, creamy cheese: in my eyes, that's perfection.

This recipe is more of an idea, followed by a recipe for hand-stretched stracciatella. If you don't wish to venture into the realm of cheesemaking, there are plenty of beautiful cheeses available that you can use as a substitute, such as buffalo mozzarella or ricotta. Even without the cheese, the tomatoes are delicious; serve them on their own, or swap in cherry truss tomatoes and serve them on top of a pizza (see page 44).

SERVES 4–6

500 g (1 lb 2 oz) in-season, ripe tomatoes (on the vine is ideal; any varieties work)
2 garlic cloves
Flaky salt
45 ml (1.5 fl oz) sweet-style cabernet sauvignon vinegar (or similar)
100 ml (3.5 fl oz) buttery olive oil
1 handful of freshly picked basil leaves
200 g (7 oz) stracciatella (see opposite)

1. Cut and slice the tomatoes into different bite-sized pieces. Pile them into a bowl.
2. Slice the garlic cloves super thin and add them to the bowl with the tomatoes. Season to taste with flaky salt and freshly ground black pepper, then pour in the vinegar and olive oil. Give it all a gentle mix with your hands, then leave to marinate at room temperature for at least 10 minutes.
3. Tear the basil leaves into the bowl and gently fold them through the tomatoes, then check the seasoning and adjust if necessary.
4. Spoon the stracciatella into a large dish, then spoon the tomatoes and their juices over the top.

Stracciatella

Stracciatella, a stretched cheese whose name means shredded, is made by stretching and tearing curds into threads and then folding them through cream and seasoning with salt. It's typically used as the filling for burrata, but is delicious in its own right, too.

For a long time, I wanted to make hand-stretched cheese to serve in the restaurants. At LP's I figured we could serve it as a starter, and it made sense to use it on pizzas at Bella Brutta. I read up on how to do it, bought books and deep-dived the internet, but I just couldn't get the curds to stretch properly. Our chef David Walster was the one who cracked the code; it wasn't even hard for him – he got it on his first try.

The cheese itself is made from cultured milk, which is set with rennet and cut into curds. As the curds sit in the whey, they ripen and become more acidic, denaturing the calcium in the milk and allowing the curds to stretch. My biggest piece of advice is not to be disheartened if your stracciatella doesn't work the first time – cheesemaking can be very temperamental, and a number of things can go wrong. Unclean equipment or even low-quality or slightly old milk can make the cheese misbehave.

Cheesemaking requires some specialist equipment. You'll need a thermometer, a small syringe (which you can buy from a pharmacy), a pH meter and micro scales. You can purchase the mozzarella culture and rennet from an online cheesemaking supplier. Please check the manufacturer's instructions for using them, as some brands vary. You'll also need a large saucepan with a lid, a colander and a bowl that snugly holds the colander. Read the recipe all the way through to get your head around the process, then dive in.

MAKES ABOUT 250 G (9 OZ)

A pinch of mozzarella culture
2 litres (35 fl oz) unhomogenised full-fat milk (the best quality you can find)
0.4 ml (0.01 fl oz) chymosin vegetarian rennet
200 ml (7 fl oz) single (pure) cream (again, the best quality you can find)
Flaky salt

1. Prepare the mozzarella culture following the instructions provided by the manufacturer.
2. Pour the milk into a large saucepan over low heat. Heat the milk to 32°C (90°F), then turn off the heat, add 40 ml (1.25 fl oz) of the prepared mozzarella culture and mix well to distribute it throughout the milk. Cover and leave the milk somewhere warm for an hour, maintaining its temperature (near the stove, but not on the heat, is a good spot).
3. Meanwhile, boil the kettle, then pour a little water into a small bowl and leave it to cool to room temperature.
4. Using a syringe, add the rennet to 4 ml (0.14 fl oz) of the cooled boiled water, then add this mixture to the warm milk and stir for no more than 20 seconds. (That's using a ratio of 0.2 ml rennet per 1 litre of milk, but always check the manufacturer's instructions.) Cover the milk and leave it somewhere warm for another hour, maintaining its temperature.
5. Remove the lid and gently touch the milk with a clean finger: it should have set into a firm curd that's similar in texture to silken tofu. If it hasn't, leave it for another 15 minutes and check again.

»

6. Take a long, clean knife and cut lines into the curd in a 2 cm (¾ in) crisscross pattern. Place the saucepan over very low heat and stir very gently (it's okay if the curds break up slightly, but no more) until the temperature reaches 42°C (108°F). Check the pH and note it down, then remove the pan from the heat, replace the lid and leave it somewhere warm for the curd to continue to mature. This will take about 3–4 hours – check the pH of the curd every hour until it reads between 5.4 and 5.2.
7. Gently stir the curd and pour off the whey. (Refrigerate the whey for up to 2 weeks to use in smoothies, whey caramel and pancakes, or to braise lamb.) Gently spoon the curd into a colander set snugly over a bowl, cover and place in the fridge to cool and drain for at least 2 hours or overnight.
8. Boil the kettle, then let the water cool to around 85°C (185°F). Tip the drained curd into a stainless steel bowl and tear it into 1 cm (½ in) pieces. Season with about ¼ teaspoon of flaky salt.
9. Prepare another large bowl filled with iced water and set it aside. Carefully pour the hot water around the edges of the curds until they're submerged. Let them sit for 3–5 minutes, then gently stir and move the curds continuously to evenly distribute the heat and make sure the curds are melting evenly. Lift up a piece of curd with your fingers and see if it stretches; if so, you're in business.
10. Carefully pour off the water, leaving the curds sitting in the bowl, then push the curds back and forth until they start sticking together. Fill and boil the kettle again (you may need latex gloves at this point), then pick up the curd and begin folding it over and back on itself so it stretches and begins to form a smooth, cohesive mass. If at any point the curd cools and starts to set, pour more hot water from the kettle into the bowl and dunk the curd back in to reheat it. You'll start to notice the surface of the curd becoming glossy. At this point, begin stretching the curd out between your hands to create a long 'rope', roughly shoulder width, then fold it in half and start stretching again. Keep stretching until you've made four ropes. Put the stretched curd in the iced water to cool completely.
11. Remove the cooled and stretched curd from the water and cut it into 7 cm (2¾ in) lengths. Take each piece and use your fingers to pull the strands apart, shredding them into fine threads. Put the threads in a clean bowl, then fold in the cream. Season to taste with flaky salt, about ½ teaspoon should do it, then refrigerate until needed (the stracciatella will keep for up to a week). If you leave the stracciatella overnight or for longer, the acidity in the curd will thicken the cream, so you may need to add a little more to loosen it before serving. If you do, be sure to check the seasoning and adjust again with salt as needed.

VEGETABLES

ROASTED PUMPKIN WITH CHESTNUTS, SAGE AND BROWN BUTTER

This is a dish that we cook when the cooler months roll around and new-season pumpkins collide with the chestnut season. Chestnuts always give me a huge sense of nostalgia, taking me back to when I ate them on the streets of San Sebastian with chef Michael Clift, or to my dad impaling them on skewers and sticking them in our fireplace at home to roast before slathering them in butter.

When chestnuts are combined with roasted kabocha pumpkin, which has delicate, sweet flesh under its rough skin, the textures of the pumpkin skin and the chestnuts almost mimic each other, bringing an extra edge to this relatively simple preparation. Crisping the sage and chestnuts in butter while it slowly turns into a fragrant beurre noisette really adds to the autumn–winter mood here. Try this with porchetta (page 136) or smoked prime rib (page 187).

SERVES 4

½ **kabocha (Japanese) pumpkin (squash)**, skin on, cut into wedges
Olive oil, for drizzling
Flaky salt
1 handful of **chestnuts** (plus a few extra to eat fresh from the oven)
½ bunch of **sage**, leaves picked
200 g (7 oz) **salted butter**

1. Preheat the oven to 200°C (400°F). Line a baking tray with baking paper. Lightly coat the pumpkin wedges in olive oil and season with a little flaky salt, then lay them on the baking tray. Roast for around 40 minutes or until soft but not collapsing. Set aside until needed.
2. While the pumpkin is roasting, carefully trim off the pointy end from each chestnut. (This allows the steam that builds up as the chestnuts cook to escape; if you skip this step, they can explode.) Spread out the chestnuts on another baking tray and roast for 30–40 minutes or until the skins are cracking and can be easily pulled off, and the flesh feels tender when poked with the tip of a paring knife. Remove the chestnuts from the oven and set aside until just cool enough to handle; I find they're easiest to peel when they're still a bit hot.
3. Peel the chestnuts, making sure there is no papery skin stuck to them, then break them into small pieces with your hands.
4. Combine the chestnut pieces, sage and butter in a wide saucepan and place over medium heat. As the butter starts to froth, keep swirling the pan to prevent the milk solids from sticking. Cook until the butter is fragrant and a beautiful golden colour, about 5 minutes. (Watch closely as it can burn quickly.)
5. If the pumpkin needs a little warming, put it back in the oven for 5 minutes. Place the pumpkin pieces in a serving dish and spoon the hot butter, sage and chestnuts over the top. Season with flaky salt and plenty of freshly cracked black pepper. Serve immediately.

BRAISED GREEN BEANS

These beans look completely overcooked, like something you'd imagine eating at your grandparents' house, but they're flavourful and moreish. The trick is to slowly cook them in olive oil with plenty of garlic cloves, which almost melt into a purée that coats the soft beans. I never tire of eating these.

SERVES 4

100 ml (3.5 fl oz) extra virgin olive oil
6 peeled garlic cloves
½ white onion, thinly sliced
600 g (1 lb 5 oz) green beans, topped, but with the tails left on
½ bunch of dill, fronds and stalks finely chopped

1. Add the olive oil, garlic and onion to a heavy-based saucepan over low heat. Increase the heat until the garlic and onion are starting to sizzle. Cook, stirring occasionally, for 5 minutes or until softened, making sure the garlic doesn't colour (if it's starting to, reduce the heat).
2. Stir the beans through the garlicky oil, season with a little salt, then cover the pan with a circle of baking paper – the aim of the game is to let the beans cook in their own steam. Cook, stirring frequently to make sure the garlic isn't sticking or burning, for 30–40 minutes or until the beans are very soft – some will have split and taken on a darker, army-green colour.
3. Remove the pan from the heat. Add more salt if you think it's needed, along with some freshly ground black pepper, then stir in the chopped dill. I like to serve the beans just like this, but if you feel like adding a little acid, some lemon juice or vinegar would work nicely.

MASH AND GRAVY

This mashed potato method has stuck with me since I first learnt it during a brief stint working at the Boathouse on Blackwattle Bay, where it was served alongside their famed snapper pie. The recipe is very similar to the one made famous by Joël Robuchon, which notoriously features more butter than potato.

Getting this right requires the cook to work quickly so the potatoes don't cool down and the starch isn't overworked, which can make the potatoes gluey. The potatoes are baked, rather than boiled, to prevent them becoming waterlogged, then the flesh is passed through a mouli or potato ricer, seasoned and combined with a lot of cream and butter (not as much as Robuchon's version, but a lot) before being passed through a drum sieve. It's quite an elaborate preparation, but the result is smooth, satiny and luxurious. If you don't have a drum sieve, it's okay to skip this step.

The gravy is based on a classic velouté or espagnole sauce, but is made with a brown chicken stock and a brown roux, with the butter replaced by chicken fat, and a little sprinkle of MSG. There are two recipes to which I'll almost always add MSG: mayonnaise, and this gravy. It makes the savouriness of the chicken stock really sing. The whole MSG argument isn't something I'm really interested in – many of the foods I enjoy have some form of MSG in them, either naturally occurring or added. I'm sure yours do, too. But don't add it if you don't want to.

SERVES 4–6

2 kg (4 lb 8 oz) scrubbed floury potatoes, such as Desiree, skin on
250 ml (9 fl oz) single (pure) cream, plus extra as needed
200 g (7 oz) unsalted butter, at room temperature

GRAVY

500 ml (17 fl oz) chicken stock (page 234)
25 g (1 oz) chicken fat
25 g (1 oz) plain (all-purpose) flour
Freshly ground white pepper, to taste
Monosodium glutamate (MSG), to taste

1. For the gravy, pour the chicken stock into a saucepan and bring it to the boil. Remove from the heat and cover with a lid to keep warm.
2. Meanwhile, put the chicken fat and flour into a saucepan. Slowly cook over low heat, stirring, until the flour takes on a dark brown colour. Be daring with this – you don't want it burnt, but it should start to smell like the unpopped kernels in a box of popcorn at the movies.
3. Once the flour is nice and dark, gradually ladle in the stock (be careful, it could splutter), whisking rapidly after each addition to prevent lumps. Once all the stock is incorporated, bring the gravy to a simmer and cook, stirring occasionally, for 20 minutes or until it coats the back of a spoon relatively thickly and there's no residual taste of flour. (You don't want to make glue, so use your judgement here.) Season to taste with salt, white pepper and a pinch of MSG. The gravy can now be cooled, kept in the fridge for up to a week and reheated later, although you may need to add some more stock to loosen it, which will require tasting and re-seasoning. If you're planning to serve the gravy straight away, keep it hot and cover the surface directly with baking paper to prevent a skin forming.
4. Preheat the oven to 180°C (350°F). Put the potatoes in a roasting tin and bake until tender, about 40–60 minutes (you should be able to insert and withdraw a paring knife easily).

5. Towards the end of the cooking time, pour the cream into a large saucepan and gently heat until it's hot (don't let it boil). Keep on low heat.
6. Remove the potatoes from the oven and, holding them with a clean tea towel, carefully cut them in half. Scoop the flesh into a mouli or potato ricer, taking care not to take any burnished skin with it. Pass the potatoes into the hot cream, keeping the heat on low.
7. Gently stir in the butter, bit by bit, until it's all incorporated, then season well with fine salt. (I find it loses some saltiness after the second passing, so you can go heavy here, or at least be prepared to adjust it later.) If you think the texture could be creamier, stir in some extra cream.
8. Set a drum sieve over a bowl and quickly pass the potato purée through the sieve, using a flexible pastry card to help scrape it through the sieve. Keep the potato hot over a double boiler or, if you're serving it straight away, transfer to a serving dish. The gravy can be served separately or ladled generously over the mash. Finish with a twist or two of freshly cracked black pepper.

PUNTARELLE WITH ANCHOVIES AND GARLIC

This recipe shows off the versatility and power of anchovies paired with garlic, a combination that also brings an edge to my creamed spinach (page 188). Puntarelle, a member of the chicory family, is only in season for a blink-and-you'll-miss-it moment. It has all the typical chicory-ish, dandelion bitterness you'd expect, and outstanding crunch to go with it. Look for it at farmers' markets, or if you can't find it you can use endive or dandelion.

The play between the bitter puntarelle, salty, umami-rich anchovies and pungent garlic, cut with the brightness of lemon juice and salt gives this dish an incredible taste and texture. It's one of my favourite things to eat each year, as good on its own as it is as an accompaniment, such as with beef tartare (page 128).

SERVES 4–6

1 large garlic clove
1 small tin (48 g/1.25 oz) good-quality anchovies in oil (I like Olasagasti)
1 tablespoon chardonnay vinegar
Juice of 1 lemon
75 ml (2.25 fl oz) buttery olive oil
1 head of puntarelle
Flaky salt

1. Slice the garlic and leave it on your chopping board. Open the tin of anchovies, pull them out of the oil and place them on top of the sliced garlic, then chop the two together to make a fine paste.
2. Scoop the anchovy mixture into a large bowl and add the vinegar and lemon juice. While mixing with a fork, drizzle in the olive oil (the mixture doesn't have to emulsify, so don't worry about drizzling too fast).
3. Pick the puntarelle into leaves with their stems attached. Wash in iced water to remove any dirt, then gently spin dry in a salad spinner.
4. Thinly slice any thick puntarelle stalks. Cut the leaves into rough strips.
5. Add all of the puntarelle to the bowl with the dressing and season with flaky salt and freshly ground black pepper. Gently fold the puntarelle over in the dressing to coat it well. Taste and adjust the seasonings; it should be distinctly punchy and sharp, but everything should be in balance. Gently layer into a serving dish and serve.

LEAF SALAD WITH PALM-SUGAR VINAIGRETTE

I love a leafy green salad. In my opinion, the best leaves you can get are the mesclun from Darling Mills Farm in Berrilee, New South Wales. I have been using these greens, which Steve Adey and his family painstakingly grow in great variety, at various restaurants for years. Every aspect of their leaves is perfection – from appearance to taste.

The other element of a good leaf salad is the dressing. I've always been in awe of Neil Perry's palm-sugar version – it's the perfect vinaigrette. And believe me, I've tried many variations on the sweet element and nothing else comes close. Something about the subtle suggestion of garlic offsets the sweetness of the palm sugar and reinforces its savouriness. This recipe is Neil's, with a slight tweak in that I've used chardonnay vinegar and hazelnut oil for a subtle shift in flavour. You'll end up with more of the palm-sugar vinegar than you need here, but you can also use it in the sweet-and-sour grilled onions recipe on page 141.

SERVES 4

250 g (9 oz) salad leaves (I like a mix of mesclun and herbs)
30 ml (1 fl oz) extra virgin olive oil
1 tablespoon hazelnut oil
Freshly squeezed lemon juice, to taste
Flaky salt
1 handful of roasted, peeled hazelnuts, roughly chopped

PALM-SUGAR VINEGAR

100 g (3.5 oz) palm sugar (jaggery)
100 ml (3.5 fl oz) chardonnay vinegar
2 g (0.1 oz) garlic, finely grated

1. Start by making the palm-sugar vinegar. Crush the palm sugar and put it into a saucepan. Moisten the sugar with water. Cook over medium heat, swirling the pan occasionally, until the sugar begins to caramelise, then turns dark and very fragrant. Be careful not to take it too far or it will burn. Remove from the heat and add the vinegar (be careful; it will spit), then stir in the garlic and let it cool completely. Once cooled, the palm-sugar vinegar can be kept in the fridge for a week.
2. Wash and thoroughly dry the salad leaves, then place them in an oversized mixing bowl.
3. Spoon 50 ml (1.5 fl oz) of the palm-sugar vinegar into the salad bowl, then add the olive oil and hazelnut oil. Squeeze in some lemon juice, season with flaky salt and freshly ground black pepper and throw in just a scattering of hazelnuts.
4. With your hands, gently lift and fold the leaves over, gently raking the dressing through them – there should never be any squeezing or closing of the hands. Taste a leaf and adjust the dressing if necessary: if it's too sharp, add some more oil; if it needs more brightness, add a tad more lemon; if it's lacking sweetness, maybe go back in with some more of the palm-sugar vinegar. Get it to the point where it ticks all the boxes for roundness, acidity, salt and fragrance, and makes your mouth water.
5. Gently lift the leaves into a serving dish, then tip the hazelnuts that are inevitably forming a posse in the bottom of the mixing bowl over the top.

CUCUMBERS AND MELON WITH HONEY AND RICOTTA

A summer salad combining two members of the same family – melon and cucumbers – which, despite their obvious differences, have a very similar scent and go well together. Look for a firmer, fragrant green melon, such as piel de sapo or honeydew, to make the most of the combination.

The ricotta here is based on a technique that was shown to me by Mat Lindsay from Ester in Sydney. It makes the most delicious ricotta with a subtle lactic tang. Be sure to use proper buttermilk, collected from the butter-making process; I like Pepe Saya brand. You'll end up with about 400 g (14 oz) of ricotta, which is more than you need for this recipe. Eat the leftovers for breakfast or with 'nduja on toast (see page 90).

Start this recipe a day ahead to allow time for the ricotta to drain. Save the left-over whey to use in braises, ragù or even granita. It will keep for up to a week.

SERVES 4–6

½ piel de sapo or honeydew melon
2 Lebanese (short) cucumbers
½ bunch of mint
2 tablespoons chardonnay vinegar
1 tablespoon freshly squeezed lemon juice
60 ml (2 fl oz) extra virgin olive oil
2 tablespoons honey
Flaky salt

BUTTERMILK RICOTTA

2 litres (70 fl oz) full-fat milk
500 ml (17 fl oz) buttermilk
250 ml (9 fl oz) single (pure) cream

1. For the buttermilk ricotta, combine the milk, buttermilk and cream in a large saucepan. Stir constantly over medium heat, gently scraping the bottom of the pan. Use a thermometer to monitor the temperature. As the mixture approaches 90°C (194°F) – don't let the milk boil or it will disrupt the curd formation – a raft of curds will begin to form on the surface. Stop stirring at this point and reduce the heat to very low. Once the curd has separated from the whey, remove the pan from the heat and let the ricotta stand for 30 minutes.
2. Scoop the set ricotta off the top with a slotted spoon, or gently spoon it into a cloth-lined colander (muslin is great here) to drain. Once it's drained, transfer it to the fridge, where it will keep for up to a week. It can be served as is, or you can firm and blend it as described below.
3. Line a colander with a clean cloth and set the colander over a bowl. Spoon 250 g (9 oz) of the set ricotta into the colander and leave it in the fridge overnight to firm up.
4. Spoon the firm ricotta into a food processor and blend until smooth. Season with a little salt.
5. Cut the melon into large chunks, then transfer it to a bowl. Slice the cucumbers into rounds and add them to the bowl.
6. Add the mint leaves to the bowl. Dress the salad with the vinegar, lemon juice, olive oil and honey. Add flaky salt and pepper to taste, then gently fold everything together with your hands. Check the seasoning and adjust if necessary.
7. Spoon the blended ricotta onto the centre of a serving dish and gently arrange the salad over the top. Serve immediately.

SMOKED BEEF-FAT ROAST POTATOES

These potatoes are the best. They're rich, but so, so good. They're first peeled and simmered in water until almost cooked through, then the outsides are roughed up before they're basically immersed in hot beef fat in the oven, where all their rough edges become crisp. This method was shown to me by one of our past chefs, Damian Trinco, who did some time in a proper pub in the UK. True to form, I added the smoking stage, which brings an extra layer of intensity to the picture.

Maintain maximum focus while you're cooking these – if you're not careful, the hot beef fat can spit while you're turning the potatoes over in the oven, making the whole thing less fun than it should be. Use either beef-fat trimmings you've collected or bought from the butcher, or dripping.

SERVES 4

250 g (9 oz) beef fat or dripping
1 kg (2 lb 4 oz) floury potatoes, such as sebago or Dutch cream
Flaky salt

1. Start your smoker for hot-smoking (see page 154), aiming to achieve a consistent temperature of around 100°C (212°F). Place the solid beef fat or dripping in a small tray in the smoker until the fat renders to a liquid (about an hour). Discard any left-over solids. Alternatively, you can melt the fat in the oven at 100°C (200°F) or even in a saucepan over low heat. Set aside the rendered fat at room temperature until needed.

2. Peel the potatoes, then cut them in half, place in a large saucepan and cover with water. Bring to a gentle boil and cook for 15–20 minutes or until a paring knife slides in easily, but they're not quite cooked through – you still want them al dente in the middle. Drain the potatoes well, then tip them onto a clean, dry tea towel. Cover the potatoes with the towel and give them a little rough-up to scuff up the edges and surfaces – this helps them crisp up in the oven.

3. Meanwhile, preheat the oven to 180°C (350°F). Pour the rendered fat into a large roasting tin and place in the oven for 10 minutes to heat up.

4. Using a spoon, gently lower the potatoes into the hot fat. Roast the potatoes for 15 minutes, then open the oven to check them: if the sides in contact with the fat are starting to look golden and crisp, flip the potatoes. Continue cooking, basting and turning the potatoes every 15 minutes, until they are golden and crisp all over.

5. Remove the potatoes from the oven and spoon them onto paper towel to drain a little. Season generously with flaky salt. If you are not serving the potatoes immediately, you can set them aside at room temperature for up to an hour, then reheat them on a baking tray in the oven.

CITRUS SALAD WITH BURNT HONEY AND PISTACHIOS

This salad is a celebration of winter. I always use as many different citrus fruits as I can: pomelos, Meyer lemons, blood oranges, cumquats, tangerines, grapefruit, limes. Each adds a different flavour, perfume and acidity.

The burnt honey vinegar offers complex honey notes without being overly sweet, the salty olives offset the sweet acid of the citrus fruits, the pistachios add texture, the fish sauce adds umami, and a good dousing of olive oil brings it all together.

SERVES 4

50 g (1.75 g) honey
50 ml (1.5 fl oz) chardonnay vinegar
2 tablespoons fish sauce
600 g (1 lb 5 oz) mixed citrus, such as pomelos, Meyer lemons, blood oranges, cumquats, tangerines, grapefruit, limes, lemons or oranges
1 handful of green Sicilian olives, pitted and halved
1 handful of pistachios, shelled and roughly chopped
100 ml (3.5 fl oz) extra virgin olive oil
Flaky salt
1 handful of Thai basil leaves

1. Put the honey in a small saucepan and place over low heat. Bring to the boil and cook, swirling occasionally, until the honey is caramelised and quite dark, but not burnt (the smell will give you some clues – it should smell sweet and like caramel, but not bitter). Once it's in the right zone, quickly arrest the cooking by adding the chardonnay vinegar and fish sauce (be careful, it'll spit). Leave to cool, adding a splash of water to loosen if it seizes up.
2. Peel all of the citrus very carefully with a sharp knife, leaving no pith on the flesh, then cut between the membranes to segment all the flesh, letting each segment fall into a bowl and then squeezing in the juice from the membranes.
3. Arrange the citrus segments in a serving dish, mixing up the colours and leaving most of the juice behind. Scatter the olives and pistachios over the top and dress with the burnt honey vinegar.
4. Dress generously with the olive oil, season well with flaky salt and freshly cracked pepper and finish with the Thai basil.

CHAPTER .SEVEN. SAUCES & STAPLES

CONTENTS

INTRODUCTION	219
BARBECUE SAUCE	220
HOT SAUCE	220
BROWN SAUCE	221
SAUCE GRIBICHE	221
PISTACHIO, CAPER AND LEMON SAUCE	222
SALSA VERDE	222
AÏOLI	223
PICKLED CABBAGE	226
CONFIT GARLIC	227
CHICKEN SPICE	227
MUSTARD PICKLE RELISH	228
BEER MUSTARD	228
QUINCE MUSTARD	229
GREEN TOMATOES	230
GREEN TOMATO CHUTNEY	230
PICKLED GREEN TOMATOES	231
PICKLED CURRANTS	232
RED ONION PICKLE	232
CANDIED CUMQUATS	233
STOCK	234
CHICKEN STOCK	234
BEEF STOCK AND BEEF JUS	235
GNOCCO FRITTO	236
MILK BREAD	237

When it comes to condiments and preserves, I often think of a quote from chef Sean Brock: 'He who dies with the biggest pantry wins.' The message? Keep your larder stocked with preserves, pickles and condiments at all times. Consider this chapter my starter pack for delicious things to go with everything else in this book.

There are pickles and preserves that can be made in peak season and kept throughout the year, mustards and sauces, spice mixes, dressings and even a recipe for a milk bread loaf to load up with slices of brisket.

Many of these are practised recipes that I've naturally refined over the years by making them again and again, slowly but surely dialling in on the flavours and attributes so they're really, really good. Add these to your repertoire and not only will they enhance most of the other recipes in this book, they'll also find plenty more places in your kitchen to call home.

BARBECUE SAUCE

I typically don't eat a lot of barbecue sauce as I find it too sweet, but it's a must-have if you're doing a chopped brisket sandwich (page 183) or if you have barbecue lovers around for lunch.

MAKES 1 LITRE (35 FL OZ)

750 ml (26 fl oz) tomato sauce (preferably Heinz Tomato Ketchup)
250 ml (9 fl oz) cider vinegar
60 ml (2 fl oz) soy sauce (preferably Yamasa brand)
10 g (0.4 oz) garlic powder
15 g (0.5 oz) onion powder
10 g (0.4 oz) smoked paprika
60 g (2.25 oz) brown sugar
45 ml (1.5 fl oz) espresso

1. Mix the tomato sauce, cider vinegar and soy sauce together in a bowl.
2. Mix the garlic powder, onion powder, paprika and brown sugar together in a separate bowl, then slowly add the tomato sauce mixture, whisking thoroughly to avoid lumps.
3. Transfer the mixture to a saucepan and bring to a simmer over medium heat, stirring occasionally to avoid burning or sticking.
4. Remove from the heat and stir in the espresso. Cool, then transfer the sauce to a jar, seal and refrigerate for up to 3 months.

HOT SAUCE

A simple fermented hot sauce that's great to have on hand as a seasoning for beef tartare (page 128), Bloody Marys, oysters and plenty more.

The xanthan gum prevents the sauce from splitting. Look for it in large supermarkets and health-food stores.

MAKES 1 LITRE (35 FL OZ)

500 g (1 lb 2 oz) long red chillies, halved, seeds removed (or left in if you want it ripping hot)
25 g (1 oz) fine salt
200 ml (7 fl oz) olive oil
200 ml (7 fl oz) cider vinegar
25 g (1 oz) white (granulated) sugar
1 g (0.05 oz) xanthan gum

1. Blend the chillies and salt to a rough purée in a food processor, then place in a non-metallic container with a lid. Cover the top of the chillies with the oil, put the lid on the container and leave at room temperature for 5–7 days to ferment, opening the container from time to time to release any gases.
2. Transfer the fermented chilli mixture to a food processor, add the vinegar, sugar and xanthan gum and blend until super smooth and emulsified.
3. Check the seasoning and adjust if necessary. Transfer the sauce to a jar or bottle, seal and refrigerate for up to 3 months.

BROWN SAUCE

Brown sauce is a must with our boudin noir (page 47), as well as being delicious with bacon or in a sausage and egg muffin. This version is an adapted recipe from London's temple of all things good, St. John.

MAKES 1 LITRE (35 FL OZ)

455 g (1 lb) peeled, cored apples
1 white onion
80 g (2.75 oz) prunes
20 g (0.7 oz) currants
220 g (7.75 oz) raw sugar
155 ml (5 fl oz) red wine vinegar
5 g (0.2 oz) ground ginger
2 g (0.1 oz) ground allspice
2 g (0.1 oz) ground black pepper
1 g (0.05 oz) ground white pepper
1 g (0.05 oz) ground cloves
10 g (0.4 oz) fine salt

1. Chop the apples, onion and prunes, then put them in a non-reactive saucepan with 55 ml (1.75 fl oz) water and the remaining ingredients. Bring to a simmer over medium heat. Reduce the heat to low and cook, stirring occasionally to prevent it catching on the bottom, for 40 minutes or until the liquid has reduced and the apples are very soft and starting to look like a purée. Remove the pan from the heat and let the sauce cool to room temperature.
2. Transfer the sauce to a food processor and blend until very smooth.
3. Check the seasoning and adjust if necessary (it shouldn't need anything, really). Transfer the sauce to jars, seal and refrigerate for up to 3 months.

SAUCE GRIBICHE

A bastardised version of a true sauce gribiche, which usually starts with an emulsion formed with boiled egg yolks. Instead, I like to start with a base of aïoli, then fold the egg through my sauce, giving it defined chunks and texture. It's a fine match with grilled beef tongue (page 176) or pig's-head croquettes (page 111).

MAKES ABOUT 300 G (10.5 OZ)

1 egg
235 g (8.5 oz) aïoli (page 223)
1 large handful of picked soft herbs (a mix of chervil, parsley and tarragon is ideal), roughly chopped
2 cornichons, roughly chopped
10 salted capers, rinsed and chopped

1. Lower the egg into a small saucepan of boiling water and cook for 7 minutes. Drain and rinse under cold water, then set aside to cool.
2. Spoon the aïoli into a bowl.
3. Peel the egg and roughly chop it into 5 mm (¼ in) dice, then add it to the aïoli.
4. Add the herbs, cornichons and capers and generously season with freshly cracked black pepper. Taste the sauce and adjust the seasoning if necessary. Sauce gribiche is best served fresh, but can be refrigerated for up to 2 days.

SAUCES & STAPLES

PISTACHIO, CAPER AND LEMON SAUCE

A very simple sauce or garnish in which the texture of the pistachios, sharp citrus and salty hit of the capers all come together to provide a welcome balance and seasoning to grilled fish (page 130), as well as grilled leeks or zucchini (courgette). This is best made on the day you want to serve it, to keep it bright and vibrant.

MAKES ABOUT 250 ML (9 FL OZ)

½ lemonade fruit or lemon
75 g (2.5 oz) finely chopped pistachios
25 g (1 oz) salted capers, rinsed
25 g (1 oz) chopped flat-leaf parsley
Juice of 1 lemon
200 ml (7 fl oz) buttery and not-so-peppery extra virgin olive oil

1. Peel the lemonade fruit or lemon very carefully with a sharp knife, avoiding the white pith. Finely dice the zest.
2. Combine the zest, pistachios, capers and parsley in a bowl.
3. Add the lemon juice, ensuring there are no seeds, then drizzle in the olive oil.
4. Stir everything together and season to taste with salt and freshly ground black pepper.
5. Keep the sauce at room temperature until you're ready to serve.

SALSA VERDE

Salsa verde, or green sauce, goes with pretty much anything, but it's especially good with roasted meats, potatoes, beef tongue (page 176), and grilled fish (page 130) or octopus (page 134). It's best made fresh, but if you know there'll be a delay before serving, hold back on adding the vinegar until the very last minute.

MAKES ABOUT 300 ML (10.5 FL OZ)

20 g (0.7 oz) flat-leaf parsley leaves
12 g (0.4 oz) mint leaves
3 g (0.1 oz) tarragon leaves
20 g (0.7 oz) salted capers, rinsed
35 g (1.25 oz) drained, tinned anchovy fillets in oil
3 g (0.3 oz) garlic
200 ml (7 fl oz) olive oil
50 ml (1.5 fl oz) good-quality red wine vinegar

1. Using a sharp knife, chop all the herbs, the capers and the anchovies quite finely (this is a rustic sauce, so don't get too carried away), then combine in a bowl.
2. Grate the garlic into the olive oil using a microplane, then gently fold the oil through the herb mixture. Generously season with freshly ground black pepper.
3. Stir in the vinegar at the last moment before serving.

AÏOLI

I love aïoli. It's got to be one of the best condiments on the planet, whether it's in a bacon sandwich or served with raw vegetables, boiled potatoes, French fries or just about anything else.

When it comes to aïoli, I do get a bit particular and want it to taste the same every time, which just shows that it's very personal. So if you make this and it doesn't taste quite right, please adjust and make it the way you prefer. I like to combine fresh garlic and confit garlic for the best of both worlds – you get the sweet richness from the confit and the sharp bite from the fresh. The final flourish is a little pinch of MSG, which (as with many popular Japanese mayonnaises) brings another dimension. If you're not into MSG, you can leave it out, just as you can leave out the garlic and make straight-up mayonnaise.

MAKES ABOUT 500 ML (17 FL OZ)

1 egg
10 g (0.4 oz) Dijon mustard
10 g (0.4 oz) confit garlic (page 227)
7 g (0.2 oz) garlic, finely grated
25 ml (0.75 fl oz) chardonnay vinegar
3 teaspoons lemon juice
Pinch of caster (superfine) sugar
Pinch of monosodium glutamate (MSG)
250 ml (9 fl oz) neutral oil, such as grapeseed oil
150 ml (5 fl oz) extra virgin olive oil (not too peppery or bitter)
30 ml (1 fl oz) hot water (optional)

1. Put the egg, mustard, confit garlic, fresh garlic, vinegar and lemon juice in a food processor. Add a small pinch each of salt, sugar and MSG and blend it all together until very smooth.
2. Mix the oils together, then slowly drizzle them into the egg mixture with the processor running. This can be a bit of a feeling-out process: you need to add the oil quickly enough that the emulsion doesn't heat up from the friction of blending and then split, but slowly enough that the egg has enough time to emulsify. Keep adding the oil until it is completely incorporated and the aïoli is thick.
3. If it looks a little too thick, blend in a small amount of hot water.
4. Taste the aïoli and adjust the seasoning with more salt, sugar, MSG and lemon juice or vinegar if needed. Fresh aïoli, made with fresh egg, will keep refrigerated for up to a week.

PICKLED CABBAGE

This pickle is a good one to keep in mind, since it's super easy and can be used for all kinds of vegetables, such as cucumber, beetroot and carrot. It's a 3-2-1 recipe, with three parts water, two parts sugar and one part vinegar. Make as much as you like, as it will keep in the fridge for weeks; you just need enough pickling liquid to cover the vegetables, and you can get creative with the seasonings.

MAKES ABOUT 500 G (1 LB 2 OZ)

500 g (1 lb 2 oz) white cabbage, very thinly sliced (a mandolin is great here)
265 g (9.25 oz) caster (superfine) sugar
135 ml (4.5 fl oz) cider vinegar
½ bunch of dill (you can use the whole bunch — the stalks and roots are delicious too)
1 garlic clove, crushed
5 g (0.2 oz) caraway seeds

1. Put the sliced cabbage in a large heatproof bowl.
2. Combine 400 ml (14 fl oz) water, sugar and vinegar in a saucepan and bring to a simmer, stirring to dissolve the sugar. Remove from the heat and add the dill, garlic and caraway seeds. Set aside until the liquid is warm rather than hot.
3. Pour the pickling liquid over the cabbage and let it cool completely before covering and placing in the fridge overnight. It will keep for up to a month.

CONFIT GARLIC

In this very simple recipe, the garlic is cooked long and slow so that it almost caramelises, becoming sweet and losing all of its fiery punch. Confit garlic has infinite uses: mash it and mix it through boiled greens, use it as a pizza topping, smoosh it on top of a resting steak, or blend it to make a dip. The oil can be used for dressings, sauces and more.

MAKES ABOUT 180 G (6 OZ) GARLIC

200 g (7 oz) peeled garlic cloves
250 ml (9 fl oz) neutral oil, such as grapeseed or vegetable oil

1. Put the garlic cloves in a small saucepan and cover them with the oil. Cook over medium heat until the oil is just bubbling along, then turn the heat down as low as possible until there's hardly any movement. Continue cooking until the garlic is very soft but still holding its shape, about 30–40 minutes. Take care to not let the heat become too intense or the garlic will colour too much and burn. Ideally, you want it to retain an ivory colour.
2. Once the garlic is super soft, remove the pan from the heat and spread the oil and garlic out on a tray or plate to cool quickly. Once cooled, transfer the garlic and oil to a jar, seal and place in the fridge, where it will keep for up to a week.

CHICKEN SPICE

This first came about as a seasoning for coating our smoked chickens to give them a thick, spicy crust, but it has many uses. We've tried it on fries and on steak, but the most delicious discovery was when one of our team used it to season some corn tortillas straight out of the deep-fryer. The flavour was reminiscent of those corn chips we all love. Give it a whirl.

MAKES ABOUT 450 G (1 LB)

175 g (6 oz) fine salt
75 g (2.5 oz) brown sugar
65 g (2.25 oz) coriander seeds
60 g (2.25 oz) smoked paprika
60 g (2.25 oz) ground black pepper
20 g (0.7 oz) dill seeds
8 g (0.3 oz) chilli flakes

1. Put all of the ingredients in a food processor and blend them to a very fine powder.
2. Transfer the chicken spice to a jar, seal and store in the pantry for up to 2 months.

MUSTARD PICKLE RELISH

A wonderful relish, reminiscent of something from your grandparents' house. It's great on a ham and cheese sandwich, and we use it regularly on our hot dogs (page 51) with a smoked frankfurter and diced onion.

MAKES ABOUT 750 G (1 LB 10 OZ)

- 350 g (12 oz) zucchini (courgette), cut into 1 cm (½ in) dice
- 1 small white onion, diced
- 400 ml (14 fl oz) cider vinegar
- 30 g (1 oz) white (granulated) sugar
- 25 g (1 oz) mustard powder
- 8 g (0.3 oz) ground turmeric
- 5 g (0.2 oz) fine salt
- 25 g (1 oz) cornflour (cornstarch)

1. Combine the zucchini, onion, vinegar, sugar, mustard powder, turmeric and salt in a non-reactive saucepan and bring to a simmer.
2. Mix the cornflour with 85 ml (2.75 fl oz) water to form a slurry, then slowly pour it into the saucepan, stirring to prevent lumps.
3. Cook, stirring occasionally, for 15 minutes or until the zucchini is tender but still holding its shape and the flavour of the cornflour has cooked out. Taste to check the seasoning and adjust if necessary, then remove from the heat.
4. Transfer the relish to a jar, seal and leave it to cool before placing it in the fridge, where it will keep for up to 8 weeks.

BEER MUSTARD

This is a sturdy mustard, meaning it can be quite pungent and will really clear the sinuses. You can use any type of beer, but we favour the pale ale made by The Grifter Brewing Co. in Marrickville, Sydney.

The longer the mustard marinates, the milder it becomes – at least that's the theory; we always end up using it before we can really test the limits.

MAKES 1 LITRE (35 FL OZ)

- 400 ml (14 fl oz) beer
- 320 ml (11 fl oz) cider vinegar
- 140 g (5 oz) brown mustard seeds
- 140 g (5 oz) yellow mustard seeds
- ½ red onion, diced
- 35 g (1.25 oz) fine salt
- 35 g (1.25 oz) caster (superfine) sugar
- 15 g (0.5 oz) mustard powder
- 10 g (0.4 oz) ground black pepper

1. Put all the ingredients in a non-reactive container with a lid and mix thoroughly, then cover and leave in the fridge for a month to marinate.
2. Strain the mixture through a fine sieve (reserve the liquid) and place the solids in a food processor. Blend until the mustard reaches your desired coarseness and texture (make it as fine or coarse as you like), adjusting the consistency with the strained liquid.
3. Transfer the mustard to a large jar, seal and store in the fridge for up to 6 months.

QUINCE MUSTARD

This recipe came about from accidentally overcooking quince, then realising we could blend it with Dijon mustard to make a delicious condiment that has just the right amount of sweetness to make it a match for terrine (page 103) or even galantine (page 112). The lower and slower the quince cooks, the more the ruby-red colour develops – we try to push it out to about 8 hours.

MAKES 500 G (1 LB 2 OZ)

500 g (1 lb 2 oz) quinces
750 g (1 lb 10 oz) caster (superfine) sugar
2 cinnamon sticks
5 fresh bay leaves
5 cloves
250 g (9 oz) Dijon mustard, approximately

1. Preheat the oven to 120°C (235°F).
2. Peel and core the quinces, reserving the skins and cores, then cut the flesh into quarters.
3. Put the sugar, cinnamon sticks, bay leaves, cloves and a pinch of salt in a saucepan with 1 litre (35 fl oz) water. Bring to the boil, stirring to dissolve the sugar.
4. Add the chopped quinces and the reserved skin and cores to an ovenproof dish, cover with the syrup, then top with a cartouche or a sheet of baking paper before covering it with a lid or a tight layer of foil.
5. Bake for about 8 hours or until the quince is tender when poked with a knife and has turned a deep ruby red. Cool, then discard the quince skin and cores.
6. Transfer the quince and syrup to an airtight container and refrigerate until you're ready to make the mustard. (At this stage, you can also use the quince to make a crumble or to top a rice pudding.)
7. Weigh the quince mixture, then transfer to a food processor and add an equal weight of Dijon mustard. Blend until smooth. Transfer the mustard to a jar, seal and refrigerate for up to 2 months.

GREEN TOMATOES

Green tomatoes, which tend to be around at the end and beginning of the tomato season, are brilliant for preserving. I've given a couple of methods here. The first, a green tomato chutney, is filled with warm spices, making it a great preserve leading into the cooler months. The pickled green tomatoes, on the other hand, make a refreshing addition to the spring table.

Green tomato chutney

This versatile chutney is just as at home on a cheese board or charcuterie plate as it is in your favourite toasted sandwich.

MAKES ABOUT 750 G (1 LB 10 OZ)

1 kg (2 lb 4 oz) green tomatoes, cored and cut into 1 cm (½ in) dice
200 g (7 oz) brown sugar
½ red onion, diced
200 ml (7 fl oz) cider vinegar
15 g (0.5 oz) mustard seeds
12 g (0.4 oz) fine salt
5 g (0.2 oz) fennel seeds
2.5 g (0.1 oz) chilli flakes
2 g (0.1 oz) ground allspice
2 g (0.1 oz) ground cinnamon

1. Combine all the ingredients in a non-reactive saucepan and bring to a simmer over medium heat. Cook, stirring occasionally to prevent catching, for about 45 minutes or until the mixture begins to thicken.
2. To test if it's ready, place a spoonful of chutney on a saucer and put it in the fridge for a few minutes. Once it's cool, check the consistency – the chutney should be slightly jam-like. Taste and adjust the seasoning if necessary.
3. Transfer the chutney to a jar, seal and leave to cool before placing it in the fridge, where it will keep for up to 8 weeks.

Pickled green tomatoes

It's not just the tomatoes you get out of this – the pickling liquid, loaded with garlic and dill, is delicious, too. I sometimes slurp a spoonful just to get a kick. Serve these with stretched cheeses like stracciatella (page 199) or warm ricotta (page 211) and plenty of olive oil, or use them in salads.

MAKES ABOUT 750 G (1 LB 10 OZ)

500 g (1 lb 2 oz) green tomatoes, cored and sliced into 5 mm (¼ in) rounds
1 white onion, thinly sliced into rings
15 g (0.5 oz) fine salt
370 ml (13 fl oz) white vinegar
90 g (3.25 oz) white (granulated) sugar
6 garlic cloves, sliced
5 fresh bay leaves
5 g (0.2 oz) black peppercorns
1 bunch of dill

1. Combine the tomato and onion slices in a large non-reactive bowl, sprinkle evenly with the salt and leave for an hour to allow the salt to draw out the moisture.
2. Combine the vinegar, sugar, garlic, bay leaves and peppercorns in a non-reactive saucepan. Add 185 ml (6 fl oz) water and bring to a simmer, stirring to dissolve the sugar.
3. Put the tomato and onion in a jar, along with the dill, then pour the hot pickling liquid over the top. Seal the jar and give it a shake to remove any air bubbles, then leave it to cool completely before placing it in the fridge, where the pickles will keep for up to 8 weeks.

PICKLED CURRANTS

These currants are delicious with pâtés and terrines, charcuterie plates and even with cheese. It's also worth giving this pickle a go with prunes or raisins, which will work just as well.

MAKES 600 G (1 LB 5 OZ)

250 g (9 oz) currants or other dried fruit (such as prunes or raisins)
280 ml (9.5 fl oz) red wine vinegar
100 g (3.5 oz) brown sugar
4 cloves
3 cinnamon sticks
1 star anise
½ nutmeg, freshly grated

1. Put the currants in a heatproof bowl. Combine the remaining ingredients in a saucepan and bring to the boil, then pour the hot pickling liquid over the currants.
2. Transfer the mixture to a jar, seal and leave to cool before placing it in the fridge. Wait at least a couple of days before serving to allow the flavours to develop. Pickled currants will keep for up to 3 months in the fridge.

RED ONION PICKLE

A recipe borrowed from the legendary Judy Rogers of Zuni Café in San Francisco. We've used these pickles for all sorts of applications: in burgers and sandwiches, with pâté and terrines, and we use them every day on pizzas at Bella Brutta. They are the absolute best.

MAKES 500 G (1 LB 2 OZ)

500 g (1 lb 2 oz) red onions
1 litre (35 fl oz) white wine vinegar
300 g (10.5 oz) raw sugar
1 cinnamon stick
2 star anise
4 fresh bay leaves
½ teaspoon ground allspice
½ teaspoon black peppercorns
½ teaspoon cloves
½ teaspoon chilli flakes

1. Peel the onions and slice them into 5 mm (¼ in) rings.
2. Combine the remaining ingredients in a non-reactive saucepan and bring to the boil.
3. Working in small batches to keep the pickling liquid boiling, blanch the onion rings for 45 seconds, then spread them out evenly on a tray or plate and leave them to cool at room temperature.
4. Let the pickling liquid cool until just warm.
5. Transfer the onion rings to a jar, then pour in the warm pickling liquid. Seal and place in the fridge, where the red onion pickle will keep for up to 8 weeks.

CANDIED CUMQUATS

Candied cumquats are a brilliant condiment to have on hand. They go very well with pâté and terrines, are brilliant with smoked duck (page 172), and I've even used them to garnish ice cream or a nougat parfait (page 248).

For a long time I was perplexed about how to cook these little fruits to vanquish their bitterness. I was soaking them in iced water, blanching them three times, trying all sorts of things. In the end I discovered the secret, so eloquently put by my business partner Elvis Abrahanowicz: 'Just put them in sugar syrup and boil the shit out of them.' Works a treat.

MAKES 650 G (1 LB 7 OZ)

500 g (1 lb 2 oz) cumquats
400 g (14 oz) white (granulated) sugar

1. Cut the cumquats in half and squeeze the seeds and juice into a sieve set over a bowl. Discard the seeds and reserve the juice.
2. Put the squeezed-out cumquats, sugar and 400 ml (14 fl oz) water in a large saucepan and bring to the boil. Reduce the heat to a low simmer and cook the cumquats for 30–40 minutes or until they're tender and jammy, but still with some resistance. Test the cumquats regularly by fishing one out of the syrup, letting it cool down and then tasting it to check the texture.
3. When you think the cumquats are ready, spoon some of the syrup onto a saucer, then place it in the fridge for a few minutes. If the syrup sets up thick like marmalade, it's ready. Remove the pan from the heat, pour in the reserved cumquat juice and stir until thoroughly combined.
4. Transfer the cumquats and syrup to a jar, seal and leave to cool completely before placing them in the fridge, where they will keep for up to 3 months.

STOCK

Stocks are a foundation of many kitchens, and a prime example of how to make use of the whole animal by taking the last remaining scraps of the carcass and coaxing liquid gold out of them. And it is coaxing: each step of stock making should be given equal consideration. It means paying attention to the bones being roasted to the right degree, to deglazing the pan thoroughly, to bringing the stock to the boil at the right pace. Each part of the process contributes to the final flavour, and if just one part is off, the stock won't reach its full potential.

There's one point I sit on the fence with, which is whether or not to add vegetables. Vegetables can add a beautiful sweetness and making stock is a great way to use up trimmings as well as herb stalks, but it depends on the final purpose of the stock. If it's being used to braise meats or for a soup, then by all means load it up with a mirepoix of carrots, celery and onions. But for stocks that are going to be reduced in order to sauce a steak or prime rib, then leaving the vegetables out really hones and accentuates the deep, caramelised meat flavours. Likewise, for a chicken stock that will be made into gravy (as for the mash and gravy on page 206), using only carcasses means focusing on getting that strong chicken flavour that makes it so appealing.

Chicken stock

MAKES 2 LITRES (70 FL OZ)

1 kg (2 lb 4 oz) raw chicken frames (or as many as you have; any meat or skin clinging on is good)

1. Preheat the oven to 180°C (350°F). Put the chicken frames in a flameproof roasting tin and roast for 30 minutes or until the bones are showing signs of colouring, then turn to colour the other sides. Continue roasting until the bones are properly browned all over and any liquid has evaporated and turned to a golden crust sticking to the tin, about 20 minutes.
2. Transfer the chicken frames to a stockpot and set the roasting tin aside. Add enough water to the pot to just cover the chicken frames. Pour any fat that has accumulated in the bottom of the roasting tin into a small bowl to use in the gravy on page 206, on roast potatoes, or even in the aïoli on page 223 for a tasty chicken-fat mayo. Deglaze the tin by adding a splash of water, placing it on the stove over low heat and using a wooden spoon to scrape off any golden crusty bits. Pour this liquid into the stockpot.
3. Heat the stock until it's just below boiling point, then reduce the heat so it's just simmering. Simmer for 1½ hours, ensuring the stock doesn't boil. Skim off and discard any foam or fat that rises to the surface.
4. Ladle the stock through a fine sieve or conical strainer into a clean pan. Taste the stock: if you'd like it to be slightly stronger, put it back on the stove to reduce until you're happy with the flavour. Let the stock cool, then pour it into an airtight container and place it in the fridge. The stock can be kept refrigerated for up to a week, or frozen for 3 months.

Beef stock and beef jus

Beef stock is a slightly lengthier labour of love, since it's best cooked slowly over a period of 8 hours. I always throw a pig's trotter in with the bones, which doesn't affect the flavour, but gives the stock or jus a slightly more gelatinous quality, a silkier mouthfeel. Ask your butcher nicely to split the pig's trotter in half for you. While you're there, ask them to cut the beef bones into pieces.

If you're making the beef jus, take care when you're reducing the stock: if you take it too far, the jus can become a thick goop resembling a preliminary stage of Vegemite. Rather than taking it to a point where it's bitter or coats your mouth, aim for a gentle viscosity and a clean flavour. This jus is great with grilled steak (page 142), smoked prime rib (page 187), roasts or anything 'beefy'.

MAKES ABOUT 4 LITRES (140 FL OZ) STOCK OR 1.25 LITRES (44 FL OZ) JUS

2.5 kg (5 lb 8 oz) beef bones, preferably knuckle and neck, cut into 5 cm (2 in) pieces
1 pig's trotter, split in half
5 fresh bay leaves
A few sprigs of thyme
Scattering of black peppercorns

1. Preheat the oven to 180°C (350°F). Put the beef bones in a flameproof roasting tin and roast for 30 minutes or until the bones are showing signs of colouring, then turn to colour the other sides. Continue roasting until the bones are properly browned all over, any liquid has evaporated and turned to a golden crust sticking to the tin, and the meaty edges look like you'd want to pull them off and eat them, about 40 minutes.
2. Transfer all of the beef bones to a stockpot and set the roasting tin aside. Add enough water to the stockpot to just cover the bones, then add the pig's trotter. If any fat has accumulated in the bottom of the roasting tin, pour it into a small bowl – this is absolute gold for roasting potatoes. Deglaze the tin by adding a splash of water, placing it on the stove over low heat and using a wooden spoon to scrape off any golden crusty bits. Pour all this delicious beefy liquid into the stockpot.
3. Heat the stock until it's just below boiling point, then reduce the heat so it's just simmering, with small bubbles rolling up from the bottom. You don't want the stock to boil. Skim off and discard any foam or fat that rises to the surface.
4. Add the bay leaves, thyme and peppercorns and let the stock tick over gently at a low simmer for 6–8 hours, constantly paying attention to the heat and skimming off any fat or impurities that rise to the surface.
5. Turn off the heat and carefully ladle the stock through a fine sieve or conical strainer into a clean pot, trying not to disturb the bones too much, which can make it cloudy. You can refrigerate the stock for up to a week, or freeze it for 3 months, or continue to the next step to make a sauce.
6. To make a reduced beef sauce, or jus, return the stock to the stove over medium heat and simmer until it has a clean, delicious beefy flavour and is thick enough that it won't run all over a plate, but still thin enough that it's not over-reduced goop. Allow the jus to cool, then store it in an airtight container in the fridge for up to a week, or freeze it for 3 months.

GNOCCO FRITTO

These crisp, deep-fried crackers make wonderful little vehicles to serve your beef tartare (page 128) on or with. We make them with Peroni Red beer to keep the Italian theme strong; you'll have to drink the remainder from the can or bottle while you make these.

Make the dough the day before cooking so it's well hydrated and rested. If you don't have a pasta machine, you can use a rolling pin.

MAKES ABOUT 24 CRACKERS

300 g (10.5 oz) plain (all-purpose) flour, plus extra for dusting
2 g (0.1 oz) baking powder
30 ml (1 fl oz) olive oil
Pinch of fine salt
140 ml (5 fl oz) beer
Vegetable oil (or other neutral oil), for deep-frying

1. Put all the ingredients in a bowl and mix with a spoon to get things going, so it's not super messy right from the start. Once the dough begins to come together, the spoon can go in the sink and you can knead the dough by hand until it's smooth and cohesive. Wrap in plastic wrap and refrigerate overnight to rest.

2. Cut the dough into quarters. Lightly dust the bench with flour and flatten each dough portion with the palm of your hand.

3. Working with one portion of dough at a time, roll the dough through a pasta machine set on the thickest setting, then continue to roll it through, reducing the setting notch by notch and dusting with flour anytime the dough feels sticky. Keep going until you reach the second-last setting.

4. Lay the dough sheet on the bench and use a fork to dock the dough all over. (This helps the gnocco bubble evenly during cooking, which prevents massive bubbles from forming.)

5. Half-fill a deep saucepan or deep-fryer with oil and gently heat it to around 170°C (338°F).

6. Cut the dough into circles with an 8 cm (3¼ in) cutter, then slip them carefully into the hot oil in batches. Once the bubbling slows down, flip them over and continue cooking until they're a nice toasty colour and the bubbling has almost stopped. Remove from the oil with a slotted spoon and drain on a wire rack set over a tray or on paper towel.

7. Once cool, the gnocco fritto are ready to eat. Store them in an airtight container to keep them fresh for up to 2 weeks.

MILK BREAD

This versatile recipe can be used to make sandwich bread (see the brisket sandwich on page 183) or milk buns, as pictured on page 157 (see the variation below). Roll them a little bigger, separate them on a baking tray and sprinkle them with sesame seeds, and you've then got burger buns for your cheeseburgers (see page 144).

Start this recipe a day ahead to allow the dough time to rest.

MAKES 1 LOAF

2 eggs
120 ml (3.75 fl oz) milk, plus extra for brushing
18 g (0.6 oz) fresh yeast
600 g (1 lb 5 oz) plain (all-purpose) flour, plus extra for dusting
12 g (0.4 oz) fine salt
30 g (1 oz) white (granulated) sugar
90 g (3.25 oz) diced butter, at room temperature
Oil spray, for greasing

1. Mix one of the eggs and the milk together, then weigh the mixture and add enough cold water to bring the total weight to 290 g (10.25 oz). Add the yeast, then pour the mixture into an electric mixer fitted with the dough hook. Begin mixing on low speed.
2. Mix the flour, salt and sugar together, then add to the mixer and mix until a shaggy dough forms. Add the butter and increase the speed to medium. Mix until the dough reaches 25°C (77°F) and is nicely elastic.
3. Transfer the dough to a container greased with oil spray, cover and refrigerate overnight to rest.
4. Line the base of a 1 litre (35 fl oz) loaf tin with baking paper and lightly spray the tin with oil. Tip the dough onto a lightly floured bench and push it out into a rough rectangular shape the same width as the tin, then roll it up as tightly as you can. Drop the dough into the tin, with the seam on the bottom. Cover with a clean tea towel and place in a warm place to prove until it has roughly doubled in size.
5. Preheat the oven to 180°C (350°F). Make an egg wash by mixing the extra egg with a splash of milk. Brush the top of the dough with the egg wash, then bake for 30–40 minutes or until the loaf has risen and the top is golden. If you check the centre with a thermometer, it should read at 95–100°C (203–212°F).
6. Leave the loaf in the tin, sitting on a wire rack, until it's cool enough to handle, then turn out the loaf and leave it to cool completely on the rack. Wrap in plastic wrap and store at room temperature for up to a week.

VARIATION

Milk buns
Roll the rested dough into 15 balls and arrange in an oiled cast-iron frying pan or small roasting tin. Cover and prove until roughly doubled in size. Brush with egg wash and bake for 20–30 minutes or until risen and golden: the centre of the buns should be between 95 and 100°C (203 and 212°F).

CHAPTER .EIGHT.
DESSERTS

CONTENTS

INTRODUCTION	241
COCONUT SORBET WITH WATERMELON GRANITA	242
STRAWBERRIES WITH ALMOND SPONGE AND CRÈME DIPLOMAT	244
NOUGAT PARFAIT WITH SALTED HONEY CARAMEL	248
TIRAMISÙ	251
POUDING CHÔMEUR	252
CHOUX AU CRAQUELIN WITH VANILLA ICE CREAM	255
VANILLA ICE CREAM	256
ESPRESSO GRANITA WITH CHANTILLY AND BISCOTTI	258
BISCOTTI	259

I may not call myself a pastry chef, but one thing I can attest to is that I love eating desserts. So while my repertoire may be short and sweet, the desserts that have stood the test of time on our menus are those that are highly geared for deliciousness, and steer away from technical wizardry in favour of simplicity and a warm, nostalgic feeling.

Maybe it's for this reason that the desserts we've served in the restaurants over the years have gained their own kind of following. (People still ask me for the recipe for the pouding chômeur we served at LP's for many years – ask no longer!)

And even if my family can tell you that I've made some of the driest cakes imaginable (which I'm pretty certain is the result of not following recipes to the letter, something that's paramount in the world of sweets), the collection of recipes in this chapter are battle-tested treats that have been practised and refined through thousands of services. Follow them closely and they'll reward you.

COCONUT SORBET WITH WATERMELON GRANITA

This coconut sorbet recipe is from Martin Boetz, who I worked under at Longrain. I've tried plenty of coconut sorbets, gelatos and ice creams over the years, but none have quite reached the heights of this one. It could be the salt, it could be the young coconut juice (specifically Cock Brand, available in Thai grocers) – all I know is that it's unfailingly delicious.

I love ice cream with granita. I can still remember the first time I ever tried the two together. It was after lunch at Jane and Jeremy Strode's Bistrode in Sydney, and was a simple combination of vanilla ice cream with a strawberry-and-rosewater granita. This was years ago, but it still sticks with me how refreshing and marvellous the two textures were together. When you play around with the pairings, you open up a whole world of flavour possibilities. Coconut with watermelon, to my mind, is about as fresh as it gets.

You'll need an ice-cream machine, and you'll need to start a day ahead so everything has time to freeze.

SERVES 6–8

100 g (3.5 oz) white (granulated) sugar
220 ml (7.5 fl oz) liquid glucose
500 ml (17 fl oz) coconut cream (preferably Kara brand)
300 ml (10.5 fl oz) young coconut juice (preferably Cock Brand)
1½ teaspoons pure vanilla essence
½ teaspoon flaky salt

WATERMELON GRANITA

750 g (1 lb 10 oz) piece watermelon
125 g (4.5 oz) caster (superfine) sugar, approximately

1. For the granita, remove and discard the watermelon rind and cut the flesh into chunks. Blend the watermelon flesh in a food processor until it becomes smooth and liquid.
2. Weigh the watermelon juice, then pour it into a bowl. Measure out enough sugar to equal one-quarter of the weight of the watermelon. Add the sugar to the watermelon juice and whisk until dissolved.
3. Pour the watermelon mixture into a tray or container and place it in the freezer. Every 2 hours, take a fork and gently move the ice crystals around as they form (this results in larger crystals in the granita, which I prefer). Continue to do this for 6–8 hours or until the granita is frozen and nicely fluffy. At this stage, it can be kept frozen, covered, for up to a week.
4. Meanwhile, start on the sorbet. Pour 200 ml (7 fl oz) water into a heavy-based saucepan, add the sugar and stir over low heat until dissolved. Add the glucose, stirring until dissolved and well combined. Remove from the heat and leave it to cool to room temperature.
5. Add the coconut cream, coconut juice, vanilla and salt to the cooled sugar mixture and stir to combine. Pour the mixture into an ice-cream machine and churn, following the manufacturer's instructions, until frozen. Transfer the sorbet to an airtight container and store in the freezer until needed.
6. To serve, spoon a large scoop of coconut sorbet into a glass and top it with a large spoonful of watermelon granita.

STRAWBERRIES WITH ALMOND SPONGE AND CRÈME DIPLOMAT

Strawberries are such a classic fruit, and I particularly love the juice that accumulates when you macerate them in sugar and a splash of liqueur – a throwback to the strawberries Romanoff recipe of old. That said, treat this light dessert (pictured on page 246) as a springboard, using whatever fruit is ripe and in season, rather than feeling like you need to use strawberries every time. I've even served it with poached quince in the cooler months.

The sponge recipe is much the same as the one you'll see in the tiramisù recipe on page 251, but with the hazelnuts swapped for almonds, which work better here. The crème diplomat, which combines whipped cream with pastry cream, is both rich and light. Fruit, creamy custard and syrupy sponge – what's not to like?

SERVES 4–6

500 g (1 lb 2 oz) strawberries
200 g (7 oz) white (granulated) sugar
100 ml (3.5 fl oz) Cointreau or other orange liqueur
Pinch of flaky salt

ALMOND DACQUOISE SPONGE

100 g (3.5 oz) roasted almonds
3½ egg whites
110 g (3.75 oz) pure icing (confectioners') sugar
Pinch of fine salt
2 eggs
30 g (1 oz) plain (all-purpose) flour

CRÈME DIPLOMAT

40 g (1.5 oz) cornflour (cornstarch)
500 ml (17 fl oz) milk
100 g (3.5 oz) egg yolks
100 g (3.5 oz) caster (superfine) sugar
1 vanilla pod, split lengthways
200 ml (7 fl oz) single (pure) cream

1. For the sponge, preheat the oven to 170°C (325°F). Line a 33 x 27 cm (13 x 10¾ in) baking tray with baking paper.
2. Pulse the almonds in a food processor until they resemble fine breadcrumbs. Set aside.
3. Using a stand mixer fitted with the whisk attachment, whisk the egg whites, 20 g (0.75 oz) of the icing sugar and the salt until soft peaks form.
4. In a separate bowl, whisk the whole eggs with the remaining 90 g (3 oz) of icing sugar until pale and fluffy. Add the ground almonds, along with the flour. Mix thoroughly to combine, then gently fold into the egg whites, taking care not to knock out excess air.
5. Pour the sponge batter onto the baking tray and use an offset spatula to spread it into an even rectangle. Bake for 25 minutes or until evenly golden. Remove from the oven, lift the baking paper and sponge onto a wire rack and leave to cool to room temperature.
6. For the crème diplomat, mix the cornflour with 2 tablespoons of the milk in a large heatproof bowl to form a smooth paste. Add the egg yolks and mix until thoroughly combined.
7. Pour the remaining 460 ml (16 fl oz) of milk into a saucepan and add the caster sugar. Scrape in the vanilla seeds and add the vanilla pod. Bring to the boil, then pour the hot milk onto the egg yolk mixture, whisking quickly as you go. Continue whisking furiously until the mixture begins to thicken and there are no lumps.
8. Return the pastry cream to the pan and stir over low heat until it's very thick, with no residual taste of flour. Transfer the mixture to a non-reactive bowl and cover with plastic wrap, pressing it directly onto the surface to prevent a skin forming. Let it cool completely in the fridge.

9. Remove the green tops from the strawberries, then cut them in half and place them in a bowl. Add the sugar, Cointreau and salt and lightly toss to coat the strawberries. Cover and leave at room temperature for at least an hour to macerate.
10. To finish the crème diplomat, whisk the cream until stiff peaks form, then fold it into the pastry cream (you may need to whisk the pastry cream first if it has set).
11. To serve, place the sponge on a board and pour over all the juices from the strawberries to soak the sponge. Arrange the strawberry halves all over the sponge, then cut the sponge into 4–6 portions, depending on how many people you're serving. Transfer to plates and serve with a large dollop of the crème diplomat.

NOUGAT PARFAIT WITH SALTED HONEY CARAMEL

This recipe (pictured on page 247) is adapted from one shown to me by the first head chef I worked under, Sandrine Urvois, an amazing Breton woman. She taught me so much at a time when I was young, a little naïve and way too keen to finish every dish with wacky garnishes. She pumped the brakes and instead showed me proper techniques, like braising, how to confit and how to make the best parfait. Basics, but so, so important. I'll forever be grateful. Two decades later, her parfait is still the one I lean on.

There are a number of schools of thought with caramel, but I like to start with the sugar fully wet so it can dissolve easily – that way, you don't get any burnt patches developing while you're waiting for the rest of the sugar to caramelise. With a wet caramel, the water reduces, then the sugar begins to caramelise evenly. Refrain from sticking anything in there to stir it or brush down the sides of the pan, such as a spoon or pastry brush – these just add to the risk of the sugar crystallising.

You'll need an 18 x 8.5 x 7.5 cm (7 x 3¼ x 3 in) terrine mould. Start this recipe a day ahead.

SERVES 6

500 ml (21 fl oz) single (pure) cream
150 g (5.5 oz) caster (superfine) sugar
150 g (5.5 oz) honey
5 egg whites

ALMOND PRALINE

100 g (3.5 oz) caster (superfine) sugar
100 g (3.5 oz) roasted almonds

SALTED HONEY CARAMEL

200 g (7 oz) honey
200 ml (7 fl oz) thickened (whipping) cream
Flaky salt

1. For the almond praline, put the sugar in a small saucepan, just cover it with water and bring to the boil over medium–high heat. Continue to cook the sugar to make a caramel; if the edges start to colour, give the pan a gentle swirl to distribute the caramelising sugar. Meanwhile, line a baking tray with baking paper.
2. Once the caramel is dark golden and reaches around 160°C (320°F) on a sugar thermometer, carefully add the roasted almonds and stir them through, then quickly but carefully pour the praline onto the baking tray. Allow to cool completely.
3. Use a rolling pin to bash up the praline, then add it to a food processor and pulse until it resembles fine breadcrumbs. Store in an airtight container until needed.
4. For the parfait, whip the cream until it forms soft, floppy peaks. Refrigerate until needed.
5. Put the sugar and honey in a saucepan and bring to the boil over medium–high heat. Let the mixture boil, swirling the pan occasionally, until it reaches 115°C (239°F) on a sugar thermometer. Meanwhile, using a stand mixer fitted with the whisk attachment, whisk the egg whites until stiff peaks form.
6. With the mixer on low speed, slowly and carefully pour in the hot sugar and honey mixture. Once it has all been incorporated, increase the speed to high and whisk until the whites are very stiff, glossy and fluffy, then reduce the speed to medium and keep whisking until cooled.

7. While the meringue is cooling, line your terrine mould with plastic wrap (I like to lightly oil the mould first to help the plastic stick).
8. Fold the chilled whipped cream and the praline into the cooled meringue with a spatula, then carefully spoon the parfait mixture into the terrine mould. Give the mould a gentle tap on the bench to make sure there are no air pockets, then cover and freeze overnight to set.
9. The next day, make the salted honey caramel. Put the honey in a saucepan and bring to the boil over medium–high heat, then continue to cook, swirling occasionally, until it begins to caramelise. It needs to reach a temperature of about 160°C (320°F).
10. Remove the pan from the heat and slowly pour in the cream (be careful, it will spit). Stir to make sure the mixture is thoroughly combined and there are no lumps. Generously season the caramel with flaky salt to taste (make sure it's cool enough before tasting it). Be daring with the salt – it's there to cut through the sugar in the parfait as well as the honey in the caramel. Once you're happy with the taste, leave the caramel to cool to room temperature.
11. To serve, turn the frozen parfait upside down onto a tray or chopping board. Cut thick slices and place them on chilled plates, then pour the salted honey caramel over the top.

TIRAMISÙ

Tiramisù is one of my favourite desserts. I always order it if I see it on a menu, and I love the balance of flavours and textures: bitter cocoa and espresso, enriched mascarpone cream, moist sponge. Just delicious. In place of the typical sponge fingers, we make this recipe with a dacquoise sponge, which is a light, aerated meringue with nuts – here, hazelnuts – folded through. The nuts add to the texture, but also lend a rich flavour.

SERVES 6

Dark cocoa powder, for dusting

HAZELNUT DACQUOISE SPONGE
200 g (7 oz) roasted, peeled hazelnuts
7 egg whites
220 g (7.75 oz) pure icing (confectioners') sugar
Pinch of fine salt
4 eggs
60 g (2.25 oz) plain (all-purpose) flour

MASCARPONE CREAM
7 egg yolks
2 tablespoons amaretto liqueur
105 g (3.5 oz) caster (superfine) sugar
770 ml (27 fl oz) thickened (whipping) cream
500 g (1 lb 2 oz) mascarpone

COFFEE SOAK
125 g (4.5 oz) caster (superfine) sugar
375 ml (13 fl oz) espresso (or brewed or instant coffee, if you're desperate)

1. For the sponge, preheat the oven to 170°C (325°F). Line two baking trays, each about 33 x 27 x 4 cm (13 x 10¾ x 2½ in), with baking paper.
2. Pulse the roasted hazelnuts in a food processor until they resemble fine breadcrumbs. Set aside.
3. Using a stand mixer fitted with the whisk attachment, whisk the egg whites, 40 g (1.5 oz) of the icing sugar and the salt until soft peaks form.
4. In a separate bowl, whisk the whole eggs with the remaining icing sugar until pale and fluffy. Add the ground hazelnuts and the flour and mix thoroughly to combine, then gently fold this mixture into the whipped egg whites, taking care not to knock out excess air.
5. Divide the batter evenly between the two baking trays, spreading it out evenly. Bake for 25 minutes or until golden all over. Lift the baking paper and sponges onto a wire rack and cool to room temperature.
6. For the mascarpone cream, whisk the egg yolks, amaretto and 35 g (1.25 oz) of the caster sugar in a heatproof bowl set over a saucepan of gently simmering water until pale and thick (you should be able to see ribbons on the surface of the mixture). Remove from the heat and let this sabayon cool to room temperature.
7. Whip the cream and the remaining 70 g (2.5 oz) of caster sugar in a large bowl until soft, fluffy peaks form.
8. Whisk the mascarpone into the sabayon to combine thoroughly, then gently fold this mixture through the whipped cream.
9. For the coffee soak, add the sugar to the espresso and stir until the sugar has dissolved. Divide this mixture in half.
10. Lay one of the sponges in a serving dish or roasting tin, making sure it goes to the edges (trim it, if needed), then pour half the espresso mixture over the top to soak the sponge. Spread half the mascarpone cream evenly over the sponge, going right to the edges, then generously dust the top with cocoa powder. Place the second sponge on top and soak it with the remaining espresso mixture, then spread it with the remaining mascarpone cream and generously dust the top with cocoa. Cover and refrigerate for 4 hours for everything to get acquainted before serving.

POUDING CHÔMEUR

I discovered this common recipe for pouding chômeur after a trip to Montreal. The dish itself comes from a time of thrift, when not too many ingredients would have been available other than pantry items and, this being Canada, an abundance of maple syrup. The name might translate to 'poor man's pudding', but over the years it's become increasingly rich, with the cream and maple syrup scaled right up. It's a bit of a twisted paradox serving this in Australia, since we don't produce maple syrup – the imported organic syrup we used at LP's was more of a luxury item, and it feels lavish using this quantity. If you ever dined with us at LP's, you hopefully know this dessert. It was a staple for years, and one of the dishes people always came back for.

SERVES 4 (OR 2, IF YOU'RE FEELING DARING)

150 g (5.5 oz) diced salted butter, at room temperature
200 g (7 oz) white (granulated) sugar
2 eggs
280 g (10 oz) plain (all-purpose) flour
1 teaspoon baking powder
500 ml (17 fl oz) maple syrup
500 ml (17 fl oz) single (pure) cream
Vanilla ice cream (page 256), to serve

1. Using a stand mixer fitted with the paddle attachment, cream the butter and sugar until they're pale and fluffy, and the sugar has dissolved. Add the eggs and mix until thoroughly combined.
2. Sift in the flour and baking powder and mix until just combined. Transfer the batter to an airtight container and refrigerate for at least 6 hours or until needed.
3. When you're ready to bake the pudding, pour the maple syrup and the cream into a saucepan and bring to the boil, stirring to combine. Remove from the heat and leave to cool to room temperature.
4. Preheat the oven to 220°C (425°F). Shape the chilled batter into pieces about the size of a golf ball and arrange them in a single layer in a roasting tin. Pour the cream and maple syrup mixture over the top.
5. Bake for 15–20 minutes or until the top is golden brown. Serve the pudding immediately, topped with vanilla ice cream.

CHOUX AU CRAQUELIN WITH VANILLA ICE CREAM

I love choux pastry. Making it has been a recurring theme throughout my career, and one of my favourite childhood memories is of eating big soggy chocolate éclairs on the weekend, when my parents went to grab a baguette from our local bakery. These are about the same level of decadence, just a little more elegant, served with chocolate sauce and my vanilla ice cream.

You'll need to start both the choux and the ice cream a day ahead.

SERVES 4

Vanilla ice cream (page 256), to serve

CHOUX PUFFS

100 g (3.5 oz) salted butter
½ teaspoon caster (superfine) sugar
½ teaspoon salt
130 g (4.5 oz) plain (all-purpose) flour
4 eggs

CRAQUELIN

85 g (3 oz) diced salted butter, at room temperature
100 g (3.5 oz) brown sugar
100 g (3.5 oz) plain (all-purpose) flour
Pinch of fine salt

CHOCOLATE SAUCE

60 g (2.25 oz) dark chocolate buttons (54%), chopped
40 g (1.5 oz) dark cocoa powder
Pinch of fine salt
115 ml (3.75 fl oz) single (pure) cream
200 g (7 oz) liquid glucose
45 g (1.5 oz) caster (superfine) sugar

1. For the choux puffs, combine the butter, sugar, salt and 240 ml (8 fl oz) water in a saucepan. Cook over low heat until the butter melts. Give it a stir, then bring to the boil over medium heat. Stir in the flour and reduce the heat to low. Cook, stirring continuously, for 5 minutes or until the dough is coming away from the side of the pan and has a sheen to it.
2. Transfer the dough to a stand mixer fixed with the paddle attachment and beat on medium speed for 5 minutes, allowing the dough to begin to cool. Add the eggs one by one, making sure each egg is thoroughly incorporated before adding the next.
3. Transfer the batter to a piping bag fitted with a 1 cm (½ in) plain nozzle and refrigerate overnight to allow the batter to rest.
4. The next day, remove the batter from the fridge and leave it to come to room temperature, which should take at least an hour.
5. Meanwhile, make the craquelin. Using a stand mixer fitted with the paddle attachment, cream the butter and brown sugar until pale and fluffy. Add the flour and salt and mix until combined, ensuring there are no lumps. Wrap the dough in plastic wrap and refrigerate for 15 minutes to rest.
6. Roll out the craquelin dough between two sheets of baking paper until it is 2 mm (1/16 in) thick. Working quickly, cut out circles with a 4 cm (1½ in) cutter, re-rolling the dough as needed (if it's getting too soft, pop the dough back into the fridge for a few minutes). The craquelin circles will be baked on top of the choux to create a delicious crust.
7. Preheat the oven to 220°C (425°F). Line a baking tray with baking paper. Pipe 4 cm (1½ in) balls of the choux batter onto the tray. (I find the best way to do this is to hold the nozzle close to the baking paper, directly above the tray, then squeeze the batter onto the tray.) Repeat this until you've used all the batter (you may need a couple of trays).

»

8. Lay a circle of craquelin on top of each choux ball. Bake for about 20 minutes, then turn the oven down to 150°C (300°F) and bake for another 10–20 minutes or until golden. The choux may be golden and inviting on the outside, but still wet inside, so check one of the choux balls by tearing it open. If it looks wet, keep cooking. If it looks nice and crisp, remove the tray from the oven and transfer the choux to a wire rack to cool to room temperature.
9. While the choux are cooling, make the sauce. Combine the chocolate, cocoa and salt in a bowl. Combine the cream, glucose and sugar in a saucepan, then bring to the boil, stirring to dissolve the sugar and glucose. Pour this over the chocolate mixture, whisking until melted and thoroughly combined. Leave at room temperature until ready to serve. (If it seizes up, give it a quick blast in the microwave.)
10. To serve, cut each choux in half and fill with a large scoop of ice cream. (You can get ahead here by filling the pastries and briefly placing them in the freezer until you're ready to serve.)
11. Make a pile of choux on a plate in the centre of the table and pour the chocolate sauce over the top. For a more refined approach, you can serve the choux and sauce on individual plates. I prefer the pile.

Vanilla ice cream

Ice cream is personal, like pizza or coffee. People have their favourites and are passionate about which is the best and how it should be served. For me, the best and most nostalgic-tasting vanilla ice cream is one that's made with crème anglaise and flavoured not with vanilla pods, but vanilla essence. I might cop it for saying it, but when it comes to dialling in on the old-school feelings, nothing comes close. Use vanilla pods for anything else – they're beautiful things – but for this recipe use essence, specifically Bingo brand if you can find it.

MAKES 1.25 LITRES (44 FL OZ)

7.5 egg yolks
500 ml (17 fl oz) milk
500 ml (17 fl oz) single (pure) cream
250 g (9 oz) caster (superfine) sugar
2 tablespoons vanilla essence

1. Put the egg yolks in a heatproof bowl with 2½ tablespoons of the milk and 2½ tablespoons of the cream and whisk them together.
2. Mix the remaining milk and cream with the sugar and vanilla in a large saucepan. Bring to the boil, stirring to dissolve the sugar, then pour the hot cream mixture into the egg yolk mixture, whisking as you go. Return the crème anglaise to the pan and cook over low heat, stirring constantly, until it reaches 83°C (181°F) and thickly coats the back of a spoon.
3. Strain the anglaise into a bowl set over another bowl of ice and stir to cool it quickly, then transfer the mixture to an ice-cream machine and churn until frozen. Transfer to an airtight container and freeze until required.

ESPRESSO GRANITA WITH CHANTILLY AND BISCOTTI

When I was 25, I was desperate to go overseas, since the only travel I'd done was between Australia and New Zealand. I remember sitting in a questionable bar very late one night with my good friends Dan Puskas and James Parry, who went on to open Sixpenny together. They were planning a trip to San Francisco, mainly to visit restaurants and to see our friend Phil Wood (now running Ursula's in Sydney), who was working at The French Laundry in Napa Valley. They invited me along on what would turn out to be a ridiculous eating trip, the kind that almost turns into 'sport eating', where you're trying to cram in as many restaurant visits as possible, to see and taste as much as you can. Back-to-back dégustations and everything else in between.

Our beacon of refuge turned out to be Judy Rodgers's Zuni Cafe, which we ended up visiting three times in the ten days we were there. Their oysters, roast chicken salad and Bloody Marys were always steadying, but this espresso granita (pictured overleaf) was something else. It's the most refreshing, delicious and light dish for when you sort of feel like dessert, sort of feel like a coffee and are unsure which to go for.

I love having this at the end of a large meal, when you can 'just' squeeze in something for dessert.

SERVES 4

250 ml (9 fl oz) espresso (be sure to use espresso rather than filter or instant coffee)
110 g (3.75 oz) caster (superfine) sugar
Biscotti (see opposite), to serve

CHANTILLY

125 ml (4 fl oz) single (pure) cream, chilled
2 teaspoons caster (superfine) sugar
Seeds from ½ vanilla pod

1. For the granita, whisk the coffee and sugar until the sugar has dissolved. Transfer the mixture to a tray or container and place in the freezer.
2. Stir the granita every 2 hours until large ice crystals have formed and the entire granita is frozen (about 8 hours in total). Because of the high proportion of sugar, the granita will have a slushie-like texture and won't freeze solid. Before serving, it will need to be mixed and folded over, as the sugar will have settled on the bottom.
3. For the chantilly, whisk the cream, sugar and vanilla seeds until light and floppy. Do not overwhip it.
4. When you're ready to serve, mix the granita to re-incorporate the sugar. In chilled glasses, layer the chantilly and the granita in equal quantities. Serve with biscotti and perhaps a small glass of Amaro Montenegro.

Biscotti

When I first started making biscotti, it was one of those hard lessons in using a timer – I used to burn the almonds at least once a week. When you perfect biscotti, they're a great vehicle for different flavours, such as nuts, citrus zests and small gestures like fennel seeds or aniseed.

MAKES ABOUT 20

30 g (1 oz) raw almonds
60 g (2.25 oz) butter, at room temperature
75 g (2.5 oz) caster (superfine) sugar
1 egg
½ teaspoon fennel seeds
1 teaspoon finely grated orange zest
2 teaspoons grappa or Cointreau
155 g (5.5 oz) plain (all-purpose) flour, plus extra for dusting
¾ teaspoon baking powder
Large pinch of fine salt

1. Preheat the oven to 180°C (350°F). Spread the almonds on a baking tray and roast for around 5 minutes (be sure to set a timer!) or until golden. Remove from the oven and leave to cool to room temperature. Reduce the oven temperature to 160°C (315°F).
2. Using a stand mixer fitted with the paddle attachment, cream the butter and sugar until light and fluffy and the sugar has dissolved. Beat in the egg until smooth.
3. Mix in the fennel seeds, orange zest and liqueur, then sift in the flour, baking powder and salt. Mix until just combined, then quickly stir in the roasted almonds.
4. Tip the dough onto a lightly floured surface and shape it into a log, then press it down lightly to make an oval shape about 4 cm (1½ in) high. Transfer the dough to a baking tray lined with baking paper.
5. Bake for 25 minutes, then lift the baking paper and cooked biscotti log onto a wire rack and let it cool completely.
6. Transfer the cooled biscotti log to a chopping board. Using a bread knife, carefully cut slices on a slight angle, making them about 1 cm (½ in) thick. Transfer the slices back to the baking tray and bake for 5–6 minutes or until the biscotti are light golden (again, use a timer). Remove from the oven and allow to cool on the tray before serving. Store the biscotti in an airtight container for up to a month.

ACKNOWLEDGEMENTS

Firstly to Tania, thank you so much for being your beautiful self. Your drive and perseverance is never ending. None of this would be possible without your love and support. To Frankie, I'm so proud of you. Thank you, Mum, for your constant encouragement on this career path. To Dad, thank you for all the pork chops. Thank you Jenny, Iain, Kerrin and Katie for always being there when needed. Thank you to Chris and Leanne.

To Justin Wolfers, for opening the door to all the possibilities – I couldn't have imagined a better person to have on this project. Thank you. To David Matthews, who finessed the words throughout these pages – you always got it. Thank you. To Justine Harding, for your meticulous and thorough sharpness – you don't miss a thing. Thank you. Thank you to Sarah Odgers for your vision and expertise, to Stuart Torkington for all your design work with the LP's brand with this book, and to Susanne Geppert for bringing it all together. To Alicia Taylor, the light whisperer (who took these amazing images), thank you for always being so precise and exact. To Jessica Johnson, for your input and styling. Thank you for being so adaptable. Thank you to Jane Morrow for making a long-time dream come true.

To all the staff at LP's, past and present, you have made LP's what it is. Thank you. To Cath, where do I begin? Thank you for everything. To Game, thank you for all your hard work and loyalty over the years. When are we printing the 'real' book? To chef Pat, the all-rounder – thank you! Thank you, Chef Izzy, it's always a pleasure. Thank you for your assistance on this book. Thank you, Dave, for your work on the shoot.

Thank you Joe, Anna, Elvis and Sarah for giving me the opportunity.

Thank you to all of my mentors, teachers and chefs: Sandrine Urvois, Kirk Jacobsen, Paul Hoather, Martin Boetz, Maria Pia de Razza, Tetsuya Wakuda, Martin Benn, Darren Robertson, Andoni Aduriz, Llorenç Sagarra, Rafa Costa E Silva, Dan Barber, Adam Kaye. Whether you know it or not, you have given me so much. Thank you.

INDEX

A
Aïoli 223
almonds *see* nuts
amaretto
   mascarpone cream 251
   Tiramisù 251
anchovies
   Creamed spinach 188
   Puntarelle with anchovies and garlic 208
   Salsa verde 222
apples
   Brown sauce 221
   Smoked mackerel nach hausfrauenart 169

B
bacon
   Bacon 158–9
   bacon, basic method 154–5
   bacon brine 159, 160
   Bacon chops 160
bacterial danger zone 31
Barbecue sauce 220
beans: Braised green beans 204
beef
   Beef stock and beef jus 235
   Beef tartare 128
   Bresaola 70
   Bresaola with parmesan custard 73
   Cheeseburgers 144–5
   doneness for 123–4
   Grilled steak 142
   Smoked beef-fat roast potatoes 212
   Smoked beef short ribs 184
   Smoked beef tongue 176
   Smoked brisket 178–81
   Smoked brisket sandwich 183
   Smoked prime rib 187
   Yorkshire puddings 189
beer
   Beer mustard 228
   Gnocco fritto 236
belly, pork
   Bacon 158–9
   Porchetta 136–7
Biscotti 259
blood, pig's
   blood bologna 39
   Boudin noir 47
bones
   Beef stock and beef jus 235
   Chicken stock 234
botulism 80–1
Boudin noir 47
Boudin noir with fried eggs and brown sauce 47
Braised green beans 204
Bratwurst 32
Bratwurst with pickled cabbage and mustard 32
bread
   burger buns 237
   Milk bread 237
   milk buns 237
Bresaola 70
Bresaola with parmesan custard 73
brines
   bacon brine 159, 160
   brisket brine 180
   chicken brine 170
   ham brine 163
   mackerel brine 166
   tongue brine 176
brining 152–3
   before smoking 150–1
   brining needles 14, 153
   equilibrium brining 152–3
   gradient brining 153
   injection brining 153
brisket
   brisket brine 180
   Cheeseburgers 144–5
   hot-smoking 150
   Smoked brisket 178–81
   Smoked brisket sandwich 183
Brown sauce 221
buns, milk 237
burgers
   burger buns 237
   Cheeseburgers 144–5
butchers 119
butcher's paper 179
buttermilk ricotta 211

C
cabbage
   Bratwurst with pickled cabbage and mustard 32
   Pickled cabbage 226
   Smoked brisket sandwich 183
Candied cumquats 233
capers
   Beef tartare 128
   Cured sardines with pickled vegetables 74
   Pistachio, caper and lemon sauce 222
   Salsa verde 222
   Sauce gribiche 221
caramel, salted honey 248
carrots
   Cotechino with lentils and salsa verde 36
   Cured sardines with pickled vegetables 74
   soffritto 36
carving, 125, 173
casings, sausage 24–5
celery
   Cotechino with lentils and salsa verde 36
   soffritto 36
chantilly 258
cheese
   Bresaola with parmesan custard 73
   buttermilk ricotta 211
   Cheese kransky 52
   Cheeseburgers 144–5
   cheesemaking 199
   Cucumbers and melon with honey and ricotta 211
   mascarpone cream 251
   parmesan custard 73
   Pepperoni pizza 44
   Pig's-head sausage muffin 56
   Smoked brisket sandwich 183
   Stracciatella 199–200
   Tiramisù 251
   Toast with 'nduja, ricotta and honey 90
   Tomato salad with handmade stracciatella 198–200

Cheeseburgers 144–5
chestnuts *see* nuts
chicken
   carving poultry 173
   chicken brine 170
   Chicken liver pâté 99–100
   Chicken spice 227
   Chicken stock 234
   crisp skin 125
   gravy 206
   Mash and gravy 206–7
   orange and pistachio terrine 104
   parsley and green peppercorn terrine 104
   Pork and chicken liver terrine 103–4
   Smoked chicken 170
chillies
   chilli oil 79
   Coppa di testa 107–8
   Hot sauce 220
   'Nduja 89–90
   Pickled mussels with chilli oil 79
   spiced saucisson 86
chocolate
   chocolate sauce 255
   Choux au craquelin with vanilla ice cream 255–6
chop, Grilled pork 140–1
chops, Bacon 160
Choux au craquelin with vanilla ice cream 255–6
choux puffs 255
chuck steak: Cheeseburgers 144–5
chutney, Green tomato 230
Citrus salad with burnt honey and pistachios 215
Clostridium botulinum 80–1
Coconut sorbet with watermelon granita 242
coffee
   Barbecue sauce 220
   coffee soak 251
   Espresso granita with chantilly and biscotti 258–9
   Tiramisù 251
cognac
   Chicken liver pâté 99–100
   port reduction 99
Cointreau
   Biscotti 259
   Strawberries with almond sponge and crème diplomat 244–5
cold-smoking 149–50, 153–4
Confit garlic 227
Cooking and storing sausages 30–1

cooking meat 119–25
   doneness for meat 123–4
Coppa 69
Coppa di testa 107–8
cornichons: Sauce gribiche 221
Cotechino 35
Cotechino with lentils and salsa verde 36
courgettes *see* zucchini
crackers: Gnocco fritto 236
craquelin 255
Creamed spinach 188
creams
   chantilly 258
   crème diplomat 244
   mascarpone cream 251
crème diplomat 244
croquettes, Pig's-head 111
Cucumbers and melon with honey and ricotta 211
cumquats
   Candied cumquats 233
   Citrus salad with burnt honey and pistachios 215
   Smoked duck à la cumquat 175
Cured salmon (or other wild-caught fish) 75–6
Cured sardines with pickled vegetables 74
cures 66, 69, 70, 75
curing 61–3
   Bresaola 70
   combined with smoking 150–1
   Coppa 69
   Cured salmon (or other wild-caught fish) 75–6
   Cured sardines with pickled vegetables 74
   curing salts 15, 81
   dry-curing 61–2
   dry-curing bacon 158
   Guanciale 66
   innoculating mould 83
   'Nduja 89–90
   Salami 80–1
   Saucisson 83–6
   saucisson sec 86
   spiced saucisson 86
   wet-curing bacon 159
   whole-muscle curing 61–2
currants
   Boudin noir 47
   Brown sauce 221
   Pickled currants 232
custard, parmesan 73

D
dextrose 15
doneness for meat 123–4
dough, pizza 44
dressings
   nach hausfrauenart 169
   palm-sugar vinegar 209
   refrito 130
dry-aged beef: Beef tartare 128
dry-aging 120–1
dry cure 158
dry-curing 61–2, 158
duck
   carving poultry 173
   Chicken liver pâté 99–100
   crisp skin 125
   Duck galantine 112–15
   orange and pistachio terrine 104
   Smoked duck 172
   Smoked duck à la cumquat 175

E
E. coli 80
eggs
   Aïoli 223
   Beef tartare 128
   Boudin noir with fried eggs and brown sauce 47
   Bresaola with parmesan custard 73
   crème diplomat 244
   Duck galantine 112–15
   galantine farce 112
   mascarpone cream 251
   parmesan custard 73
   Pig's-head sausage muffin 56
   Pork and chicken liver terrine 103–4
   Pouding chômeur 252
   Sauce gribiche 221
   Strawberries with almond sponge and crème diplomat 244–5
   Tiramisù 251
   Vanilla ice cream 256
   Yorkshire puddings 189
equilibrium brining 152–3
equipment 14–15
   brining needles 153
   for cheesemaking 199
   for smoking 149, 151, 153–4
Espresso granita with chantilly and biscotti 258–9

F
fat
   Bacon chops 160
   Bratwurst 32

Cheese kransky 52
Chicken liver pâté 99–100
Cotechino 35
Frankfurts 51
gravy 206
kangaroo mortadella 39
Mash and gravy 206–7
Mortadella 38–9
'Nduja 89–90
Pepperoni 43
Salsiccia 26–8
Saucisson 83–6
saucisson sec 86
Schinkenwurst 48
Smoked beef-fat roast potatoes 212
spiced saucisson 86
Yorkshire puddings 189
fennel
Biscotti 259
Pepperoni pizza 44
Salsiccia 26–8
spiced saucisson 86
fermentation 63
fermentation chambers 15
'Nduja 89–90
Salami 80–1
Saucisson 83–6
saucisson sec 86
spiced saucisson 86
fibrous casings 25
fish
cold-smoking 154
Creamed spinach 188
Cured salmon (or other wild-caught fish) 75–6
Cured sardines with pickled vegetables 74
Grilled fish 130–1
grilling 123
Pil pil 133
Puntarelle with anchovies and garlic 208
Salsa verde 222
Smoked mackerel 166
Smoked mackerel nach hausfrauenart 169
flounder: Grilled fish 130–1
forcemeats 22
Frankfurts 51
fruit, buying 193, 195

G
galantine, Duck 112–15
galantine farce 112

garlic
Aïoli 223
Confit garlic 227
gherkin
Cheeseburgers 144–5
Smoked mackerel nach hausfrauenart 169
girello, beef: Bresaola 70
glaze, maple and mustard 164
Gnocco fritto 236
gradient brining 153
granita
Coconut sorbet with watermelon granita 242
Espresso granita with chantilly and biscotti 258–9
watermelon granita 242
grapefruit: Citrus salad with burnt honey and pistachios 215
gravy 206
Green tomato chutney 230
Green tomatoes 230–1
Grilled fish 130–1
Grilled octopus 134–5
Grilled pork chop 140–1
Grilled steak 142
grilling 121–3
Cheeseburgers 144–5
Grilled fish 130–1
Grilled octopus 134–5
Grilled pork chop 140–1
Grilled steak 142
Sweet-and-sour grilled onions 141
Guanciale 66

H
ham
ham brine 163
Maple and mustard glazed Christmas ham 164
Schinkenwurst 48
Smoked ham 163–4
hazelnuts *see* nuts
honey
Citrus salad with burnt honey and pistachios 215
Cucumbers and melon with honey and ricotta 211
Duck galantine 112–15
galantine farce 112
Nougat parfait with salted honey caramel 248–9
Pil pil 133
salted honey caramel 248

Smoked duck 172
Toast with 'nduja, ricotta and honey 90
Hot dogs 51
Hot sauce 220
hot-smoking 150, 154–5

I
ice cream, Vanilla 256
ice, crushed 15, 23
injection brining 153

J
jowls, pork
Boudin noir 47
Guanciale 66
orange and pistachio terrine 104
parsley and green peppercorn terrine 104
Pig's-head sausages 55
Pork and chicken liver terrine 103–4
jus, Beef stock and beef 235

K
kangaroo mortadella 39
knives 14
kransky, Cheese 52

L
lamb: doneness for 123–4
lard: Bacon chops 160
Leaf salad with palm-sugar vinaigrette 209
legs, pork
Maple and mustard glazed Christmas ham 164
Smoked ham 163–4
lemonade fruit: Pistachio, caper and lemon sauce 222
lemons
Citrus salad with burnt honey and pistachios 215
Pistachio, caper and lemon sauce 222
Sweet-and-sour grilled onions 141
lentils: Cotechino with lentils and salsa verde 36
limes: Citrus salad with burnt honey and pistachios 215
livers
Chicken liver pâté 99–100
orange and pistachio terrine 104
parsley and green peppercorn terrine 104
Pork and chicken liver terrine 103–4
loin, pork: Grilled pork chop 140–1

M

mackerel
  mackerel brine 166
  Smoked mackerel 166
  Smoked mackerel nach hausfrauenart 169
Madeira
  Chicken liver pâté 99–100
  port reduction 99
Maillard reaction 121
man-made casings 24–5
maple syrup
  Maple and mustard glazed Christmas ham 164
  Pouding chômeur 252
mascarpone cream 251
Mash and gravy 206–7
maturating chamber 15
meat
  buying 119
  carving 125, 173
  cooking 119–25
  doneness for 123–4
  tempering 121
  see also beef, chicken, duck, kangaroo, pork
melons
  Coconut sorbet with watermelon granita 242
  Cucumbers and melon with honey and ricotta 211
  watermelon granita 242
microscales 14
Milk bread 237
milk buns 237
mincers 14
Mortadella 38–9
mould-ripened: Saucisson 83–6
moulds 81
muffin, Pig's-head sausage 56
mussels: Pickled mussels with chilli oil 79
mustard
  Beer mustard 228
  Mustard pickle relish 228
  Quince mustard 229
myosin 23

N

nach hausfrauenart, Smoked mackerel 169
natural casings 25
'Nduja 89–90
neck, pork: Coppa 69
nitrates 15, 81
nitrites 15, 81
Nougat parfait with salted honey caramel 248–9
nuts
  almond dacquoise sponge 244
  almond praline 248
  Biscotti 259
  Boudin noir 47
  Citrus salad with burnt honey and pistachios 215
  Duck galantine 112–15
  galantine farce 112
  hazelnut dacquoise sponge 251
  Leaf salad with palm-sugar vinaigrette 209
  Nougat parfait with salted honey caramel 248–9
  orange and pistachio terrine 104
  Pistachio, caper and lemon sauce 222
  Roasted pumpkin with chestnuts, sage and brown butter 203
  Shaved zucchini with hazelnuts and mint 196
  Strawberries with almond sponge and crème diplomat 244–5
  Tiramisù 251

O

octopus, Grilled 134–5
oil, chilli 79
olive oil 195
olives: Citrus salad with burnt honey and pistachios 215
onions
  Red onion pickle 232
  Sweet-and-sour grilled onions 141
oranges
  Biscotti 259
  Citrus salad with burnt honey and pistachios 215
  Duck galantine 112–15
  galantine farce 112
  Maple and mustard glazed Christmas ham 164
  orange and pistachio terrine 104
oven thermometers 14

P

palm-sugar vinegar 209
parfait: Nougat parfait with salted honey caramel 248–9
parmesan custard 73
parsley and green peppercorn terrine 104

pâtés 95–6
  Chicken liver pâté 99–100
Penicillium nalgiovense 83
Pepperoni 43
Pepperoni pizza 44
pH meters 14
Pickled mussels with chilli oil 79
pickles
  Mustard pickle relish 228
  Pickled cabbage 226
  Pickled currants 232
  Pickled green tomatoes 231
  pickling liquid 74, 79
  Red onion pickle 232
pig's head
  Coppa di testa 107–8
  Pig's-head sausage muffin 56
  Pig's-head sausages 55
  see also jowls
pig's trotters
  Beef stock and beef jus 235
  Coppa di testa 107–8
  Pig's-head croquettes 111
Pil pil 133
pistachios *see* nuts
pizza
  Pepperoni pizza 44
  pizza dough 44
poaching sausages 30
pomelos: Citrus salad with burnt honey and pistachios 215
Porchetta 136–7
porchetta seasoning 136
pork
  Bacon 158–9
  Bacon chops 160
  blood bologna 39
  Boudin noir 47
  Boudin noir with fried eggs and brown sauce 47
  Bratwurst 32
  Bratwurst with pickled cabbage and mustard 32
  Cheese kransky 52
  Coppa 69
  Coppa di testa 107–8
  Cotechino 35
  Cotechino with lentils and salsa verde 36
  doneness for 123–4
  Duck galantine 112–15
  Frankfurts 51
  galantine farce 112
  Grilled pork chop 140–1
  Guanciale 66

Hot dogs 51
kangaroo mortadella 39
Maple and mustard glazed
    Christmas ham 164
Mortadella 38–9
'Nduja 89–90
orange and pistachio terrine 104
parsley and green peppercorn
    terrine 104
Pepperoni 43
Pepperoni pizza 44
Pig's-head croquettes 111
Pig's-head sausage muffin 56
Pig's-head sausages 55
Porchetta 136–7
Pork and chicken liver terrine
    103–4
Salsiccia 26–8
Saucisson 83–6
saucisson sec 86
Schinkenwurst 48
Smoked ham 163–4
Smoked sausages 165
spiced saucisson 86
Toast with 'nduja, ricotta
    and honey 90

port
Chicken liver pâté 99–100
Duck galantine 112–15
galantine farce 112
Pork and chicken liver terrine 103–4
port reduction 99

potatoes
Grilled octopus 134–5
Mash and gravy 206–7
Smoked beef-fat roast potatoes 212
Smoked mackerel nach
    hausfrauenart 169

Pouding chômeur 252

poultry
carving 173
see also chicken, duck

praline, almond 248
prime rib: Smoked prime rib 187

prunes
Brown sauce 221
Pickled currants 232

puddings
Pouding chômeur 252
Yorkshire puddings 189

pumpkin: Roasted pumpkin with
    chestnuts, sage and brown
    butter 203
Puntarelle with anchovies and
    garlic 208

Q
Quince mustard 229

R
rack, pork: Bacon chops 160
Red onion pickle 232
reduction, port 99
refrito 130
reheating sausages 31
relish, Mustard pickle 228
resting 125
rib-eye: Grilled steak 142
ribs: Smoked beef short ribs 184
rice: Boudin noir 47

ricotta
buttermilk ricotta 211
Cucumbers and melon with honey
    and ricotta 211
Roasted pumpkin with chestnuts,
    sage and brown butter 203

roasting 121, 124–5
Porchetta 136–7

S

salads
Citrus salad with burnt honey
    and pistachios 215
Cucumbers and melon with honey
    and ricotta 211
Leaf salad with palm-sugar
    vinaigrette 209
Puntarelle with anchovies and
    garlic 208
Shaved zucchini with hazelnuts
    and mint 196
Tomato salad with handmade
    stracciatella 198–200

salami 80–1
Saucisson 83–6
saucisson sec 86
spiced saucisson 86

salmon: Cured salmon (or other
    wild-caught fish) 75–6
Salsa verde 222
Salsiccia 26–8
salt 15
salted honey caramel 248
sandwich, Smoked brisket 183
sanitising sprays 15
sardines: Cured sardines with
    pickled vegetables 74

sauces
Aïoli 223
Barbecue sauce 220
beef jus 235
Brown sauce 221
chocolate sauce 255
gravy 206
Hot sauce 220
Pil pil 133
Pistachio, caper and lemon sauce 222
Salsa verde 222
Sauce gribiche 221

saucisson
Saucisson 83–6
saucisson sec 86
spiced saucisson 86

sausages 19–23
and crushed ice 23
blood bologna 39
Boudin noir 47
Boudin noir with fried eggs and
    brown sauce 47
Bratwurst 32
Bratwurst with pickled cabbage
    and mustard 32
Cheese kransky 52
chilling 31
cooking 21–2, 30–1
Coppa di testa 107–8
Cotechino 35
Cotechino with lentils and
    salsa verde 36
Frankfurts 51
Hot dogs 51
kangaroo mortadella 39
Mortadella 38–9
'Nduja 89–90
Pepperoni 43
Pepperoni pizza 44
Pig's-head sausage muffin 56
Pig's-head sausages 55
poaching 30
ratio for making 22
reheating 31
Salami 80–1
Salsiccia 26–8
Saucisson 83–6
saucisson sec 86
sausage basics 22–3
sausage casings 24–5
sausage fillers 14
sausage sizzle 31
Schinkenwurst 48
Smoked sausages 165
smoking 30
spiced saucisson 86
storing 31
Toast with 'nduja, ricotta and
    honey 90

scales 14
Schinkenwurst 48
seasonality 193
seasonings 121
    Chicken spice 227
    cures 66, 69, 70, 75
    for vegetables and salads 195
    porchetta seasoning 136
    spice kits 26, 32, 35, 38, 43, 47, 48, 51, 52, 55
    see also brines
Shaved zucchini with hazelnuts and mint 196
short-ribs: Smoked beef short ribs 184
shoulder, pork
    Boudin noir 47
    Bratwurst 32
    Cheese kransky 52
    Cotechino 35
    Frankfurts 51
    hot-smoking 150
    Mortadella 38–9
    'Nduja 89–90
    orange and pistachio terrine 104
    parsley and green peppercorn terrine 104
    Pepperoni 43
    Pig's-head sausages 55
    Pork and chicken liver terrine 103–4
    Salsiccia 26–8
    Saucisson 83–6
    saucisson sec 86
    Schinkenwurst 48
    spiced saucisson 86
skin
    Cotechino 35
    crisp 124–5
    Duck galantine 112–15
    Pil pil 133
Smoked beef-fat roast potatoes 212
Smoked beef short ribs 184
Smoked beef tongue 176
Smoked brisket 178–81
Smoked brisket sandwich 183
Smoked chicken 170
Smoked duck 172
Smoked duck à la cumquat 175
Smoked ham 163–4
Smoked mackerel 166
Smoked mackerel nach hausfrauenart 169

Smoked prime rib 187
Smoked sausages 165
smoking 149–55
    Bacon 158–9
    Bacon chops 160
    cold-smoking 149–50, 153–4
    combined with curing 159
    dos and don'ts 153
    equipment 151, 153–4
    hot-smoking 150, 154–5
    Maple and mustard glazed Christmas ham 164
    sausages 30
    Smoked beef-fat roast potatoes 212
    Smoked beef short ribs 184
    Smoked beef tongue 176
    Smoked brisket 178–81
    Smoked brisket sandwich 183
    Smoked chicken 170
    Smoked duck 172
    Smoked duck à la cumquat 175
    Smoked ham 163–4
    Smoked mackerel 166
    Smoked mackerel nach hausfrauenart 169
    Smoked prime rib 187
    Smoked sausages 165
    smokers 15, 149, 151, 153–4
    smoking 101 152–5
    types of 150
    woodchip method 155
sodium nitrate 15, 81
sodium nitrite 15, 81
soffritto 36
sorbet: Coconut sorbet with watermelon granita 242
spice kits 26, 32, 35, 38, 43, 47, 48, 51, 52, 55
    adding 23
spiced saucisson 86
spinach, Creamed 188
sponges
    almond dacquoise sponge 244
    hazelnut dacquiose sponge 251
squash: Shaved zucchini with hazelnuts and mint 196
stocks 234–5
    Beef stock and beef jus 235
    Chicken stock 234
storing sausages 31
Stracciatella 199–200
Strawberries with almond sponge and crème diplomat 244–5
Sweet-and-sour grilled onions 141
synthetic casings 25

T
tangerines: Citrus salad with burnt honey and pistachios 215
tartare, Beef 128
tempering meat 121
terrines 95–6
    Coppa di testa 107–8
    Duck galantine 112–15
    orange and pistachio terrine 104
    parsley and green peppercorn terrine 104
    Pork and chicken liver terrine 103–4
thermometers 14
Tiramisù 251
Toast with 'nduja, ricotta and honey 90
tomatoes
    Green tomato chutney 230
    Green tomatoes 230–1
    Pepperoni pizza 44
    Pickled green tomatoes 231
    Tomato salad with handmade stracciatella 198–200
tongue, beef
    Smoked beef tongue 176
    tongue brine 176
trotters *see* pig's trotters

V
Vanilla ice cream 256
vegetables, buying 193
vinaigrettes
    refrito 130
    palm-sugar vinegar 209
vinegars 195

W
walnuts *see* nuts
watermelon
    Coconut sorbet with watermelon granita 242
    watermelon granita 242
wet-curing bacon 159
woodchip method for smoking 155

Y
Yorkshire puddings 189

Z
zucchini
    Hot dogs 51
    Mustard pickle relish 228
    Shaved zucchini with hazelnuts and mint 196

Published in 2024 by Murdoch Books, an imprint of Allen & Unwin

Murdoch Books Australia
Cammeraygal Country
83 Alexander Street
Crows Nest NSW 2065
Phone: +61 (0)2 8425 0100
murdochbooks.com.au
info@murdochbooks.com.au

Murdoch Books UK
Ormond House
26–27 Boswell Street
London WC1N 3JZ
Phone: +44 (0) 20 8785 5995
murdochbooks.co.uk
info@murdochbooks.co.uk

For corporate orders and custom publishing, contact our business development team at salesenquiries@murdochbooks.com.au

Publisher: Justin Wolfers
Design Manager: Sarah Odgers
Design Concept: Stuart Torkington, Tork Design
Designers: Susanne Geppert and Sarah Odgers
Editorial Manager: Justin Wolfers
Editor: Justine Harding
Writer: David Matthews
Photographer: Alicia Taylor
Stylist: Jessica Johnson
Production Director: Lou Playfair

Text © Luke Powell 2024
The moral right of the author has been asserted.
Design © Murdoch Books 2024
Photography © Alicia Taylor 2024

Murdoch Books acknowledges the Traditional Owners of the Country on which we live and work. We pay our respects to all Aboriginal and Torres Strait Islander Elders, past and present.

All rights reserved. No part of this publication may be reproduced, stored in a retrieval system or transmitted in any form or by any means, electronic, mechanical, photocopying, recording or otherwise, without the prior written permission of the publisher.

ISBN 9 781 76150 038 1

 A catalogue record for this book is available from the National Library of Australia

A catalogue record for this book is available from the British Library

Colour reproduction by Splitting Image Colour Studio Pty Ltd, Wantirna, Victoria
Printed by 1010 Printing International Limited, China

OVEN GUIDE: You may find cooking times vary depending on the oven you are using. This book was tested using a fan-forced oven. For conventional ovens, as a general rule, set the oven temperature to 20°C (35°F) higher than indicated in the recipe.

TABLESPOON MEASURES: We have used 20 ml (4 teaspoon) tablespoon measures. If you are using a 15 ml (3 teaspoon) tablespoon add an extra teaspoon of the ingredient for each tablespoon specified.

IMPORTANT: Those who might be at risk from the effects of salmonella poisoning (the elderly, pregnant women, young children and those suffering from immune deficiency diseases) should consult their doctor with any concerns about eating raw eggs. Please ensure that all seafood and beef to be eaten raw or lightly cooked are very fresh and of the highest quality.

DISCLAIMER: It is essential to follow all instructions for the preparation and fermentation of meat products with the utmost accuracy, and in clean and sanitary conditions. When using sodium nitrite or sodium nitrate, always be sure to strictly follow the manufacturer's instructions. While we try to keep all information up to date and correct, the author and publisher do not assume and hereby disclaim any liability for any loss, damage or disruption caused by errors or omissions, whether such errors or omissions result from negligence, accident or any other cause.

10 9 8 7 6 5 4 3 2 1